CONNECTION TRAINING

THE HEART AND SCIENCE OF POSITIVE HORSE TRAINING

Hannah Weston
and Rachel Bedingfield

First published in 2019 by Connection Training

ISBN: 978-1-9162101-0-3 Print - Full Colour
ISBN: 978-1-9162101-1-0 Print - Black and White

Cover Design: Tanja Prokop
Interior Formatting: Tracy Atkins

Connection Training / Hannah Weston and Rachel Bedingfield

www.ConnectionTraining.com

This book is dedicated to the memory of Willie Dawson, who saw the start of its creation, but, sadly, not the end. He was the most supportive horsey husband and father we could have wished for (did we ever thank you enough for selling your Honda Africa Twin bike to buy us a horsebox?!).

We miss you.

CONTENTS

FOREWORD

As a clinical animal behaviourist and university lecturer I am regularly asked for recommended reading around equine training and the science behind it. This text would definitely be on my essential reading list. Crafted into a volume that seamlessly combines the science of behavioural ethology with the practice of training, this book consistently champions the ultimate aim: to provide optimally for the welfare of our domesticated equines in all our interactions with them.

This book introduces itself as an accessible, useable and reliable aid for the horse owner, trainer, rehabilitator, competition rider and beyond to help their equines develop and express agency and competence in all areas of their lives. Within the first few Chapters the reader is engagingly led through the science of equine ethology and behaviour which is demystified through clear prose and real-life examples that every horse-person can relate to. The 'getting to know your horse' exercises in Chapter 2 are hugely valuable for every horse owner and a fundamental precursor to successful connection and training. So many horse-human relationship issues (and many problem human-human relationships) hinge upon a lack of understanding around each others' core personality traits, prior experiences and, crucially, how these make the horse (and us) feel; with resultant mishaps in communication. Taking time to work through these exercises will be a sure 'lightbulb' moment for many owners in bridging the gap.

As the book progresses Hannah and Rachel take the reader through the Connection Training philosophy in a practical yet scientifically evidenced way, highlighting the preparation important for training success, the valuable skills of the trainer and the importance of recognising each equine as an individual with unique experiences, preferences and the odd quirky attribute!

Further Chapters of this book go on to provide detailed guidance on basic handling techniques, ground and ridden work training as well as resolving often seen behavioural issues. At all times the fundamental precepts of training and behaviour modification, namely consideration of *context*, *intensity*, *duration* and *distance* (alongside gradual development of these factors), are faithfully observed to reinforce calmness and ensure that at all times the horse or pony remains below threshold (the point at which the animal can not cope emotionally with the situation). It is a delight to see these principles of ethical equitation being so deftly and practically dealt with in this book.

The significant advances that have been made in the scientific study of equine behaviour, learning and memory that have taken place over the last couple of decades have undoubtedly led to the potential for high welfare training and management of equines. This book champions those scientific advances around ethical and positive training and thanks to the enlightened work of those such as Hannah and Rachel these are demonstrated through the teaching of their practical application. As such, those who study this text and follow its ethos will not only be contributing to the growing group of high welfare owners and trainers, but will also no doubt come away with a desire to truly connect with their equine and a real drive to develop mindful and positive training with their equines.

Loni Loftus

MSc, BSc(Hons), PgAEd, CAB

Loni is a Clinical Animal Behaviourist with over 17 years experience in the training and behavioural rehabilitation of equines. She has undertaken numerous prominent roles within the equine behaviour and welfare field including Head of Department roles within UK Universities, Head of Equine Operations at the RSPCA and is currently a Post-graduate lecturer in Animal behaviour and welfare at a number of UK universities where she is actively engaged in equine research specialising in 'affect' and emotional wellbeing. She is a full member of the Association of Pet Behaviour Counsellors and an Animal Behaviour and Training Council registered Clinical Animal Behaviourist and Animal Training Instructor.

VIDEO RESOURCES

Throughout this book, you will find references to relevant video resources which amplify or illustrate the text.

VIDEO RESOURCE

THE WAY HORSES FEEL

Rachel explains all of the emotional brain systems in horses, with plenty of footage to see the behaviour is real life situations.

THESE CAN BE FOUND AT:

WWW.CONNECTIONTRAINING.COM/VIDEO-RESOURCES

BIBLIOGRAPHY

We have compiled a list of source material and recommended reading.

THESE CAN BE FOUND AT:

WWW.CONNECTIONTRAINING.COM **/BIBLIOGRAPHY**

INTRODUCTION

WHAT IS CONNECTION TRAINING?

Why have you picked up this book? Are you looking for a gentle way to work with your horse, and build your relationship together? Do you have a difficult problem with your horse and are looking for techniques that might help? Maybe you feel there's a better way to help you and your progress in a way that you both enjoy. Perhaps you are a first-time horse owner, or parent of one, and are learning everything you can. Whatever your reason for reading this book, our reason for writing it is to help you. We want to help you to train your horse in a way that is rewarding for both of you and which creates an amazing partnership between you.

Our mission is to teach you how to train your horse to become a happy all-rounder, who is your equine partner. Our focus is threefold:

- to teach you a proven, effective way for you to train your horse for all your needs;

- to promote healthy postural engagement so that your horse can be sound for a long life;

- to foster confidence and joy in both you and your horse.

These will give you everything you need for a desirable leisure horse. From trail rides to dressage rings; from playing over obstacles to joining the Riding Club jumping class, you will have a horse who is happy and relaxed. If you want to go further into a particular discipline, you will have a solid foundation to take into more focused training, while also knowing how to keep your horse sound and happy for life.

WHY GOOD TRAINING IS VITAL

Effective training is one of the cornerstones of good animal welfare. It is just as important as providing the correct environment, companions, healthcare, and nutrition. A lack of effective training can cause difficulty in care routines, such as hoof trimming and veterinary visits., making daily handling stressful for both you and your horse. It also limits the activities you can enjoy together.

You've probably seen that, although people have horses for leisure and relaxation, many owners struggle with anxiety, frustration and tension when dealing with their horse. Positive and effective training makes these daily interactions easy and safe and works with all horses, whether young, old, green or problematic. Whatever kind of horse you start with, our aim is for you to have a horse who:

- Is easy and safe to handle.

- Is fun to spend time with.

- Moves correctly for good health and physical well-being.

- Enjoys whatever tasks you want to focus on.

- Lives a happy, healthy, enriched life.

To accomplish this, we use reward-based training, underpinned by equine ethology and the science of emotions. This approach has been shown scientifically to be the most effective and fair way to train animals. Through years of hands-on experience with horses, we have established how to use it most effectively to get the best results, the happiest horse, and the strongest partnership.

HOW DOES CONNECTION TRAINING WORK?

Connection Training is based on 3 elements:

1) Making training rewarding, which encourages and enthuses your horse;

2) Clear communication, which relaxes your horse and creates confidence; and

3) Fostering a close bond between you and your horse.

WHAT THIS BOOK WILL TEACH YOU

We begin by looking at what it means to be a horse and how your horse learns. Then you'll

discover how to use the Connection Training principles and techniques to address any training situation you encounter. Our principles and philosophies in the book are fully supported by our full training programme which you can follow online.

Throughout our work, the emotions of your horse and your relationship together will be prioritised and strengthened. Good horse training takes time, so you won't find quick fixes through our approach. But you will find deep and permanent fixes. The journey itself is fascinating and rewarding as you feel the deepening bond between you and your horse.

Our strongest goal is to teach you to be empowered as an independent trainer. Once you understand the scientific principles behind the training and have learnt good practices, you will be able to train any horse, anywhere, to do anything they have the capability to do. Learning Connection Training will give you all the skills and confidence you need.

WHO ARE WE?

Connection Training is a collaboration between Rachel Bedingfield and Hannah Weston, a mother and daughter team. We are experienced horse trainers who live and work in the UK and Spain. We have created the Connection Training Club, which is an online Membership Site, where students from all over the world learn to train their horses using our video courses. We have a global team of Certified Coaches and focus on providing individual support to Members so that their training is successful and fun.

HANNAH WESTON

My love of horses shone through at an early age. I started riding at age three, then spent my childhood hanging out at the stables. I got my first pony, Toby, when I was ten and loved competing in show-jumping and eventing with him.

During my teens, I began to explore alternative horsemanship, along with traditional British riding. In 2004, I discovered reward-based training and noticed that my horses learned new behaviours quickly and their levels of joy and motivation were much higher than ever before. This led me to study reward-based training in depth and train everything in this way, both on the ground and in the saddle.

I developed a strong interest in creating sound, healthy movement in horses, mainly as I struggled to keep Toby sound. I qualified as an equine bodyworker using the Equine Touch technique, studied rider posture and alignment, and learned about classical dressage exercises for straightening and strengthening horses.

My greatest joy comes from the creativity of bringing together skills and knowledge from different areas into fun and practical exercises to create healthy, happy horses.

As well as training my own horses, I teach in the UK and abroad, working with horse owners and rescue centres. I launched my first online training site, Clix College, in 2010, teaching members from around the world. This evolved into Connection Training in 2014.

RACHEL BEDINGFIELD

At the age of forty, I became a 'born-again' horsewoman, led back to horses through Hannah. I became passionate about understanding equine behaviour and creating the best life possible for our domestic horses. I organised courses so that I could study with the best horse trainers and behaviourists I could access. I developed extensive knowledge and experience about horse welfare and management, studying areas such as hoof trimming, saddle fit, and field management. In 2004 I started working as an equine nutritionist.

I founded and ran both the Natural Horse Group and the Natural Horse Company, which provided events and products aimed at improving the quality of life for domestic horses.

After breaking my back in a simple riding fall, I recognised that I had completely lost my confidence in riding. Determined not to give up, I found approaches that would help me. This was predominantly a combination of developing my own body awareness, posture and breath-work both in and out of the saddle, and improving my use of reward-based training to establish better communication with my horses. In this way, I overcame my fear and became a confident rider again. I now love to work with anxious horse-owners to build their confidence and joy with their horses.

Connection Training is strongly grounded in science, and I am responsible for bringing up-to-date science into our teaching. This has led me to study modern neuroscience to understand the emotions of horses, how horses learn best, and how to foster good feelings in training and horse life.

Along with Hannah, I pioneered online learning for positive horsemanship. In 2012 and 2013 we ran the world's first dedicated Equine Clicker Conferences, hosting international panels of speakers, who are leaders in the field of equine reward-based training. I am also a partner in Positive Horse Training, Spain, which hosts residential training courses teaching Connection Training.

VIDEO RESOURCE

HEAR OUR JOURNEY STORY

Listen to our story about how our horses have led our journey all the way in this podcast interview with Tracy Malone on Come Along for the Ride.

www.connectiontraining.com/video-resources

This book brings together our deep and wide-ranging knowledge and experience. We hope you enjoy it and that it inspires you to create even better relationships with your horses. They are our true inspiration and have led our journeys all the way. We'd like to thank them all for teaching us everything we know about building close bonds and joy with equines everywhere.

Rachel working with Roisin, while the rest of the herd wait for their turn! Connection Training creates horses who love to work and be with you, which is the best feeling in the world.

CHAPTER 1

THE EMOTIONAL HORSE

Good training is needed both for the well-being of horses and for us to be able to communicate with them and have fun together. However, good training is an addition to a healthy lifestyle, not a replacement for it. Therefore, we must begin by looking at the management of the horse.

If you start with a relaxed horse, happy in her life, the training will be rewarding and straightforward. But if your horse is already stressed—maybe through separation from herd mates, or being shut in a stable for long hours, or gut pain from having the wrong diet—your training will also be stressed and much less effective. We believe that horse owners have a duty to keep domestic horses in a way that meets their natural needs. These can be summarised with three F's: friends, freedom, and forage. In this Chapter, we look at the horse's natural behaviour and emotions, how we can best meet these needs in domesticity, and their impact on learning.

ETHOLOGY: THE SCIENCE OF NATURAL LIFE

Ethology is the study of animal behaviour and society in their natural habitats. It's vital to understand horses in their ecological niche so that we can create the best environment for their emotional and physical well-being. When we cannot provide a copycat environment for domestic horses, ethology helps us to understand their needs and provide for them in alternative ways.

Ethology is a rapidly growing area of science. Fascinating studies are being published each year, continually challenging us to improve our horse-keeping practices. We will focus on the basics in this book so that you can easily provide what your horse needs to be calm and relaxed for training. First, let's take a look at the basic needs of horses.

ENVIRONMENTAL NICHE

By the late 1970s there were no truly wild horses left in the world. The horses we generally call 'wild' are, in fact, feral, meaning that they were once bred by humans and have since escaped or been released from domesticity. Feral horses live in a broad range of environments, from high deserts to seashores. However, their common characteristic is that they prefer open spaces where they can see possible predators. Horses are good digesters of fibre, so they can live in areas where the grazing is sparse. They are social mammals, living in a group to survive predator attacks and to satisfy their emotional needs.

FRIENDS

Mares live in family bands with long-term bond mates, who provide security and companionship. Each family band has one stallion, or sometimes two. The surplus males form their own bands, called bachelor groups, which provide security and companionship for each other. Stallions will be ousted from family bands as they age or become weak, but generally the mares stay together, with some movement between bands.

Bands are not territorial. Several bands can share large home ranges and enjoy interacting as they encounter each other around the ranges, for example at water holes. Within the band, horses have complex social lives, as befits a highly developed social mammal. Constant communication goes on within the herd, as seen with ear positions, body alignment, spatial arrangements, tail swishing, and more obvious behaviours such as mutual grooming, mating, playing, caring for young, or males challenging each other for supremacy.

If a TV documentary truly showed horses' lives, it would be too boring for most people; most of the footage would show horses grazing peacefully. You'd need expert commentary to explain the subtle but constant communication between the horses. In a one-hour episode, fifty-five minutes would consist of relaxed grazing interspersed with short sleeping episodes. You'd get about five minutes of action, such as mutual grooming, play, or sexual behaviours. Rarely would you see any high-drama stallion fights, since the vast majority of horse behaviour is about creating and strengthening their social bonds and collaborating to ensure the success and survival of the group.

FREEDOM

Feral horses, from birth, move about fifteen to twenty miles per day. The prime motive for moving is nutrition. If the grass is lush, they will move less; if sparse, they will move much more.

Movement is highly important to horses' health. The four hooves act like miniature hearts, since the expansion and contraction of soft tissues in the hoof creates the necessary blood circulation in the lower legs. Movement is also important socially, as horses play, fight, and court with lots of movement.

Freedom also means that horses get to explore and experience different sounds, smells, tastes and sights. Through all the movement and travel, feral horses are constantly encountering new things in their environment.

FORAGE

A horse's digestive system needs a constant supply of high-fibre, low-sugar forage. Horses need to eat for sixteen to eighteen hours per day to keep their digestive system functioning correctly and prevent issues such as stomach ulcers and colic.

It is natural for the weight and condition of feral horses to fluctuate. They will lose a lot of weight in winter, then put weight on quickly in the spring as the fresh grass arrives. Then they will lose weight again during the summer months as the grass gets sparser and the foals more demanding. Stallions will lose weight during the mating season too, but autumn brings another flush of grass, and with lower demands, horses can build up weight again to be ready for the winter.

NATURAL MANAGEMENT

For the well-being of your horse, you need to provide as much of a natural life as possible through pasture, herd, diet, and lifestyle management. This can be difficult to do. Domestic horses are prone to laminitis, colic, and stomach ulcers due to the diets and lifestyles we provide. Giving constant access to rich grazing, for example, can make horses fat and therefore prone to laminitis, if we are unable to provide sufficient movement as well. Any separation from bond mates can cause sufficient stress for stomach ulcers to form, and lack of free movement, along with stress, can make horses prone to colic.

So, forage, friends, and freedom must be provided as a basic condition of keeping a horse. The science of ethology has provided us with the evidence. As this realisation has been accepted by horse owners, new guidelines for keeping horses are being shared. For example, more and more horse management systems enable horses to chew forage for many more hours per day than traditional systems and daily turnout with other horses is prioritised. Innovative concepts such as 'Paddock Paradise', track systems, Equi-Central, and high-tech 'smart' stables all aim to create a more natural lifestyle and provide the basic requirements for equine well-being.

THE SCIENCE OF EMOTIONS

Once you have provided the basic requirements for your horse, how do you know if he is truly happy? As a horse owner, you know your horse has feelings. You know what he likes and what he doesn't, when he's playful, and when he's frightened. For a long time, the scientific world has disregarded these suppositions because no one has been able to 'prove' them. To say your horse felt this or that was to be 'anthropomorphic' and unscientific. But science is changing. The developments coming from neuroscience are supporting what we already knew as owners. Horses do have feelings; we recognise them, and they respond to our feelings too.

The scientific word for emotional feelings is 'affect' (from the same source as 'affectionate'). The branch of science that studies the brain is neuroscience, so the scientific term for the study of emotion in the brain is 'affective neuroscience'. We have found that studying this science has given us an excellent framework for understanding our horses' emotions and associated behaviour. Connection with your horse is an emotional connection. Trying to avoid being anthropomorphic, explaining everything without that emotional component, does not reflect the truth of our experience. On the other hand, understanding the horse emotionally enhances connection.

As a new science, affective neuroscience includes competing theories about what actually happens in the brain. As this is a book about horse training, we are going to focus on the work of just one prominent scientist, but, if you are interested to explore further, it is a rich and fascinating field. We use the work of Jaak Panksepp as our guide.

Neuroscience is showing us that horses' emotional brain activity is very similar to humans. Therefore, we think it is entirely valid to ascribe emotions to their behaviours. Panksepp clearly demonstrated that *all learning and behaviour has emotion at the base*. If something feels good, the animal will work for more of it; if it feels bad, the animal will work to avoid it. Instead of 'What is my horse doing and what do I want him to do?' the primary question we ask is 'How is my horse feeling and how would I like him to feel?'

PANKSEPP'S METHODS

Panksepp studied the emotional systems in mammalian brains. By system, he meant particular structures, chemistries, and neuronal patterns that are consistent when a mammal displays behaviours associated with specific emotions.

Since many people are still sceptical about animal emotions, it is important to know that Panksepp's work is meticulous and robust. It has been published in top scientific journals and subjected to critical scrutiny by other members of the scientific community, who search for flaws in the work. If flaws are found, the scientist goes back and rechecks the data until everyone is satisfied that the work passes scrutiny. In science there is no 'proof', but instead the notion of probability and reproducibility—that is, can other scientists demonstrate the same results? Panksepp's work passed all these critical tests.

To determine which emotions animals experience, Panksepp applied electrostimulation (a painless procedure) to particular areas of the brain, then observed the animal's behaviour. He compared this behaviour to the feelings humans reported when the same brain pathway was stimulated. For example, stimulating one area caused humans to report feeling great fear. Rats, stimulated in the same area, demonstrated fear by trying to run away. When another brain area was stimulated, humans expressed great loss and guinea pigs made distress vocalisations. Brain stimulation caused animals to consistently show certain behaviours: fear behaviours, such as freeze or flight; angry behaviours, such as spitting or hissing; and caring behaviours, such as licking their young. Given the same stimulation, the feelings that humans verbally reported correlated closely to the animals' behaviour. In this way, Panksepp was able to understand how emotions work in the brain and identify which systems were involved in the feelings associated with particular behaviours.

DOES THIS FEEL GOOD TO YOU?

Panksepp also needed to scientifically demonstrate whether the emotions the animals showed felt good or bad to them. For this, he used a common scientific assessment called 'conditioned place preference or conditioned place aversion'. In other words, does an animal go back to a place where the trial was done, or does it avoid it next time?

To test this, the electrostimulation process was carried out in a particular place. Once this had been done a few times, the animal is given the choice to return to that place or go to a neutral place, not associated with the trial. If the animal returns to the trial site, it is demonstrating conditioned place preference, suggesting the effect was pleasant and the animal would like more. Alternatively, if the animal avoided the trial site and chose the neutral environment, it was demonstrating conditioned place aversion, or avoidance. You have probably observed that your horse demonstrates place preference for a feeding area and place avoidance for a fearful area, such as a horse trailer. Panksepp used this simple approach as part of demonstrating which emotions felt good or bad when stimulated.

Neuroscientists have shown that the brain has no 'neutral' state. Panksepp's brain stimulation felt either positive or negative from the animal's viewpoint. Emotional systems that feel good are known as 'appetitive'—that is, the animal has an appetite for them. Systems that feel bad are known as 'aversive'—the animal would avoid them if it could.

Rowan showing place preference for being inside the horse box. Following a progressive training programme, Rowan has experienced relaxation and lots of rewards inside the horsebox and now chooses to go inside.

This horse is showing place avoidance for the trailer as he does not want to step inside. He would leave the area completely if he could.

PANKSEPP'S SEVEN EMOTIONAL BRAIN SYSTEMS

Panksepp identified seven distinct emotional brain systems: SEEKING, RAGE, FEAR, PANIC/GRIEF, CARE, LUST, and PLAY. Place preference was shown for SEEKING, CARE, PLAY, and LUST. Place avoidance was shown for FEAR, RAGE, and PANIC/GRIEF.

Place Preference | Place Aversion
SEEKING CARE PLAY LUST | FEAR RAGE PANIC/GRIEF
FEELS GOOD | FEELS BAD

You may be wondering why the labels for these systems are written in capital letters. Panksepp deliberately capitalised them to differentiate them from our typical use of these words. He wanted people to understand that he was talking about distinct brain systems, different from each other in terms of brain structures and neurochemistry. These primary emotional systems are present in the brain at birth. That is, these emotions *do not have to be learned*. The structures involved are deep in the brain and arrived early in the evolutionary process. These systems are innate (inborn) and lead to instinctive behaviours. They are also the systems that are fundamental for the animals' life learning. Panksepp called them 'the tools for life'.

These emotional systems have evolved along with the physical behavioural systems too. For example, the SEEKING system's deepest structure is very close to the olfactory (scenting) system. It appears that the first search systems were based on scent. Following a scent led to sniffing and forward-moving behaviours, which are also characteristic of the SEEKING system. FEAR is closely related to pain, and RAGE to blood-pressure sensors in the arteries. These systems cannot be separated from the physiology of animals. The brain and body are one system, and the emotional systems are at one with physiological systems that try to keep the body stable and functioning well.

INSTINCT: INNER EMOTIONS DRIVE EXTERNAL BEHAVIOURS

Instinct is behaviour that new-borns don't have to learn. The mammal performs behaviours, such as searching for the nipple, from some sort of innate programming. These behaviours are not a response to an external environment stimulus. But what drives the behaviour? This is a key question scientists have been trying to answer for a long time.

Certainly, searching for milk is often the first behaviour we see. In species like horses, that requires a lot of other behaviours: getting up, moving around, and finding the sweet spot. We know the behaviour is not driven by hunger or thirst. Why? Because new-borns normally arrive in a good blood-sugar state. It is an evolutionary advantage to be well-fed at birth, since getting the next meal is a risky business. The better nutritional state the animal is in at birth, the more chance it has of surviving.

If searching for the nipple is not caused by a feeling of hunger, what else could drive the behaviour? Panksepp liked to call these innate impulses 'ancestral memories': information passed down through the generations that contains the instructions for survival for that species. Therefore the foal is "pre-programmed" to get to its feet and find the nipple to drink.

The emotional system that is highly active in this process is the SEEKING system. It is associated with sniffing and forward movement. The first voluntary move the foal makes is to lift its head. This behaviour is triggered by the arousal of the SEEKING system.

At just 8 hours old, Maverick is already standing and suckling competently.

No external environmental stimulus is required to initiate the head lift. The brain's SEEKING system gets aroused by internal brain instructions, and the associated behaviour is to lift the head and scent the air. The SEEKING system feels good; it is appetitive. In other words, the brain chemistry involved with the arousal of the SEEKING system creates good feelings in the brain, arising mainly from the release of dopamine. Therefore, the search for food resources, even before the actual reward of finding the food, feels good.

As a foal starts to move her head voluntarily, following instinct, learning immediately happens. The scientific term for learning is 'conditioning'. As soon as the foal lifts her head, the muscles, tendons, and nerves that are required for head lifting start to get conditioned—in other words, more efficient at the behaviour. The brain connections to this behaviour also get conditioned. Certain neurons fire up and start to create pathways in the brain, which is part of the process of making behaviours more efficient. This learning is taking place in a feel-good brain state, so these movements will feel good. The end point of these behaviours is to drink milk, which is the food reward. But all along the way to gaining that reward, the foal's brain is being rewarded by having an aroused SEEKING system: by the increasing intensity of the milk smell, by the protective bulk of her mother's body (which stimulates the CARE system too), and then by the muzzle touch at the udder. It is the brain that is being rewarded, by the release of dopamine and other feel-good chemicals. The brain will note which behaviour caused a dopamine release and will instruct the body to repeat those behaviours, so the foal learns how to find the milk quicker and quicker. Each time the foal drinks some milk, the search is over and the SEEKING system powers down momentarily.

At the same time, the foal is struggling. She lifts her head, but then gets tired and drops it again. She finds the teat, but the mare moves and she loses it again. These problems stimulate the feel-bad systems: PANIC/GRIEF when she loses track and RAGE when she fails and gets frustrated. These systems stimulate the release of the chemicals associated with feeling stressed, such as norepinephrine. The brain is receiving punishers as well as rewards.

What we can conclude from this is:

• Behaviours are always associated with innate emotional states. Every behaviour has a "feels good" or "feels bad" history in the brain

• All learning, therefore, is associated with these emotional states, good or bad.

• Learning often involves both good and bad emotional states. Frustration, for example, is usually part of the learning process.

• For horses to enjoy learning, it is important that the good-feeling emotional states are aroused much more than any associated bad-feeling emotional states.

• Animals' brains are designed to cope with bad-feeling emotional states, provided they are relieved from the stress, too. Not getting relief creates chronic stress, especially in flight animals who are primed to react to acute stressors for survival, but not chronic stressors. Chronic stress leads to physiological changes which may develop into illness.

The Connection Training approach mimics these innate natural behaviours that come packaged in the foal. For example, one of the first things we teach the horse is to touch an object with his muzzle. This stimulates the SEEKING system and mimics the foal's search for the nipple, or an older horse's search for a tasty plant. When the muzzle touches the object, we deliver a reward, exactly as milk is delivered when the foal's muzzle reaches the udder or when the horse finds a special leaf amongst the grass. Our aim is for the training to feel good overall and thus for the horse to feel good about us. They associate us with feeling good, and so the beginning of the connection is made.

Now let's look at the seven systems in more detail and see how they create behaviour and affect training.

THE APPETITIVE EMOTIONAL BRAIN SYSTEMS

The positive-feeling systems are SEEKING, CARE, LUST, and PLAY. When these brain systems are triggered, they will make your horse feel good. He'll repeat anything that triggered them, from returning to a specific location to repeating a certain rewarding behaviour. At Connection Training, we work to maximise the SEEKING, CARE, and PLAY systems during training so that our horses find training rewarding and desirable.

SEEKING SYSTEM
The SEEKING system is responsible for making animals 'get up and go' to search for what they need to survive and thrive. An activated SEEKING system feels good to animals because it drives them forward to what they want and need. The behavioural

characteristics of an active SEEKING system are moving forward, sniffing, searching, exploring and problem-solving with varying degrees of excitement. The SEEKING system is also employed in finding solutions to aversive events, such as escaping a predator.

Although the SEEKING system is always aroused to some extent, chronic stress and traumatic experiences can cause it to operate at a very low level of arousal. This is actually depression. The horse has little interest in the world and is not curious about the training, the environment, or perhaps even food treats. Generally, in this case, we say the horse is 'shut down'. It can be caused by chronic pain, some medical conditions, loss of a beloved companion, living conditions or by "learned helplessness".

Naturally, your horse's SEEKING system is engaged when he is browsing, searching, and exploring.

Learned helplessness often occurs with punishment-based training when the horse has learned that it is futile to try any behaviours because the response is always punishment. For example, a horse who tried to avoid bit pressure by opening his mouth. The human then attaches a flash noseband, preventing this, and the horse cannot then find a release from the

pain. So they learn that they are helpless in that situation and their best option is to withdraw and not to try at all. Systems of horsemanship that say 'I don't want my horse to think' or 'I want my horse to obey my commands without question' may create learned helplessness. Horses trained this way look robotic when they are with their trainers, do everything that is asked of them without question, and are mentally closed to environmental stimuli. Their SEEKING systems will be operating at a low level of arousal during training and they are likely to be shut down in other situations.

In training, activating the SEEKING system is a key element of your horse's curiosity, mental engagement and problem-solving.

CARE SYSTEM

In many mammals, the CARE system is activated primarily in mothers when they have young, but also in fathers who are involved in care giving. It is also the system for bonding in herd mammals, such as horses. Behaviours associated with this system are licking, mutual grooming, touching, close spatial arrangements, mimicking others' behaviour, sharing food, and eating together. These bonding behaviours are driven by oxytocin release in the brain. This feels good, and horses will prefer to spend time with other horses and humans they have experienced CARE with. This is an important part of training and building a bond with your horse - you want him to come running when he sees you, rather than be indifferent or try to avoid you.

Simply hanging out with your horse is a lovely way to build your bond, including grooming and scratching if your horse enjoys it.

In herd life, the CARE system shows up through behaviours such as mutual grooming, nuzzling and being in close proximity.

When watching horses, the easiest way to determine pair bonds and thus the action of the CARE system is to observe their spatial arrangements. Pair-bonded horses will graze closely together, usually mimicking each other's stance, such as leading with the same foot. They often graze with muzzles almost touching. They will loaf together and stand head to tail so they can keep each other free of flies. They will lie close together, or one will lie down with the other standing over in a close and probably guarding way.

PLAY SYSTEM

The PLAY system is strongly active in young mammals, who will exhibit play behaviours if they are relatively secure. In adults, play is generally continued more by males and is associated with fight behaviours such as play-fighting. Horses also play by running together, rearing, prancing, bucking, and leaping. The mares enjoy this type of play, especially when it's sexual play. There is also object play, which naturally occurs when horses are exploring something new, such as picking up sticks or splashing around in water. In domestic horses, object play is seen in behaviours such as chasing balls and picking up objects.

The PLAY system is designed so that young animals learn to perfect the innate behaviours they are born primed to perform. For example, running play helps young foals strengthen their limbs, condition their muscles, and become better at balance, transitions, negotiating rough terrain and moving in sync with the herd.

Play can take many forms for horses, such as running, posturing and playing with objects. Male horses love to playfight; older horses like Pegaso will spend time playing with colts like Tiny.

Play also performs a vital social function in social mammals, since it is through play that young animals create their relationships with each other. Play in young males is important for them to learn fighting skills and who they can fight with and who they should avoid. One study showed that stallions played up to 6 times more with their sons than other young stallions in the bachelor herds. This will confer an advantage on the sons who will be more likely to succeed in winning a band and passing on their genes.

How you incorporate PLAY with your horse will depend on your horse's personal preferences. Hannah's pony, Toby, has always loved to run and posture with her, but play could include fun puzzle-solving, object games and exploration or other movement-based exercises your horse enjoys.

LUST SYSTEM

Clearly, the LUST system is there to initiate procreation. Lust is a high-energy emotion and creates lots of the play behaviours we love in horses: the high-stepping movement, poses, rears, and collection. It also creates many unwanted behaviours in domestic horses, such as posing and rearing when we're not asking for it and distraction, spookiness, and increased separation anxiety.

Sexual relationships form strong cohesive behaviours, so the LUST system will be affectively positive. For the neighbouring bands of bachelor stallions, however, it is presumably a frustrating emotion. They can smell mares in season and watch sexual behaviours but cannot join in. Thus, they will fight with other stallions if they think there is an opportunity to mate, despite living happily in bachelor herds. Research has shown that, in domesticity, stallions housed in groups, rather than singularly as we tend to keep them, are more relaxed and virile than lone stallions.

Dealing with the consequences of sexual behaviour in domestic horses creates a moral dilemma for horse owners, and it's a debate that needs to be continually addressed. As far as the LUST system is concerned, being able to enjoy and express it creates an enriched life, but not allowing full sexual behaviour creates frustration. In the rest of our discussion, we'll leave the LUST system out because it is not an emotional system we typically engage with for training. However, the effects of the LUST system do create issues in training, such as the unpredictability of a mare in season or when working with stallions and some geldings. We need to be aware of these issues, and there may be direct behaviours arising from the LUST system which we do have to manage through training. An example would be teaching stallions to be quiet and relaxed around other horses when being ridden.

Although the LUST system leads to mating, there are many other behaviours associated with it, such as sniffing, posing, squealing and nipping.

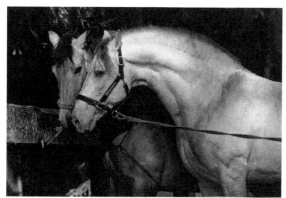

Awareness of LUST-related behaviours in stallions, geldings and mares is important when managing or handling horses in a domestic situation.

THE AVERSIVE EMOTIONAL SYSTEMS

The aversive emotional systems of FEAR, RAGE, and PANIC/GRIEF feel bad. When these emotional systems are activated, horses will demonstrate place avoidance and will use their SEEKING system to find a way to escape what triggered them. When the FEAR, RAGE, and PANIC/GRIEF systems are triggered over and over again through aversive training or management, they create stress and illness in horses. With Connection Training, we actively work to minimise the presence of these emotional systems and certainly do not base training on activating them.

FEAR SYSTEM

Designed to keep the animal alive, the FEAR system is all about the fear of losing one's life. It is triggered by pain or the anticipation of pain. The tell-tale behaviours of this system include freezing in place, listening and looking intently to find the source of the fear, orienting the body to the source of the fear, and running away—in other words, freeze and flight behaviours.

When humans have their FEAR system electrically stimulated, they report feeling great dread, as if in fear of their lives. Rats who have had their FEAR system stimulated will demonstrate avoidance for the place where it took place. If they have no way to escape, they will behave fearfully: clinging to the side walls, hiding where possible, and sniffing for danger. Horses, too, exhibit place avoidance where they have felt fear. They may baulk at going down a path where they previously got a fright or show anxiety when the vet turns up because she inflicted pain last time.

Activation of the FEAR system is commonly used in many horse training methods. These include using a lunge whip behind the horse to get him moving forward, waving a rope under the horse's chin to get him to back up, or using spurs to inflict pain to create forwards movement. Needless to say, Connection Training does not use these methods.

As prey animals, the FEAR system is easily aroused in horses and leads to spooking and flight.

Spooking is also caused by arousal of the FEAR system. As prey animals, horses have a sensitised FEAR system. This means that the neuronal connections are fast and that smaller stimuli create big responses. Horses are quick to feel fearful and spooking is the cause of many behavioural problems in horses. As horse owners, we need to teach our horses to feel confident and relaxed in novel or potentially spooky situations.

The FEAR system is often deliberately activated in some horse training methods to activate the flight response and make the horse move. In this picture, you can clearly see how the horse is extremely tense as she tries to avoid the unpleasant situation.

RAGE SYSTEM

Whereas the FEAR system promotes a freeze or flight response, the RAGE system is responsible for fight. With horses, its purpose is usually defensive, to fight off a predator or another threat such as entrapment, frustration, or irritation. When the RAGE system is stimulated, the mammal will express it outwardly; humans report feeling angry and needing to blame someone. It seems to be impossible to feel RAGE without also needing something or someone to blame, hence the outward expressions towards the environment.

In horses, the sensitivity of the RAGE system is likely to be less than that in predators. Being herbivores, they are more

peaceable. Donkeys, though, will turn and fight on many occasions, so their RAGE system is probably more sensitised than that of horses. This is an example of how the brain evolves along with the body in response to different environmental niches. Horses evolved to use running away on open plains as their go-to strategy, so their FEAR system is highly sensitised. Asses evolved in higher, rocky places, where running away was more difficult and there were more possibilities to get trapped. Therefore, they evolved with a higher fight response to predators, which in the brain means a more sensitised RAGE system. Although we are not aware of any brain studies that show this (and it would be difficult!), we infer it from the different behavioural responses to predators between horses and donkeys, and from understanding their different evolutionary niches.

When a horse's FEAR system is activated, he'll want to run away. If he's trapped or caught and can't escape, the RAGE system will be activated and the horse will instead fight for freedom. The RAGE system inhibits the FEAR system, resulting in the strength and determination that comes from 'blind rage'. A common example is a horse who fights the vet or farrier when he is afraid and is not allowed to escape.

In their natural environments, horses perform many more affiliative behaviours between each other than they do aggressive behaviours. This makes sense because their individual survival depends on their inclusion in the herd, so they create strong bonds that are maintained by the affiliative behaviours. However, the RAGE system is responsible for inter-male dominance behaviours and for resource

RAGE includes defensive behaviours such as this mare guarding her foal. Horses generally only attack when they feel the threat is extreme.

When a horse is fearful but not allowed to flee, the RAGE system can be activated causing horses to bite, threaten and kick. This response is often seen when being treated by a vet or when being groomed, rugged or tacked up. This zorse (zebra x Arabian) came to his owner with a strong aversion to saddles and blankets, leading to dangerous behaviour when approached with one. You can see how we helped him to overcome this in Chapter 7.

guarding, such as when a mare keeps others away from her foal.

Compared to feral horses, the RAGE system in domestic horses is probably at a much higher arousal level due to the artificial competition for food and personal space. Domestic horses are kept in stables and small paddocks, and even when they are in larger fields, the fence usually appears before they have run out of natural ranging space. This means they will feel frustration, which is part of the RAGE system. Domestic horses also experience a great deal of entrapment. We confine them with halters and ropes to tie them up and hold them still, shut them in stables for extended periods of time, and use gadgets such as nosebands, martingales and tethers to restrict their movement. All of these can arouse the RAGE system since they are unable to escape the situation when they wish.

Domestic horses are often subject to fearful stimuli where they are not allowed to express their natural flight response, so the brain then switches on the RAGE system. An example of this is a horse fighting desperately to get out of a horsebox when he is fearful and has been shut inside, unable to escape. Another expression of the RAGE system commonly seen in domestic horses is resource guarding, where they defend their access to food, water, friends and other valuable resources. In domesticity this resource-guarding often leads to the formation of a pseudo-dominance hierarchy. The horses learn who guards the feed buckets most fiercely and learns to avoid aggressive encounters by avoiding interactions. For example, an individual may wait for enough feed buckets for all the other horses before eating.

However, it's important to know that this observation is not a true dominance hierarchy. If the horses did not have to compete for any resources then this behaviour would not happen. No dominance hierarchies have been seen in feral herds and dominance behaviours in feral horses are very much the minimum. Their survival depends on staying together, so their behaviour is mainly for promoting bonds.

PANIC/GRIEF SYSTEM

Panksepp originally labelled this system PANIC as its stimulation caused the same behaviours as young animals exhibit when they are separated from their mothers. However, he realised that this was the system which creates the feeling of grief when a human loses a loved one, so he decided to give it both names. Because it is innate in horses to stay with their herd,

PANIC/GRIEF is seen in horses throughout their life and is the cause of separation anxiety.

Associated behaviours are distress vocalisations, searching for the lost companion, and returning to the place they last saw their bond mates. A common example in training is horses who shout when they are taken away from their companion. The companion who is left behind will often shout back and pace the field or stable in an attempt to be reunited.

Separation anxiety feels bad to the animal and is physically closely linked to the gut. The stress of separation anxiety is a probable cause of many horses having stomach ulcers, in both horses taken away and their companions left at home.

One of the most important parts of Panksepp's work was the discovery that there are separate systems for the general expression of fear and for the anxiety arising from loss. Generally, we tend to lump fear, anxiety, and panic together as one thing. The significant difference is that the FEAR system is about the fear of physically losing your life, including fear of pain and injury. The PANIC/GRIEF system, on the other hand, is about social loss, about being alone in the world without emotional support. In many social mammals, such as horses, being alone is effectively a death sentence because it makes them susceptible to predators, so it is highly sensitised in these animals.

Feral horses live as a herd, so the PANIC/GRIEF system will be activated only in extreme circumstances, such as a trapped or injured horse who cannot keep up. It will also be seen briefly when a foal realises he's strayed too far from his mother but will be quickly rectified when he gallops back to her. In domesticity, however, distress vocalisations are all too common. Horses are expected to tolerate being separated and alone, either permanently or temporarily when they are stabled alone, ridden out alone, travelled alone, or turned out alone. Horses who are under the expression of this emotion become dangerous to themselves because its power is so strong.

Since humans can be entirely happy when alone, the horse's distress is often ignored, belittled, and generally not taken seriously, unless it is so extreme that something has to be done. A common example is the way many foals are weaned in domesticity. A baby foal, far younger than the natural weaning age, is abruptly removed from his mother. He is shut up in a stable without her, with no possibility of escape. He will cry and cry. Although this is frequently distressing to the humans around, they squash the feelings by saying, 'It won't last long. He has to learn to be alone. He'll soon get used to it.'

The horse's PANIC/GRIEF system kicks in if they are separated from the herd. Their survival depends on them staying together, so this is strong in horses throughout their life.

In fact, the foal goes through a massively painful process of arousal of the PANIC/GRIEF system. He cries and cries, waits and listens. His SEEKING system is working overtime trying to find an escape, so he wheels round and round the box, trying to get out and back to his mother. But as his attempts fail, his SEEKING system gets progressively shut down, which means he gets quieter and quieter.

He seems to be 'getting used to it'. In fact, he is in a state of despair and then depression. This loss will then have sensitised his PANIC/GRIEF system in the brain, meaning that all future social losses will be felt much more deeply and keenly than nature intended.

This type of management, in which the animal has no possibility of escape from the aversive experience, is known as 'flooding'. The subsequent quietness is, in fact, learned helplessness. This means that the aversive situation cannot be avoided or escaped, so the SEEKING system cannot find a solution and is dampened down. The animal gives up trying, but the internal emotional state is depression from grief, not relaxation. Simply changing the weaning practise can help foals to be separated without trauma and be much more confident horses for the rest of their lives. Best practise is to gradually wean the foal, starting at seven months at the earliest. The foal spends increasing time away from his dam and with a group, ideally composed of young and older horses. It then becomes quite easy to simply increase the separation time until the foal is weaned.

Horses vary widely in how sensitive they are to separation. This is a function of personality but is probably highly modified by their life experiences, such as how they were weaned. There are some horses who are naturally more confident and content when on their own. Through careful training, you can help most horses with average separation anxiety become much more relaxed with herd separations. However, in our opinion, some horses experience separation anxiety so painfully that the fairest approach is to ensure they always have an equine companion when being trained or taken out.

In domesticity, horses often feel strong separation anxiety when left alone or taken away from their herd mates. They will stare after and call to their companions, often pacing and searching for a way to reunite.

EMOTIONAL SYSTEMS WORK TOGETHER

While we've looked at the emotional systems in isolation, in reality they all work together at various levels of arousal. For example, when horses are grazing together, their SEEKING systems are active at a relaxed level as they forage through the grass, picking and rejecting various plants. Meanwhile, their CARE systems are activated as they graze side by side with their bond mates. Maybe a mare is coming into season, and today she is grazing close by her favourite gelding, who is also triggered to stay close to her by arousal of his LUST system, too. Then another mare comes alongside. The first mare pins her ears and swishes her tail as her RAGE system triggers resource guarding to protect her mate. Soon another gelding comes along. They all graze for a while and then start to snooze in the sun. The two geldings mutually groom, their CARE systems aroused. This grooming session stimulates the PLAY system, and they indulge in a bit of bitey boy-play.

Suddenly a farm dog appears out of the hedge. The horses spook, their FEAR system going from low to high arousal in an instant. They gallop off and then turn and look to see what scared them. They realise it's the dog they know, and the mares engage in the game they play with him: they start to chase him, and they all end up running around together.

Next, a person comes along and takes away the first gelding. Although the mare in season is left with companions, she doesn't like to be left by him. Her PANIC/GRIEF system is aroused. She wants to get to the gelding, but she can't, so stays at the gate where she last saw him. Although she isn't shouting for him, she can't settle back to grazing and paces up and down. When the gelding appears back in sight, she whinnies in greeting and then follows closely behind him as he walks back into the field. Now the PANIC/GRIEF system powers down, and the mare's CARE and SEEKING systems are able to return her to a relaxed state.

HOW THE EMOTIONAL SYSTEMS AFFECT EACH OTHER

As you can see, the emotional systems are affected by what is going on around the horse. In addition, some emotional systems have the effect of stimulating or inhibiting others.

For example, arousal of the CARE system acts as an antidote to the FEAR system. In human medicine, trials have shown that when people hold the hand of a loved one during treatment, their fear indicators, such as an increased heart rate, sweaty palms, and higher adrenaline levels, are greatly reduced. Oxytocin (the 'bonding' hormone) is released with the CARE system, and this hormone calms and reassures us.

The RAGE system can also inhibit the FEAR system. A horse who starts to feel scared in a horsebox can quickly turn to fighting to get out. Initially, the SEEKING system works with the FEAR system to find a way of escape. When that fails, and if the fear arousal is high enough, the brain will activate the RAGE system. At an elevated level of RAGE arousal, SEEKING is inhibited. The horse stops looking for solutions in a rational way and instead gets into a 'blind rage', willing to do anything to escape, even at the cost of injuries to himself.

OVER-SENSITISED EMOTIONAL SYSTEMS

A healthy brain can experience and deal with *all* these emotional systems, and this leads to a rich life. However, if one system has been over-sensitised—such as the PANIC/GRIEF system with early-weaned foals—then the brain will find this system difficult to cope with whenever it is aroused. Even a small trigger of an over-sensitised system will create a big response.

We often see that rescue horses have difficulty maintaining moderate emotional states. They may be very fearful of humans when they first arrive. Through careful training and a better environment, they begin to lose some of their fear, but it can often be triggered much more easily throughout their life than a horse who has not suffered the same fear-inducing trauma.

Overcoming fear and building trust with rescue ponies can take some time and expertise, as shown by CT Coach, Megan Hines. They may still remain more highly sensitised to fearful experiences.

EMOTIONAL RESILIENCE

Being able to function well under the influence of the painful emotional systems is known as 'emotional resilience'. This is the ability to feel some fear, rage, or panic, but be able to stay calm enough to think and make a useful response during the situation and to return quickly to a calm emotional state when the arousing stimulus has passed. Emotional resilience is vital for any animal. It allows animals to live a confident and happy life as they learn to deal with challenges calmly and competently.

Domestic horses often have very little chance to build emotional resilience and problem-solving abilities due to the way they're managed. Everything they need is easily accessible to them, and they have little choice in their diet, companions, or exploring further than their paddock. We think it's important to create as much choice and complexity in your horse's life as possible. This is known as "enrichment" and involves providing simulations of natural challenges and opportunities, to enrich an animal's life. In addition we like to train emotional resilience too. As a result, horses become better equipped to deal with difficult situations such as vet visits, travelling, or meeting something unexpected while out hacking.

THE CONNECTION ZONE—STAYING BELOW THRESHOLD

All the emotional systems can be aroused at different levels. Panksepp showed this by increasing the electrical currents during electro-stimulation. For example, at low levels of current in the FEAR system, animals may freeze or sniff the air. At high levels, though, they may run around, desperately seeking a way out of the situation; they are in "flight" mode. So, we need to take into account the level of arousal of the emotions in training too.

When the positive emotional systems are over aroused, the horse will be too excited to think. When the aversive emotional systems are over aroused, the horse will be too scared, anxious, or angry to think. Either way, when the horse's emotional states are over aroused, it is known as being 'over threshold'. Horses that are over threshold are unable to think, make

decisions, learn, or focus on you or the training.

In Connection Training, we aim to keep the emotional arousal levels high enough for the horse to be motivated to try, but low enough for the horse to stay below threshold. We call this the Connection Zone. It is a key factor in successful training.

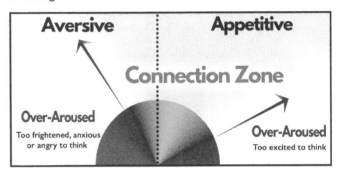

Engaged with the training and below threshold, the horse can make behavioural choices. If the horse can think, she can solve problems calmly. The brain is then clearer about what behaviour worked and what didn't. Those learning memories will then be stored in the brain in a way that makes them easier to access when the horse is faced with the same decision again. Choosing the same behaviour will create further success for the horse, so the memory will be placed even more strongly and the learning will be even more effective. We have found that learning within the Connection Zone is more effective and more reliable than any other learning. Our primary focus is to create positive-feeling training that is also relaxed, calm, and connected with you.

THE EMOTIONAL NATURE OF LEARNING

Learning is occurring at all times in the brain to help the animal succeed and stay safe. The brain pays attention to significant cues - such as places, objects, sounds, and situations - that predict a certain outcome, which creates either good or bad feelings. Basically, the brain begins to create a pathway between receiving the cue and the behavioural response. These pathways are strengthened each time the behaviour is repeated in association with the cue.

Pavlov's dogs are a notable example. Pavlov rang a bell just before the dogs got fed. Initially, the bell meant nothing to the dogs; it was just another noise in the environment. They did not salivate when the bell rang, but only when they got their food. But as soon as the ringing was followed by food, the bell left a trace in the brain cells, like making a faint mark with a pencil. The next time the bell was followed by food, the trace was strengthened, like adding another pencil stroke to the original mark.

The delivery of food increased the level of dopamine in the brain. Dopamine has many functions, one of which is to signal pleasure or the anticipation of pleasure. Each time the bell was followed by food, the trace got stronger because the brain is designed to pay attention to cues that predict a desired outcome, such as food. Essentially, this is what learning is: the brain learning to pay attention to cues that predict good feelings (rewards) or bad feelings (punishers).

With Pavlov's dogs, the sequence in the brain initially was:

Hear bell → Smell food → Release dopamine

After enough repetitions, the association with the bell was strong enough for the pattern to change. The sound of the bell had become such a reliable predictor of reward that the brain sequence became:

Hear bell → Release dopamine

Pavlov was unable to examine the brain to see this pathway in the way scientists can now. But he saw the dogs salivating as soon as the bell rang and *before* the food arrived. The salivating was the symptom of the dopamine release in anticipation of food, which feels highly rewarding to the animal.

Pavlov's experiments are a notable example of "classical conditioning". The bell came to be associated with the food. The cue of the bell predicted that a reward was on its way. The SEEKING system primes the brain to be aware of any cues in the environment that will lead to food. With repetition, the sound of the bell becomes associated with food. This means that the dogs will increasingly pay attention to the bell; the cue is getting strengthened as the pathway in the brain gets more defined and permanent, through a process known as "myelination". This means that the neurons involved in this pathway get a coating of "insulation" each time the behaviour is repeated. This makes the message quicker and more reliable, just as good insulation improves electric signals in cables. However, not only is the bell a cue to predict a reward, it becomes rewarding in its own right. At first the bell meant nothing to the dogs. It was a "neutral stimulus" and was not marked by the brain as significant. But as it began to be associated with the food and became a reliable predictor that food was on its way, the dogs would get a rewarding shot of dopamine in their brains at the sound of the bell. The reward of dopamine was released in the brain when the bell sounded, before the food was delivered.

A cue that predicts aversive outcomes can also be reinforced. For example when a horse is exposed to an electric fence for the first time. The horse reaches across the fence to get to the grass on the other side and receives a shock. This pain stimulates the FEAR system and the horse will snort, spook or run away. It has been punished by the shock which means the brain has had a shot of aversive neurotransmitters in the arousal of the FEAR system. The horse approaches the fence again. The grass is irresistible and he didn't realise it was touching the fence that caused the pain. He repeats the behaviour and gets shocked again. The brain reviews what happened just before the pain and may decide it was that particular place. So the horse moves away from there and repeats the behaviour at a different place. He gets another shock. This time the brain starts to link the fence with the pain and FEAR, The next time, the horse approaches cautiously. He reaches out with his muzzle, exploring the fence. His whiskers sense the charge and the horse snorts and moves away. Now the fence is a cue. If the horse avoids touching it, he can avoid the aversive.

As there is no neutral in the brain, the horse has to feel something when he sees the fence. The fence cue arouses the FEAR system, which is why the horse continues to avoid it. This is negative reinforcement. The negative part means that something that feels bad is taken away, like subtracting a number in mathematics. So the horse sees the fence, feels the FEAR system arousal, which is aversive, and moves away, which switches off the fear arousal. In order for the horse to learn to avoid the fence *he needed to feel the aversive feelings first* in order to learn the cues that predict them and do the behaviour which avoids them.

In this way, it's easy to see that all behaviours have a feeling attached to them. If a behaviour is learned with rewards, like reacting to the sound of the bell, the feeling in the brain will be good. If the learning happened through punishment, as with the electric fence, the feeling will be bad.

RELIEF IS NOT A REWARD

When choosing how to reward your horse, remember that relief of pressure is not the same as a reward. For example, let's say that you're working on improving your horse's trot, looking for more impulsion in his movement. If you're creating that trot by chasing him forward with a whip or spur, he feels coerced into it. The situation triggers his FEAR and RAGE emotional systems. His SEEKING system is aroused to help work out how to escape these bad feelings. When he finds the correct answer, you stop coercing him and release the pressure. This causes the RAGE and FEAR systems to "dial down" which creates a calmer, more relaxed brain. Exterior signs of calming, such as licking and chewing, accompany this relief of pressure. That is not reward. That is relief of discomfort. This way of training is called "negative reinforcement". Your horse soon learns that the only way he can get rid of these feelings of fear and rage is to go forward more. He does learn to give you an improved trot, but the emotions associated with those cues are frustration and fear.

PRIMARY AND SECONDARY REINFORCEMENT

Back to Pavlov's Dogs. The food reward they got is known as a "primary reinforcer". The brain did not have to learn that food is rewarding. It is innately programmed that way.

However, after the associative learning, the sound of the bell now releases a shot of dopamine, the sound of the bell itself has become rewarding. *This shows that a cue that predicts a reward becomes rewarding in its own right.* The bell is known as a "secondary reinforcer". The brain had to go through a learning process to gain the dopamine reward from the bell which is why it is known as "secondary". As opposed to the "primary" reinforcer, where no learning was needed for the reinforcer to be rewarding. .

If the bell started to not be followed by food, the dopamine release when it was rung would diminish over time, until it disappeared completely. The brain now learns that the bell doesn't mean a reward. This is known as "extinction". The interesting fact is the brain creates a new pathway to learn that the bell is not rewarding. It does not erase the original pathway where the brain learned that the bell was appetitive. It creates a whole new pathway to learn that the bell has no significant meaning.

As the brain is never neutral, this new pathway is created by punishment. The bell rings, dopamine is released, no food follows so the animal experiences disappointment, or arousal of the RAGE system. Thus, the sound of the bell starts to create an aversive affect. Repeated bell ringing will produce less dopamine as the brain creates this new association of hearing it with the feeling of the RAGE system. This is a different pathway from the original learning. It is easy to re-condition the original pathway by just following the bell once with a reward. This will trigger the old pathway and it will quickly be back in action.

HOW THE EMOTIONS OF LEARNING AFFECT HORSE TRAINING

Plainly, the brain is sorting out cues that predict rewards or punishers all the time. Therefore, there is always an emotional tone to any learning. Because the brain has no neutral state, all learning is driven by either looking for rewards - which arouses the SEEKING, CARE, and PLAY systems - or avoiding punishers to

minimise the arousal of the FEAR, RAGE, and PANIC/GRIEF systems.

So every behaviour your horse does feels either good or bad when it is being learned. For example, at feeding time, it is common for horses to learn the cues associated with the feeding process. Your arrival at the gate is a cue. The open stable door is a cue. The feed bucket is a cue. As the horses approach the feed, knowing they are going to get it, they will have lots of dopamine rushing around their brains and will be in a state of happy anticipation, with the SEEKING system highly aroused. They will demonstrate place preference for the feeding location, and it may be difficult to take them away from it. After sufficient repetitions, dopamine will be released earlier and earlier in the sequence of predictable cues. Soon your horses will get a dopamine rush when you appear, and you will have become a conditioned (learned) cue for rewards. Your horses are then likely to demonstrate 'conditioned person preference' and will whinny when you appear, since you are a predictor of rewarding feelings.

On the other hand, a horse who has needed a lot of veterinary treatment may start to feel anxious at the sight of the vet arriving. Her brain has learned to associate the cue of the vet with the fearful feelings the veterinary procedures create. She will try to get away to avoid the aversive feelings. Her FEAR system is highly aroused, and all her focus is on escaping. She is demonstrating place avoidance. Soon she will start to feel anxious at the sound of the vet's car arriving, and she'll try to escape then. If the vet comes before you've brought her in, she could be difficult to catch. She will demonstrate 'conditioned person avoidance' and avoid that vet as much as she can.

Horses will also make associations with different objects. For example, it's common for horses to come running when they see someone approach the field with hay nets, but run away if they see a person approach with a halter. This is because they associate hay nets with feeling good and halters with unpleasant feelings they'd rather avoid.

Your bond with your horse will strengthen the more you are associated with good feelings, built through spending relaxed time together, grooming, providing interest and excitement as well as the usual 'good stuff' like feed buckets and special treats.

Basically, training choices are as simple as that. You can either use methods that stimulate FEAR, RAGE, and PANIC/GRIEF or choose those that stimulate SEEKING, CARE, and PLAY. The simple question is:

Would you rather chase your horse, stimulating the flight response, to get him to move, or engage his curiosity so he moves forward under the arousal of the SEEKING system, in happy exploration? Connection Training is all about the latter. It is new and different for horse training, but the brain science completely supports it as the most rewarding and efficient method of training. It is also the fairest and the one that will create a happy, relaxed, and safe horse.

Unfortunately, many training systems are based on arousing the FEAR system. Furthermore, many horses live in systems where RAGE is stimulated by entrapment in stables, forceful handling, and competition with other horses for resources such as hay or water. They may also have an aroused PANIC/GRIEF system if they are left alone or are separated from their preferred companions.

In those cases, training based on arousing the positive emotions will help to relieve stress a bit, but it is no substitute for a better lifestyle. Creating a horse-friendly management system is the foundation of creating a happy, healthy horse who is ready for training.

VIDEO RESOURCE

THE WAY HORSES FEEL

Rachel explains all of the emotional brain systems in horses, with plenty of footage to see the behaviour is real life situations.

www.connectiontraining.com/video-resources

CHAPTER 2

YOUR HORSE'S EMOTIONS

As we discussed in Chapter 1, we need horses to be emotionally in the "Connection Zone" in order to train them successfully. This is a place where they are interested yet calm, motivated to learn and not so excited, angry or fearful that communication is difficult. In this Chapter we'll look more closely at understanding horses' emotions and some techniques to help you assess the best training approaches for your own horse.

ASSESSING YOUR HORSE

Before you start training we recommend you begin by assessing your horse, evaluating her temperament, her natural preferences and understanding your current relationship. First of all, you need to get a handle on how reactive or phlegmatic your horse is. How likely she is to get over-aroused or to be very fearful. Or maybe you have a horse who is pretty laid-back or is difficult to motivate and interest in her work.

Then it's good to know how much of a pair-bond you and your horse have already created. Maybe your horse is new to you and you're just getting to know each other. Or maybe you have a long history together and a great relationship to build on. Or, perhaps you've had long-term issues which you've tried to solve using various approaches. By assessing your horse's temperament and reactions to you, you'll be able to tailor the training to her needs to be successful from the very first session.

OBSERVING EMOTIONAL STATES

Since the acceptance that horses have feelings is relatively new in the scientific world, it's not surprising that there has been little study into how they express their feelings. This is something that most horse owners have a good 'feel' for, although they may find that their feelings get dismissed by professionals, such as some vets, transporters, farriers or trainers, when they are trying to explain their concerns. Since the scientific world is now accepting the emotional side of animal life, more work is being done to objectively identify emotional states. Here are some of the methods being used.

PHYSIOLOGICAL SIGNS

Heart rate is the easiest indicator of stress, excitement, or relaxation. Heart rate variability can give us useful insight into the internal balance of the horse. For example, it can tell us whether they are reacting 'normally' to stressors, or are not adapting well, indicating a lack of coping with the situation. Other techniques used include measuring changes in eye temperature, salivary, urinary, faecal, hair and blood cortisol levels. Although accurate measures of physiological changes, these are not practical for daily monitoring when handling and training. For that, we need to look at behavioural signs you can observe in your horse.

HORSE GRIMACE SCALE

When mammals feel pain, their face shows this with a classic pain grimace. With non-verbal humans or with animals, practitioners needed a way to assess the level of pain being experienced. The Pain Grimace Scale was developed as a 10-point scale, from relaxation and feeling no pain (1) to the highest level of pain (10).

Recently, the Pain Grimace Scale has been developed for horses. Horses, like other prey animals, need to hide their weaknesses or they will be selected by predators, so they tend not to show the level of pain they are feeling. The Horse Grimace scale is useful alongside other measures for vets and owners to see just how much pain the horse may be feeling despite a lack of more obvious behavioural signs.

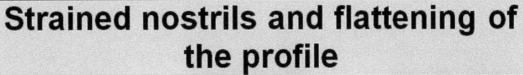

Strained nostrils and flattening of the profile

Not present (0)	**Moderately present (1)**	**Obviously present (2)**

Nostrils look strained and slightly dilated, the profile of the nose flattens and lips elongate.

An extract from the Horse Grimace Scale. There are 6 sections detailing different aspects of facial expression in relation to pain. Dalla Costa E, Minero M, Lebelt D, Stucke D, Canali E, Leach MC (2014) Development of the Horse Grimace Scale (HGS) as a Pain Assessment Tool in Horses Undergoing Routine Castration. PLoS ONE 9(3): e92281. https://doi.org/10.1371/journal.pone.0092281

Scientists are now working on an equine 'Happiness' scale. This will allow owners and vets to understand how positive a horse is feeling. Recently, an equid ethogram has also been validated in order to assess levels of pain when a horse is being ridden.

BEHAVIOURAL SIGNS

An excellent full study of behavioural signs and their place in horse life can be found in *The Equid Ethogram* by Dr Sue McDonnell. The author has compiled studies of feral, semi-feral and domestic horse behaviour to create a comprehensive field guide. This enables researchers, students and horse-owners to have a common language for behaviours. For example, in describing the "stand alert" pose, the head, ear and eye positions are all defined. The comment then notes what follows the pose, such as approach or withdrawal from the object of interest or a return to previous activity.

CALMING SIGNALS

One form of equine behaviour has been called "calming signals". Horses are highly social and communicative mammals, and they have a large suite of behavioural signals that let others know how they are feeling. For example, if a horse is feeling anxious, these signals tell the other horses in an interaction, 'Hey, back off a little so I can relax.' Hence, they are known as calming signals. They help keep horses from going over threshold of fear and anxiety. They maintain calm and cohesion between horses, which is vital for herd animals who must stay together for survival.

Calming signals have been discussed in dog training for about twenty years now but are only beginning to be applied to horse training. Rachaël Draaisma is a leader in this field and is the author of the book *Language Signs and Calming Signals of Horses: Recognition and Application*. They are useful to know and understand as they give us detailed information about how our horses are feeling. We can then respond appropriately, which builds communication and trust with our horses. Studies have shown that horses in domesticity are always trying to communicate with humans, for example, to ask for a gate to be opened. Once we start responding to them, these studies have shown that their communications increase. Once they have our attention, they have a lot to say!

An example of calming signals in action is licking and chewing. Science tells us that it is a typical mammalian reaction to relief from stress. When the Sympathetic Nervous System is activated by a stressor, salivation ceases, resulting in a dry mouth, a tight throat, and tight lips. When the stress has passed, there is a switch back to the Parasympathetic Nervous System, or a state of relaxation. Salivation starts up, the throat softens and the animal swallows and often licks their lips. In horses, this gives us the typical licking and chewing behaviour.

Many people are taught that licking and chewing is a good thing—that it shows that the horse understands what you are teaching and is processing the learning. However, it is a calming response to having experienced a higher level of stress and now relaxing a bit. Licking and chewing is a simple reflex reaction to the switch between the sympathetic and parasympathetic nervous systems. Other behavioural responses seen can be itchiness, yawning, stretching and, usually quite obviously, a sigh (strong out breath).

In training systems where the FEAR system is deliberately aroused, say by chasing the horse with a whip, the sympathetic nervous system is aroused. When the whip is removed because the horse has started moving, the relief of stress causes the switch to the parasympathetic nervous system. This causes the accompanying behaviours of licking, chewing etc. It is the *relief* of an aversive which we are witnessing. The behaviours we see are symptoms of physiological calming. Therefore, we can call it a calming signal.

READING YOUR HORSE

What does a calm and relaxed horse look like? The more skilled you are in reading your horse's body language, the better your training will be as you will notice the small signs of his emotional state and will be able to adapt your training sooner in order to get the best response.

Leonera is very relaxed as Rachel puts on her fly mask. Note Leo's droopy lips, long nostrils and "soft" eyes.

A truly relaxed horse will walk beside you quietly. Her head is likely to be in a low to middle position, so not high headed. She will have her attention to you and the situation you are in, and not be scanning the environment anxiously. Her ears will be soft, neither pinned back nor intensely pricked looking intently ahead. Her lower lip will be relaxed with a soft-looking chin. Stressed horses hold their lips tightly together and the chin becomes quite prominent and distinctive. Her eyes will be more almond-shaped than round, which gives them a soft look. And she'll feel relaxing to be near.

Manuela is showing all the signs of a relaxed walk with Rachel. Her body is soft, her head is at the horizontal, her ears are soft and attentive to Rachel and she's maintaining her position at liberty

In contrast, this horse is showing many signs of tension. His head is high, his muscles are tense, his mouth and nose are tight and his attention is on the environment rather than his handler. It is also clear that the handler needs to use the bit to maintain position and control.

A good way to assess how calm your horse is to ask yourself, who would I let handle my horse in this moment? Would you feel safe to let a 5-year-old child take the lead? How about a 12-year-old? A novice adult? No-one except your instructor?!

These pictures are a guide to assessing your horse's emotions. They were all taken in just one session and show how changeable horses' emotions can be.

Rowan on alert. Her head is high, her focus on what's alarming her. You can see how tight her lip is, and there is tension through her jaw and neck, too.

Rowan is spooking here at a low arousal level. Her attention has been caught by something to her left and she has disconnected slightly from Hannah to look at it.

Rowan is more relaxed here. You can see her head is in a relaxed, horizontal position, her ears and mouth are soft and her muscles and stride and fluid and relaxed.

Rowan's focus here is on Hannah as she reconnects with her in a long, relaxed walk.

Rowan is tense here, showing more signs of frustration than fear as her ears are pinned. Her nostrils are flared and her jaw and lips tense.

Here, Rowan is in a perfect state of relaxed enthusiasm. She is soft, her muscles, ears and face are all relaxed. Yet, she is also focused on Hannah and the work they're doing, with energy, engagement and willingness.

TRAINING *YOUR* HORSE

The most important thing to understand is that every horse is different. Some are confident or even pushy, others timid and shy. Some are not interested in people or food; others live to eat or be fussed over. All these basic differences affect how you approach the training, what you should be looking for, the rewards you will use, and when you will reward. These variations will set your horse up for success as you will choose the best exercises, location, rewards to help create the best emotional state in your horse during training.

You probably already have a good idea of your horse's personality. Whether he's spooky or calm; how food-oriented he is; how happy he is to leave the herd or if he feels a high level of separation anxiety. However, we suggest a quick and easy assessment of these factors using an enrichment exercise before you start training. This means you have a reference to go back to, to check if your horse's general attitude is changing for the better. To see if he is becoming calmer, more motivated, braver and better at solving puzzles.

This exercise is a good way to observe your horse and you can repeat it at intervals to assess how your horse is changing as he develops through the reward-based training. It is known as the "Enrichment Exercise"

ENRICHMENT EXERCISE

Watching how your horse searches for treats can give you a lot of useful information about how to approach the training. How much work a horse puts in to search for treats is a good way of assessing the activity of their SEEKING systems. A horse who gives up easily may be under-aroused or anxious. Another who gets very excited and high-energy, or even frustrated, may be prone to over-arousal. Watching them search freely for treats gives you a good clue of what to expect when you use treats in the training and can help you to decide the best approach to take. We use a simple exercise, where treats are placed in a safe space where your horse can be at liberty.

THE EXERCISE

1. Use a space where your horse can be released at liberty. Typically, an arena is a good place or a fenced-off corner of a paddock. It should be a familiar place where your horse is used to going and has no fear of being there.

2. Place food in various places. You can scatter it about or place it in buckets as we have here. They should be familiar objects so your horse is relaxed with them. Start placing them about 10 steps away from the gate so you can see if your horse is happy to leave the gate and explore, or not.

3. Place a variety of treats at each station. You can even leave a couple of buckets empty. You can use low value feed, such as hay, through medium value treats such as alfalfa or grass nuts and high value treats such as apples, carrots and parsnips and big chunky horse feed nuts.

4. Bring your horse in and let her be at liberty. You can step back from the fence to watch. You want her to realise that she is free to leave you and explore.

Then simply observe what your horse does. It's good to take a video so that you can watch it back and look out for any calming signals, changes in behaviour, reactions to certain objects or specific areas and be able to evaluate it over time too.

CASE STUDY: ENRICHMENT WITH HANNAH AND RACHEL'S HERD

We scattered large pony nuts around the sand paddock and let the whole herd in. We'll focus on India, the skewbald, Khalil the grey Arab and Copper, the Shetland pony. This was their first position.

After a few mouthfuls of food, Copper decided to go and explore. India and Khalil stayed calmly searching where they started, though India was pawing, showing low levels of frustration as she searched.

Copper began to check out all of the buckets and obstacles as he already associated these with treats. The other horses stayed calmly where they were as there were plenty of nuts to be found.

But Copper had to check even further and went down to join the other horses. Maybe they had found something really good?!

All this time, Khalil and India had stayed in their original positions, calmly searching and eating in that place. This exercise clearly reflected how the horses reacted around food in the training.

India and Khalil had always been calm around the food and easily learned to take treats politely and to not mug us. Copper, on the other hand, had been the opposite. He easily got over-aroused around food treats and we had to work hard to train him to take treats politely. We began to use more scratches and hay as rewards to help him to stay calmer.

What do you think your horse would do? Have a go at this exercise and use these questions to guide your understanding of your horse. Remember to capture it on video so you can really see what happens.

OBSERVATION

1. Does your horse go to the first bucket immediately or wait at the gate?

2. This gives you an indication of how relaxed your horse is at liberty and on his own.

3. Does your horse take a straight line towards the bucket or curve towards it?

This gives you an indication of how aroused the SEEKING system and FEAR systems are. A straight line indicates the horse has little fear and is mainly in search mode. A curved approach suggests the horse has some fear active and is approaching more cautiously

1. How calm is your horse when eating at the bucket? Scale it from 1-3:

1= Stands quietly and calmly. Keeps her head down and eats the food in a relaxed way.

3= Cannot stand still. Paws at the bucket or kicks it, noses it around. Can't seem to eat quickly enough.

2. How focused is your horse on the other buckets?

Does he focus on the bucket he's eating from or is he already anticipating the next one? Does he finish one bucket before moving on to the next, or does he leave some feed in it?

A horse who focuses on the next bucket while eating at the first bucket is likely to be easily over-aroused by food and impatient to perform behaviours to get rewards. They may be more prone to resource-guarding you and the treats during training and possibly try and block you from leaving when their sessions end. A horse who just eats one bucket at a time is likely to be calmer around the treats in training.

3. Do your horse's emotions stay stable throughout or are there changes?

You want to note if your horse gets calmer as they work through the session or do they start to get more aroused? Is that fear arousal, so maybe they start to look around and be more distracted by what is going on around them? For those horses, shorter sessions would be advisable at the start. Or does your horse get more relaxed as they get into the session? For those horses, longer sessions or doing something else (such as this exercise) before you start training could be useful.

Overall, the Enrichment Exercise is a great way to assess your horse's personality and emotions. It gives you useful guidance for how to introduce the training, in terms of rewards to use, length of sessions and place of training.

You can repeat this exercise any time you like. Your horse will enjoy it and you can learn about her changing emotions as you progress.

EMPOWER YOUR HORSE

The Empowerment Exercise is another good exercise to help you determine how spooky or fearful your horse is. It is similar to the Enrichment Exercise but this time you introduce a novel object into her environment and watch her response. This is done at liberty in a place where your horse can move away from the object if she needs to. We learned this exercise from Rachaël Draaisma.

THE EXERCISE

1. Use a space where your horse can be released at liberty. It should be a familiar place where your horse is used to going and has no fear of being there.

2. Place a familiar object and a novel object in the space. Place them well away from the gate so your horse can choose to go and explore them or stay at the gate and feel she's at a safe distance.

3. Place high value treats you know your horse enjoys at or on each object. We like apples, carrots and parsnips and big chunky horse feed nuts.

4. Bring your horse in and let her be at liberty. You can step back from the fence to watch. You want her to realise that she is free to leave you and explore.

Then simply observe what your horse does. It's good to take a video so that you can watch it back and look out for any calming signals, changes in behaviour, and be able to evaluate it over time too.

As you leave your horse with the spooky object, closely watch what he does. Does he go straight up and explore it? Does he take one look and turn away from it, keeping as far away as possible? Does he approach cautiously, circle it, check it out from distance and slowly and carefully go nearer?

The next part is to go in with your horse. Keep the video going! Observe how this changes your horse's attitude, if at all. Usually bold horses stay bold, but more timid horses may get a lot of confidence from you being with them. Often, you will see them happily approach the object with you, or at least get closer and engage with it more. If your presence doesn't give your horse more confidence, then that is an indicator you should keep working on easy exercises where no fear arousal is involved. You want to build her connection with you before you start working with fearful situations. However, if your horse does get comfort from your presence, you can use that connection to help her become bolder in general.

EMPOWERMENT CASE-STUDY WITH LEONERA

Rachel and Centre Director, Claire Waldron, worked on this at their training centre, Positive Horse Training Spain, when Rachaël Draaisma visited. We worked with rescued mare, Leonera (AKA Leo), who is generally a spooky horse. We want to build her self-confidence and tolerance for new objects. She had demonstrated fear with saddle pads, fly masks and blankets. So, we set up a project to discover the depth of her fear, how she responded to human presence and a way to help her to become less fearful. Here's the case study:

We placed a dog blanket in the arena. Beside it we put a familiar surface, a blue bag we use to carry hay. We put apples on each. Then we let Leonera into the arena to see what she would do. Her choice was to stay by the gate and wait with the humans. She did not want to explore the scary object on her own.

When she got no help from Rachaël, she walked down the fence towards Rachel, who was filming. You can clearly see her attention is divided. She has an ear and eye on the novel object, to her left. Her right eye and ear are looking towards Rachel, holding the camera. Receiving no encouragement from Rachel either she continued down to the corner of the arena, as far away from the novel object as she could get. It confirmed what we knew about Leonera's innate spookiness and gave us a good baseline to work from.

The next day we repeated the exercise with exactly the same set-up. This time, Leonera examined the novel object from about half-way up the arena and then walked past it and stood looking over the fence, with her back to the blankets.

Rachaël explained that Leo was actually giving a calming signal to the blankets. This meant she wasn't ignoring it, but she was examining the scary blankets from a safe distance. With her equine vision, she could clearly examine it, looking backwards.

After standing like this for over five minutes, she turned around and presented her flank towards the object. Presenting flank is the next stage as levels of anxiety decline. This creates more engagement with the scary object than presenting hind-quarters. But it's still a safe distance for Leo. You can see that she is also rubbing her nose on her leg. This is a classic displacement behaviour. In this context, it shows that her general level of anxiety was reducing from the higher level she had felt when presenting her hind-quarters.

Leo also started licking and chewing and then started to blink slowly, all clear calming signals. She stood in this way for over 5 minutes, so we decided to end the session there and brought her out of the arena.

The fact that she was expressing calming signals shows that she had been experiencing a higher level of tension beforehand. However, remember that this is all under her control. She could have stayed at the gate with the people or gone back to the corner where the hay was. But she chose to explore the object. This was great progress from the day before, when she hadn't gone this far in engagement at all. As with us, when a horse is learning to overcome fear, they need to feel it a little but not so much that they get too scared. By giving Leo all the control over the situation, she was able to explore within her own levels of comfort and curiosity. In this way, we empower the horse to start to deal with fear in a more useful way for them, than simply being anxious all the time.

When she came in on day 3, she walked round the object at her safe distance and then clearly and deliberately came over to the fence where Claire, Rachaël and Rachel stood. This time we decided to help her out. She was obviously not keen to explore the object on her own and we felt it was a good time to see how much difference some human support would make.

Support from someone she trusted made all the difference for Leo. Claire reassured her with a scratch and voice praise, and then moved closer herself and crouched down, all to give Leo more confidence. Finally, she was confident enough to eat the apples off the blanket.

As she ate and began to relax, Claire slowly melted away. She stopped at the point when Leo began to show signs of tension, and then finished that session when Leo walked back to join her.

The next day, Leo came in brimming with confidence. She immediately left Claire at the gate and went straight to the object to eat apples.

This simple exercise told us a lot about Leonera's spookiness. She was very anxious about the cloth and it seemed to be a lot about the feel/texture of it as well as it blowing in the breeze. She felt braver when Claire was with her. Therefore, we knew that when she was scared with her human being there, such as carrying the saddle, pad, it was a really deep fear, as she couldn't even take comfort from her human.

By the end of the week we were able to introduce a new material into the exercise and she went straight up to it and ate the apples from it. She had generalised the idea of this being safe and rewarding, to a new situation. We had empowered her and increased her self-confidence. We noticed the following week that she was much more interested in novel objects around the yard and field and would go and explore them rather than avoid them.

We recommend you try this exercise with any new horse or one where you are trying to find ways to build self-confidence. It's a fun game, too, for all horses, and you can set up new puzzles and trials for them to explore while you do other jobs such as mucking out. It is another great way to provide enrichment too.

REVIEW AND EVALUATION

After you've tried this, reflect on what happened to assess how best to help your horse in training. These questions can guide your reflection.

1. Was your horse more anxious than you thought? Or more relaxed? Or did she respond exactly as you expected?

2. How important were the treats? Did you think your horse maybe explored a bit further, despite her fearfulness, in order to get the treats? Were you surprised that your horse's level of fear meant that she didn't eat the treats at all?

3. What about how your horse responded to your presence? If he was calmer, why? Is it because of your close bond? Were you surprised? Is it because your horse isn't used to exploring on his own and maybe your presence gave him confidence?

Generally, this exercise helps us to determine how the horse Is likely to react to training. If the horse was bold and food-oriented and got excited by the exercise, this tells us we must approach the feeding part of the training with caution to ensure he stays relaxed with the addition of food. It might be better to train with hay as the reward, rather than exciting carrots. It could be important with a horse like this to include a lot of movement in the early exercises, so he can keep returning to calm through walking quietly. We'll be especially looking for these horses to be able to stay calm and relaxed in the presence of food and in exciting situations, such as at higher gaits.

On the other hand, if your horse was very anxious and even the food didn't overcome this, then you will need to take things very slowly. This horse is likely to want a lot of repetition of simple exercises to gain confidence. If this anxious horse was more worried with you close by, as is often the case for horses who have a troubled past, such as rescued horses, then you'll have to be aware of keeping your movements slow and predictable and setting up your training to help your horse become more confident around people. However, if your anxious horse gained confidence with your presence, you can support that through scratching and having calm "hanging-out" times together. Your objective with this horse will be to build self-confidence and help the horse to be more relaxed around previously spooky situations.

VIDEO RESOURCE

EMPOWERING YOUR HORSE

Watch the whole case study here with commentary by Rachaël and Rachel.

www.connectiontraining.com/video-resources

WORKING WITH HORSES WHO GET OVER-EXCITED OR TENSE AROUND FOOD

Through the above exercises, you may have discovered that your horse has a tendency to get very excited in the presence of food and new objects. If you observe your horse exploring the food and objects with very high energy, rushing from one to another; or showing signs of frustration such as pawing the ground while looking for treats, it's a sign that your horse feels tension around food and problem-solving. These are common responses in domestic horses, which can result from situations such as food deprivation and scarcity, such as being stabled without sufficient forage for long periods of time.

Personality also plays a part, with some horses more prone to over-excitement and frustration around food. These triggers can create horses who have learned to be aggressive or tense when food is presented. Since we're always looking to create the best emotional response in our horses, including high levels of relaxation, extreme tension in the presence of food can be detrimental, triggering the negative emotional systems. In these cases, you need to do some work to create a calmer horse before you proceed with the training.

CASUAL CONNECTION TIME

It's easy to spend all of your time with your horse busy with something – training, riding, care routines and chores take up a lot of time. However, you'll get the most from your training and your horse if you prioritise some relaxed time with your horse. Casual connection time is beneficial for all horses and we use it regularly throughout all our training sessions.

CASUAL CONNECTION TIME EXERCISE

Begin in a situation where your horse is already at his most relaxed, such as just after he's come into his stable, or in a corner of his field, or even standing tied if that is a situation he is used to and is genuinely relaxed and happy there. Introduce food into this situation. You want it to be as low-value as possible, so begin by offering your horse a hay-net, or a bucket of chaff or hay chop. If you are in a field, you can allow your horse to graze.

To begin, don't ask your horse to do anything, or groom him or clean around him. You want to create a really calm, safe space together. Sit or stand close to your horse, talking to him calmly. Observe his behaviour: is he calmly eating the hay or grass or is he grabbing and pulling at it? Is he worried about movement, or other horses, or is he settled and relaxed?

If he's eating calmly, move closer to him. Does he show signs of tension when you approach such as eating faster or resource-guarding behaviours such as pinning his ears? Can you touch, groom and stroke him as he's eating?

If your horse is showing tension, grabbiness or anxiety at this stage, practice this exercise daily, simply spending calm time with your horse as he eats quietly. Gradually move closer towards him and away again, until he is relaxed about you being near him while he eats and moving away again. Ensure that he has enough time to eat and feel satiated, so spend at least 20 minutes per day on this exercise and ensure your horse isn't hungry before you start. If your horse has a normal routine, you can add this exercise into it, such as after he's been ridden or come in from the field. Choose the calmest times of day and situation to begin with, and then try it at different times and in different locations so that you practice spending very relaxed, calm time with your horse and your horse begins to associate being with you and food as something relaxing.

This part of the exercise helps your horse learn to be more relaxed around you and food, an important skill for daily well-being and ensuring successful reward-based training.

The next stage of the exercise is to introduce some more problem-solving aspects into it for your horse. You have a few options here. One way is to repeat the basic enrichment exercise with your horse, giving him a variety of objects to explore. This time, instead of using high-value rewards, use hay, chaff or another very low-value food reward around the objects. You want your horse to begin exploring and problem-solving in a softer and more relaxed way, so you want to arouse his curiosity without making it too exciting. If your horse is confident with exploring these objects, you can start to make the challenges trickier, such as hiding the rewards in a bucket covered with a cloth that he has to remove, building your horse's problem-solving abilities.

You can also try this exercise with novel objects but without the food and monitor your horse's curiosity with different textures, shapes and smells, such as brushes from unknown horses, essential oils or plastic bags. Other casual connection exercises include walking with your horse as you explore your environment together, grooming with a selection of brushes to see which your horse enjoys, massaging your horse, scratches and cuddles or simply hanging out by him while he snoozes or grazes.

Casual Connection Time can include any time you spend with your horse in a relaxed way, with no expectations. Joining your horse in his environment is a lovely way to connect.

The aim of casual connection time is to help your horse to feel more relaxed around problem solving, new objects and food. It strengthens your relationship and you'll learn more about your horse's preferences and reactions. It will also set your horse up perfectly emotionally as you progress into more focused training sessions.

TAILORING YOUR TRAINING

These assessments and exercises have given you insight into your horse's brain and behaviour. As we proceed through the book we give examples and suggestions for horses whose FEAR system is easily over-aroused and for those whose SEEKING system is easily over-aroused. Now that you know if your horse fits one of these categories, you can look out for these differing suggestions to improve your training. If you find that you have a generally calm horse, you will probably find the training quite straight-forward and make progress quickly. As long as you keep the focus on relaxation, though, you will eventually create a calm, happy-to-learn horse, no matter where you start emotionally.

CHAPTER 3

THE CONNECTION TRAINING FOUNDATION

This training approach is likely to be different to your horse from any previous training. You'll need to teach him how Connection Training works so that he's relaxed, polite, confident and eager to learn. We do this through teaching some basic behaviours including Stand Quietly Together, Walk Together, Stay and Targeting. These essential lessons create a solid foundation on which to build your training as you refine your communication and connection with your horse. They contain the core of Connection Training as you learn how to train with an emphasis on your horse's emotions, cognitive abilities and relationship together. Taking time at this stage to make good preparations will help you get off to the best start and speed up the long-term process.

PREPARING FOR YOUR FIRST SESSION

Getting started in the right way establishes the emotional associations your horse will make with this new way of training. From the exercises in Chapter 2, you already have a good idea how relaxed or otherwise your horse is going to be around food rewards, new situations and you. Use this information to make the best decisions for your horse within the training, such as the location, rewards and behaviours you use. This will help to create feelings of interest, joy, trust and relaxation.

WHERE AND WHEN TO TRAIN

Choose your training area to help set your horse up for success. Since you want your horse to be relaxed, work in an environment that will support this. This could mean having your horse's herd mates nearby or working at a specific end of your arena or field where your horse is most comfortable.

Minimising distractions will also help your horse to stay focused in the session. It will be much harder to keep your horse's attention if you work them somewhere new, or if there are lots of novel objects to explore or lush grass to eat.

Your training area needs to be big enough that you can comfortably walk a circle together, but can be in a barn, yard, arena or field. It is also ideal if the area is fenced so that you can work your horse without a lead rope on. However, if you don't have this option, it's fine – you can certainly introduce Connection Training successfully using your lead rope sensitively.

When you train your horse will also impact your session. If your horse is expecting to be fed or turned out, you will be more likely to have a distracted, tense horse, so choose a time that is quiet for your horse. This could be after a ride, or when he's brought in from the field or after he's been fed. You know your horse and his routine best, so pick a quiet time to train. Take into account external factors such as what's going on around you and the weather. If it's a windy day and your yard has a show on or it's farrier and vet day etc., then you will be more successful if you wait to train at a quieter time if your horse is reactive to the busy environment. Alternatively, if you struggle to motivate your horse, choose a time of day when he's higher in energy and keen to work.

Eventually, you want to be able to train your horse at any time of day and in a variety of locations, but working with your horse's natural rhythms in the beginning will get you both off to the best start. It's generally a lot easier to build enthusiasm and motivation than it is to create and sustain relaxation, so err on the side of a satiated or sleepy horse than one who is over-excited. You can always change and adapt the training in future to build the energy and motivation. Like everything emotional, this is about reaching a balance. It's wonderful to see your horse come up to you with pricked ears, nickering gently in anticipation of spending time with you and enjoying the training. It's only a problem if it escalates into over-excitement, frustration, and tension.

WHAT YOU'LL NEED

You don't need much equipment to get started with Connection Training, so bring your horse into the training area in just a headcollar and lead rope. The two items you will need are a **marker** and **rewards.**

WHAT IS A MARKER?

When you're training your horse, timing is everything. The marker is a sound or signal that means 'Yes! What you just did was correct, and you've earned a reward.' Being able to communicate clearly to your horse like this allows your horse to understand exactly what you want. Because it also predicts that a reward is coming, the horse learns to listen out for

the marker signal and pay attention to what he was doing at the time. This is how the marker creates clarity and accuracy which helps the horse to learn quicker and better. For the marker, you can use a whistle, a pat, a certain word or specific noise, such as a 'click'.

The marker signal is also called a 'bridge' signal. It's called this because it bridges the time gap between when your horse does the right thing and when you can reward him. For example, if you're teaching your horse to pick up the correct canter lead, you can't feed him some treats the moment he does it. However, you can mark the moment, which tells the horse exactly what movement was the right one. Then you can bring him down from canter to halt and reward him then. Although the reward is given at halt, your horse's brain will have registered what he was doing at the time the bridge signal was given, and this will be the behaviour he learns to repeat. Throughout the book, we use 'marker' most often, but 'click' or 'bridge' mean the same thing.

CHOOSE YOUR MARKER

Choose a marker that stands out enough for your horse to pay attention to it, but that feels natural to you and doesn't cause tension in your horse. A common marker signal is a clicker, a small box which makes a sharp 'click-click' noise when pressed. This has the value of being precise and distinctive, but the sharpness can be alarming or exciting for some horses. We like to use a specific word, such as 'good' or 'yes'. We also use a click noise, but prefer to make the noise with our mouth as it's a little softer than a mechanical clicker. We actually use different markers at different times, and you can certainly have a few different markers that your horse responds to, such as a click when you need precision when teaching something new and a verbal marker when you're rewarding your horse for a well-known behaviour.

Horses quickly generalise the click, whether you use a mechanical clicker or a tongue-click and they respond well to both. The mechanical clicker is useful to really bring your awareness to your timing in the training and helps to keep consistency, especially if the horse is being trained by different people. The tongue-click leaves your hands free to work with your horse and is a softer noise, which can help with horses who startle at the abrupt sound of the mechanical clicker.

Although we often use a clicker in our training, we tend to describe our training as Positive Reinforcement Training (PRT), which has been properly defined scientifically. 'Clicker training' is a well-known term, but it is a casual expression with no agreed definition and, as such, is used in different ways by different people. We emphasise emotions before behaviours and focus entirely on the connection between you and the horse, looking for relaxation, joy and fun. So, the specific marker is less important to us in the training, as long as the communication is open and clear.

WHICH REWARDS ARE BEST?

By now, you know that food is a primary reinforcer and that all animals repeat behaviours that earn them food. This makes food a powerful training tool, as long as it's used with understanding of learning and awareness of the emotional state. Through the exercises in Chapter 2, you have assessed your horse's emotions regarding food and begun to make any changes to ensure that your horse feels relaxed around food and problem-solving. We will take that process deeper throughout the training.

Hannah working with Rowan with a treat bag full of pony nuts. Although Rowan was pushy and nippy around food when she arrived with Hannah, these lessons taught her to be relaxed and polite when being trained with food.

BUT ISN'T HAND-FEEDING HORSES BAD?

Teaching your horse to take treats calmly and politely is part of introducing CT to your horse.

You may have been told not to hand-feed horses or use treats in training because it leads to pushy or dangerous horses. Well, it can, if you don't do it properly. In fact, many people accidentally train their horses to be pushy around food because they don't understand how easily horses associate food with other behaviours. For example, if you give your horse his bucket when he's kicking the stable door, you're actually training him to kick the door. If you put your horse's hay net in the stable even when he's pinning his ears, you're training him to be aggressive around food. If you hand-feed your horse a treat when he's gently nuzzling at your pockets, you're training him to mug for treats and it could easily escalate into pushing or nipping.

The first thing we do with horses in Connection Training is teach them how to be calm and polite around food and treats as begun through the casual connection exercise. We'll strengthen that behaviour and relaxation through the first exercise we train: standing calmly beside you, keeping his head away from the treats. By rewarding the horse when he's standing in a relaxed, neutral position, you will strengthen this behaviour and associated calmness.

The rewards will not come when the horse is mugging for treats or showing tension. This relaxation is important for your safety, your horse's well-being, and the success of the training. It means you can use this effective and powerful reward to shape your horse's behaviour for the better, and your horse will be relaxed and polite around buckets, at feeding time, and during hand-feeding.

CREATING RELAXATION AROUND FOOD

In positive dog training, the typical protocol is to feed one small treat at a time. With horses, it's better to feed handfuls for your rewards when you feed. Horses are grazing machines! They bite and chew, passing the food back in their long mouths while they take the next bite. If we just feed a small treat the brain may not register that food is being consumed. You'll remember from Chapter 1 that we are stimulating the SEEKING system when we start training with food. The horse is in SEEKING mode, sniffing for the food, exploring with his muzzle and whiskers. Interestingly, it is not the search for food that triggers the learning pathway in the brain, but the *consumption* of it. Just at the moment the food is consumed, the SEEKING system switches off momentarily. It is this moment that the brain registers as achieving the reward.

In humans, this understanding is applied to many diet programmes that focus on 'mindful eating'. When you eat, as you fill your fork, you are in SEEKING mode. If you keep scooping up more, you are not letting your brain register that food has been received, and so you eat more and more. Mindful eating programmes teach you to put your fork down and concentrate on the food you are chewing, which switches off the search mode. Then when you finally swallow, you pick up the fork and begin the cycle again. This helps your brain and stomach to communicate on when you have eaten enough.

If you feed a single pellet or slice of carrot at a time in quick succession, your horse's brain is unlikely to register the consumption. Therefore, the SEEKING system does not get powered down and the horse is likely to get over-aroused and overexcited. As a result, the horse gets frustrated and anxious about the treats, which can lead to ear-pinning and resource-guarding behaviours. In males, continued over-arousal of the SEEKING system can trigger the arousal of the RAGE system and the LUST system. He drops his penis and gets grabby with his mouth, often pinching your hand as he takes the treats or even biting you.

Feeding horses generously, giving them time to chew and spacing out the rewards promotes relaxation. In the beginning, we often use hay or chaff as the food reward to promote this chewing. While the horse is chewing, it gives us time to just be with our horses, without always asking them to do something and work for treats. It slows the whole training session down and helps to make it less about the food. By focusing on relaxation in this way and giving your horse time to chew to switch off the SEEKING system, you will keep your horse in the Connection Zone and will prevent over-arousal.

Rachel is using hay to reward Pegaso when teaching him to accept fly spray.

WHAT FOOD IS BEST FOR TRAINING?

Since you will be feeding handfuls of food at a time you will use a lot of feed. For this reason, we recommend using low-energy, high-fibre horse feed. Branded horse treats are unnecessary and will become very expensive.

We all know how enthusiastic horses can get about buckets and treats. Since the aim is to teach polite behaviour and relaxation around food, start with the lowest-value, or most boring, reward you can find, such as hay or plain chaff. This is usually tasty enough to keep your horse's interest, but not so exciting that they get totally focused on the food rather than you, or get excited, pushy or frustrated in the session. Once you've established softness, manners and relaxation when working with food, you can increase the value of the rewards for your horse as necesssary. Other treat options include high-fibre grass pellets, hay cubes, alfalfa (Lucerne) pellets, and feed created for laminitic horses. These are usually a little tastier than hay or chaff, so can be used if you need a bit more motivation with your horse.

All these are suitable to add to your horse's daily diet, but be aware of your horse's nutritional state. You can use his daily feed ration as the training treats if you don't want to feed extra and seek advice for horses with particular nutritional requirements. Do not use molasses feed or cereal grains, as they tend to make horses overexcited. However, such tasty feed and fresh fruit, such as apples, are good to use with shy or timid horses and those who are not too interested in food.

The physical form of your treats can be vital for anxious horses or others prone to choke (obstruction of the oesophagus). Ensure the treats you use are safe to hand-feed and focus on relaxation throughout the training so that your horse spends relaxed time chewing after each reward. Young horses may struggle to take treats politely so larger nuts can help them to learn to take food gently without nipping. They may also vary in what they like over time, as their teeth change, so be aware of that too. When working with food treats, always have fresh water available for your horse, and encourage drinking breaks.

NON-FOOD REWARDS

Food is a powerful training tool. It will create a huge amount of motivation and joy in your horse. You can often change his emotions from resistance to enthusiasm just by adding food. But food is just one piece of the puzzle.

Variety keeps your horse more motivated and more strongly focused on you. We recommend you use as many other rewards as you can in your training, right from the start. For example, your horse can be rewarded by scratches or head rubs, taking a break, walking over a pole, exploring an object, and so on.

Pegaso loving a scratch reward during the same fly-spray acceptance session.

The use of rewards other than food enables you to tailor the training to your horse's personal preferences. As you progress with the training, you'll find your horse has certain behaviours he naturally loves, and you can use these as rewards. Find out where your horse loves to be

scratched—manes and tails are the usual favourites. A forward-going horse might enjoy trotting next to you, while another horse may prefer to take a walk. Rewards can also change from day to day or season to season as your horse's mood and energy levels change. For example, many horses love to be scratched when their coats are shedding in spring but dislike it at other times of the year. On a windy day, when your horse is full of energy, he may love the chance to pop over a jump, but on a hot, sunny day he may find it more rewarding to have a head rub in the sun. As you incorporate different rewards and variety in your horse's training, you'll strengthen your bond as you open this two-way communication.

Rachel working with 5-month-old mule foal, Maverick. As he learned basic handling at a young age, he was rewarded with much-loved scratches and the opportunity to explore new objects – at this age, they are curious about everything!

SAYING "YES!" TO YOUR HORSE

One of the main benefits of using a marker and rewards is that you will look out for and notice all the best moments your horse offers. Simply looking for things to say 'yes' to adds positivity and joy to your time with your horse. You both feel better when you realise how many things you did well in each session. You'll also both be clearer about what the right answer is and be eager to repeat it next time. Training sessions should be joyful, fun, and progressive. Saying 'yes' to your horse helps you both feel great about your training sessions and really does mean both of you look forward to your time together.

THE FIRST CONNECTION TRAINING SESSION

OK, let's dive in and see what Connection Training looks like in practice! We've found that the best length of sessions is 20-40 minutes. This gives your horse time to settle into the training and plenty of time to work on some exercises. This time will be split into mini sessions, which will include casual connection time, relaxed breaks, time spent on easy exercises and time spent on more difficult exercises. The pace of your training should be slow and the energy relaxed, interspersing more intensive challenging exercises with plenty of relaxation and connection.

BEGIN WITH CASUAL CONNECTION TIME

As explained in Chapter 2, casual connection time is a way to establish relaxation in your horse around you, food and problem-solving. Always begin your sessions in a way that helps your horse to relax and begin to connect with you by choosing the best exercise for your horse today. For example, if she's already had a hay net or just come in from the grass, she might prefer to be groomed or explore some novel objects together. If she's feeling energetic, maybe she'll relax best if you go for a walk. Or maybe standing together at a hay net is the best way to soften and connect.

Take this time to assess how your horse is *today*. Does she seem relaxed and content or high energy and spooky? Is she keen to explore or does she stay with you? This will give you useful information that you can use to adapt the training and set your horse up for success. For example, if your

horse is spooky about one corner of the training area, you can avoid that corner as you begin until she is more relaxed and focused. Or, if your horse is whizzing about enthusiastically, she'll be likely to find standing still difficult so you might begin with plenty of steady movement until she settles.

Take this time to assess how you are today, as well. Do you feel rushed? Are you really present with your horse or do you have problems and to-do lists running through your mind? Do you feel clear and confident about your training plan or vague and anxious? Take some deep breaths and allow your tension and any worries to melt away; for this moment, you're here with your horse and everything else can wait. As you watch your horse and assess her mood, become tuned into her world. We call it 'horse time' and it's a little different from human time as they don't follow clocks and have different priorities. Slow down and find horse time! Take a moment to plan what you're going to work on with your horse in this session so that you're clear in your training.

These exercises are all about becoming present and getting connected with your horse. Your horse will respond to your tension, relaxation, focus, presence and confidence so get started on the best foot by taking 5-10 minutes at the start of the session to establish your innate connection with your horse. It's all too easy to become overly focused on training 'stuff 'and to teach your horse that as soon as you arrive it's intensive, highly focused training time. This can lead to horses who struggle to relax in your presence and get over-excited, tense or frustrated in the training. Beginning with casual connection time, and including regular breaks this way throughout your sessions, ensures you prioritise the relationship and communication between you. It also makes the training much easier, too, because you and your horse are both calm, connected and ready to train as soon as you begin.

INTRODUCING THE MARKER AND FOOD

You have introduced food to your horse in a relaxed way through casual connection time, but now you're going to begin pairing the marker with the food. As discussed, using low value food rewards, especially at this stage, helps your horse to stay calm and to transition smoothly into this way of training. The best way to start this is by throwing a handful of hay or chaff into a bucket and just quietly standing with your horse while they eat. Then, you can add in the marker, pairing it with food and giving it some meaning to your horse. To do this, simply mark as you throw the food into the bucket. Your horse will come to associate the marker with the arrival of food.

There are two main aims of this exercise; the first is to begin to teach your horse that the marker has good associations and is something they should pay attention to as it means the food is coming, and the second is to pair feelings of softness and relaxation with the marker, the food and the

training. The emphasis here is on 'being' rather than 'doing'. You're not looking for you horse to do anything specific, just to relax. You can help your horse to relax by talking gently to him, stroking him and so on. It's also important that you're marking and throwing food into the bucket at moments that your horse is relaxed, such as when they are gently eating from the bucket. If your horse gets tense, spooky or focused on the food you have in your treat bag, rather than the bucket, just talk quietly to him and redirect his focus back to the bucket. When he drops his head and softens again, you can mark and throw more feed into the bucket.

Hannah works with Lady, a rescue horse at Hope Pastures rescue centre, in her first Connection Training session.

VIDEO RESOURCE

HOW TO START CONNECTION TRAINING PART 1: INTRODUCE THE MARKER

Watch Hannah introducing the marker to Lady and Tino (who you'll meet later in this Chapter) with the emphasis on relaxation and connection.

www.connectiontraining.com/video-resources

STAND QUIETLY TOGETHER

Once you have spent a few minutes pairing the marker and the food for your horse, you can begin to train your first behaviour – for your horse to just stand quietly and politely next to you. The first behaviours you train this way are usually the strongest and the ones your horse will revert to in times of confusion, so standing quietly next to you is a great place to begin.

When you're training your horse to do any behaviour, break it down into tiny steps and build from there. These steps are called 'successive approximations'. Approximations are informed guesses towards the behaviour, and they are successive because they gradually become more accurate. For example, if you are teaching your horse to stand quietly beside you, the most common issue is horses turning their head to you to look for treats. So, you will begin by rewarding your horse as soon as they turn their head away from the food even an inch, then a little further and a little further until they are clearly keeping their head away from the treats.

This entire process is known as "shaping a behaviour". The more you teach your horse, the better you will become at breaking big goals down into small steps so you can progressively train your horse towards your end goal.

INTRODUCING CONNECTION TRAINING CASE STUDIES

Put into practice, the process does vary from horse to horse, so here are 2 case studies from Hope Pastures Rescue Centre, showing Hannah introducing Connection Training and teaching stand quietly next to her:

LADY

Lady is a Dales mare in her late teens who came to the Rescue Centre when her owner's widow could no longer care for her. Although she had some work when she was younger, it had been some years since she'd had much handling and she had lived alone for a large portion of that time, too. The staff reported that she seemed very unaware of people and could be quite pushy around food.

I began with casual connection time, turning her loose in the arena. Lady immediately left me to explore the arena, sniffing poo piles and talking to the other horses. She didn't return to me at all and seemed quite oblivious to me, just as the staff had reported.

Since I'd been told Lady could be pushy around food, I was extra careful to begin with, feeding her plain chaff in a bucket when I marked. After a few minutes, Lady actually lifted her head from the bucket and greeted me, which was fantastic!

I followed this with a casual connection break, where Lady was free to explore on her own again, before I went back in with my treat bag for another training session. This time Lady came over straight away, which was lovely to see – she was starting to pair me with good things!

This time, I began to wait until she'd finished the food in the bucket. This is the point when your horse really begins to problem-solve – what behaviour will get you to throw more food in the bucket? Wait for your horse to stand quietly by your side, and then mark and reward in the bucket. For most horses, you're looking for them to keep their head in their own space or turn their head away from you slightly.

However, with Lady I had the opposite problem as she struggled to stay focused on me, wasn't pushing for the treats and kept wandering away. So, instead, I waited for her to stand quietly but with her focus and attention on me, which often meant a slight head tilt towards me. She was still relaxed and polite, but I really wanted to draw her attention to and reward those moments where she connected with me. So, when she stood quietly with me, her attention on me, I marked and threw another handful of food in the bucket.

We practiced this with 2 buckets, which was great for Lady as she had to follow me between them, which further emphasised her focus on me. As we progressed, I also began to occasionally feed her by hand. It didn't take long before she was able to stand quietly next to me without a bucket.

This was Lady's entire first session. It lasted approximately 30 minutes and included 3 breaks of casual connection time and about 20 minutes of training broken up into 5-10 minute mini sessions. It was a great introduction to Connection Training for Lady, especially as she didn't know me at all when we began. She disconnected and walked away from me many times throughout the session, but these became less frequent and she returned sooner as the session progressed. When training, you're always looking for improvements, not perfection – if it's getting better, keep going!

Tino was a 2-year-old colt who had come to Hope Pastures in terrible condition, starved, unable to stand and with ulcerated eyes. The staff did an incredible job of nursing him back to health, though he did lose one eye. Despite all this, Tino was a very friendly horse, who loved attention and scratches. Due to his age and his experience of food deprivation, Tino was a prime candidate for getting over-aroused in the training. Young horses have high energy, get excited easily and the males can also get sexually aroused quite easily, too, or bring 'boy play' into the training, such as nipping, striking or rearing. I was very aware of all of these factors, and made sure it was a relaxed experience for Tino.

I began working him in a small paddock next to his herd mates so that he would feel comfortable and, since I knew he enjoyed scratches, began some casual connection time scratching him.

To break it up a bit, I simply asked him to follow me to different areas of the paddock and scratched him for short periods of time before asking him to move on.

Tino was completely different from Lady as he was totally focused on me right from the start. I began introducing the marker to him, following it with being scratched since it was clearly a strong reward for him. This is still an effective way of giving the marker meaning because it's being paired with something the horse values. Just like when I waited for Lady to stop eating to let her figure out the solution to get more food (stand quietly with me), I did the same with Tino only this time I stopped scratching him. Because he wanted more scratching, his first response was to lean or step into me more, but I quietly ignored that and reassured him with my voice. The moment he tried the opposite – moving his head away from me and keeping to his own space, I marked and scratched him again. He quickly learned that the best way to get scratches was to wait quietly beside me.

He did really well with this, so I worked with him for a few more minutes and then gave him a break, before beginning another mini session where I introduced food. I began with chaff and a bucket in a similar way to Lady but, because Tino had already practiced standing quietly for scratches, we moved onto hand feeding that behaviour quite quickly. He did find the addition of food, even plain chaff, a little more exciting than the scratches, so I worked on lowering my energy, deep breathing and talking gently to him to help him relax. I made sure that he was standing still and feeling softer before I marked and rewarded him and he picked it up quickly.

As well as waiting for Tino to stand quietly before marking, I also made sure that he was standing quietly and politely before I rewarded him, too. When you begin, it's best to give the reward quickly after you mark because you want the horse to associate the reward with the marker. However, after the first few minutes your horse will have made this connection. From then on, it is more important that your horse remains calm, relaxed, and polite while you give the reward. If you mark and your horse swings his head around and starts pushing you for the food, just wait until he turns his head away again before giving him the reward. This will teach him to wait patiently for his treat.

I also continued to scratch Tino in the session once I'd added the food. However, he showed me that he didn't want to be scratched if there was food available by backing up away from my hand when I tried to stroke or scratch him in this situation. This is a common pattern, but it's one to watch out for because it's a sign that your horse is overly focused on the food rather than the relationship and connection between you. If your horse usually likes to be touched, but refuses it when you're training with food, you can work on this to show your horse that it's okay, doesn't mean the food is leaving and that they can relax in the sessions, too. I worked on this with Tino by lifting my hand to stroke his neck when he was standing quietly next to me. If he backed up, I gently backed up with him, talking softly to him to help him relax. As soon as he stopped with my hand on his neck, I marked and rewarded. It only took a few repetitions before he realised that he could get a scratch AND a food reward and was again happy to let me touch him all over during our session.

Touch, such as scratching, stroking or grooming (avoid patting/clapping him, however—it has the opposite effect) is an effective way to stimulate your horse's CARE system, helping them to relax and strengthen the bond between you. Oxytocin, nicknamed the 'cuddle hormone', is released under the influence of touch. Scratching, stroking, and grooming activate the CARE systems of both you and your horse by giving you both an oxytocin boost. This will help to relax your horse even more and will turn down the SEEKING system further, creating a mini brain break. Your bond and trust are strengthened, and your touch ensures that training is not just about food, but about spending enjoyable time together and building connection. Use of your voice in a gentle and soothing tone also helps your horse to relax with you.

By the end of the first session, Tino was happy to stand quietly next to me while I stroked or scratched him both with and without food. When I had food on me, he stayed relaxed and polite. Again, the entire session lasted for around 30 minutes and we switched between casual connection time and more formal training mini sessions.

STANDING TOGETHER, BUT NOT QUIETLY!: WHEN TENSION CREEPS IN

Through standing together, you've taught your horse that the way to get food is to turn her head away from it instead of pushing, nipping, or mugging. However, without focus on relaxation, this can turn into an extreme behaviour, as if the horse is saying 'I'm turning away! I'm doing it, I'm doing it!' She may keep her inside eye intently upon you, desperately waiting for you to mark. Then when you do mark, she swings around to grab the treat.

Extreme head turned-away is the 'calming signal' head position and is a sign of anxiety from one horse to another. Of course, we don't want our horses to feel anxious in our relationship. We want them to feel calm and confident and trust us. Therefore, we move quickly to rewarding a natural head forward position, rather than the more extreme head away. This will help your horse feel more relaxed and comfortable next to you.

To help your horse relax, take some deep breaths yourself. Talk to your horse and reassure him, or give him a stroke or a scratch. When you notice your horse relax—perhaps by exhaling, lowering his head, softening his eyes, ears, and mouth, and generally quieting a little—mark and reward that moment to strengthen those feelings of softness and relaxation. Like all training, this is a progressive process. So, if your horse is very high-energy to begin with, just reward the moments that are a little softer and more relaxed, and you will see it improve in time.

VIDEO RESOURCE

HOW TO START CONNECTION TRAINING PART 2: STAND TOGETHER

See how to teach your horse to stand quietly with you in this video.

www.connectiontraining.com/video-resources

TEACHING WALK TOGETHER

Walking with your horse is a fundamental part of training and interacting with your

horse and this exercise is all about maintaining connection and softness in movement. Horses are physical animals designed to move a lot and incorporating plenty of movement into your sessions right from the start will help your horse to stay calm and soft in your sessions. This exercise also teaches soft polite leading to your horse, which is necessary for basic handling as well as being the foundation of so many other behaviours such as lunging, in-hand work and riding.

Incorporating walking together into your sessions alongside standing together is very easy. You will naturally ask your horse to stand still for a few moments, maybe have a bit of a cuddle and a scratch, then to follow you a short way before asking them to stop and stand quietly again. As you do this, your horse will begin to anticipate the rewards for standing quietly next to you when you stop, and will show this by getting into that position and staying in it as much as possible, even when you're walking, coming into a lovely leading position by your side.

You can then build on this by marking the best moments when walking together. This could be as you feel your horse soften and come into step beside you or, perhaps, if you have a horse who rushes, when you notice them slow down and wait for you, or if you have one who gets tense when they breathe out, lower their head or soften their ears.

Tino gets rewarded for standing by Hannah's side. As they practice walking on and halting, he anticipates getting into this position and begins to stay there even as they walk together. Hannah can then mark and reward those moments as the leading position improves.

SYNCHRONY AND COMMUNICATION IN MOVEMENT

Ethologist, Lucy Rees, has done some fascinating studies of feral horses, showing how they synchronise their movements with each other as they graze, play and run. This is practice for staying safe in a stampede away from danger, but also enhances their communication and relationships. Walking with your horse taps into this natural bonding through movement and helps you to establish a strong connection with your horse.

While walking with your horse, aim to connect with him by synchronising your movements. To begin, follow your horse's pace to find his natural rhythm. This might mean slowing or speeding the pace or rhythm of your walk or adjusting the length of your strides to start to walk more in time with your horse. Following your horse's natural rhythm helps your horse to relax and soften and the connection deepens as you move together and begin to mirror each other.

As you continue, you can gently start to adjust your stride and see if your horse follows. Experiment with slowing down, speeding up and turning. Avoid abrupt changes of pace or direction as that is likely to bring tension to your horse, so take a few strides to make any changes to give your horse time to adjust while staying relaxed and connected.

This process should be a conversation between you, as you both work to match your movements. You can intersperse walking together with standing quietly, practicing keeping the connection and softness in both walk and halt. Mark and reward moments when you feel you and your horse are working well together, or when your horse makes a good effort to stay connected and in sync with you, for example if you are standing quietly and your horse thinks you're about to walk off, but then stops and waits when she realises you're not.

VIDEO RESOURCE

HOW TO START CONNECTION TRAINING PART 3: WALK TOGETHER

Watch Hannah teaching 'Walk Together' and see how it works with 'Stand Together'.

www.connectiontraining.com/video-resources

EQUIPMENT

During your session, work your horse both with and without a head collar and lead rope. Observe your horse to see if his behaviour changes. Is he more relaxed/connected/tense/ distracted with or without a head collar and lead rope? Does he try and avoid the head collar and lead rope or is happy to wear it? This is fantastic information about how your horse feels about both being loose and his head collar. Many horses have experienced unpleasant situations when in a head collar and lead rope, so will often show avoidance or tension when worked in one. Sometimes they have learned that lead ropes mean no choice, so they become very compliant but are not really present and engaged with the situation.

Alternatively, some horses have had negative experiences when worked at liberty, such as having their FEAR system stimulated by being chased in round-penning or free-lunging. Hannah has also worked with rescue horses who were strays in populated areas and had many experiences of being herded or chased by people before coming to the rescue centre. These horses are often more tense when worked at liberty and relax when on a headcollar, because they've had much more positive associations in that situation.

Ideally, you want your horse to feel exactly the same whether they have a headcollar on or not – relaxed, willing and knowing they have a voice that will be listened to. Working your horse with and without equipment in each session is a brilliant way to teach your horse that the kit doesn't matter and that the relationship and communication remains the same both ways. Stay soft, sensitive and respect your horse, even when working on a rope. Many clicker trainers advocate working at liberty as much as possible, because then your horse has the choice to leave. However, if you're paying attention to your horse's emotional state and threshold, you will know just as clearly whether he's relaxed and happy or not, even if he's on a rope. It's up to you to pay attention to what your horse is telling you and adjust your training accordingly to bring positive emotions to the situation.

Even if your horse does show some tension in particular equipment, gently persevere in working him both ways each session, making it very rewarding for your horse. You'll notice a change in your horse's attitude as he learns that the interactions with you are positive and fun, regardless of the equipment used. This also sets your horse up to be handled happily in daily life and a variety of interactions.

Hannah working with Ned, a rescued donkey with big leading issues. He showed clear tension when presented with the headcollar at first and had a history of biting and barging when being led. Hannah worked Ned both with and without the lead rope from the first training session and he quickly became much more relaxed and happy to lead either way.

VIDEO RESOURCE

GENTLE LEADING: HOW TO STOP BARGING AND PULLING

Watch Ned's training and see how these basic exercises can improve leading through gentle and soft techniques..

www.connectiontraining.com/video-resources

NO-FOOD MINI SESSIONS

Incorporating mini training sessions without food right from the start teaches your horse that working without food is fun and rewarding, too. Many people get worried about, or stuck on, feeding all the time for every behaviour and, if they've established this pattern with their horse, it does take a little longer to teach them to be relaxed when working without food. Horses get confused and frustrated when we set up expectations and then change them abruptly, so including training time without food right from the start prevents these negative emotions because they haven't learned to expect anything else. It's simply part of the process. This makes it much easier for you or other people to handle your horse without food outside training sessions as well as making it a smoother transition as you fade out the markers and rewards for behaviours your horse knows.

The best way to add in a no-food mini session is to include it within your full session. After a casual connection time break in your session, return to your horse without food on you. Simply ask them to follow you a few steps and stand quietly with you as you have been doing. You can mark for good moments and scratch your horse if suitable, or simply mark and praise your horse. Repeat this once or twice more, walking only a few steps and standing quietly for a moment. Then, return to the edge of your training area and give your horse a jackpot on the ground or in a bucket, followed by a short break. This mini session will only be a minute or two long to begin with. You are teaching your horse that working without food is no big deal and that they will get a high value food reward at the end if they work calmly with you. From here, you can begin to increase the duration and complexity of your no-food mini sessions, though always keep them easier and shorter than the

sessions with food because they are challenging in a different way.

By establishing this as part of your training and handling routine right from the start, your horse will expect it and be happy to work with or without food rewards. This gives you more flexibility in your training, teaches your horse to be relaxed with variety and prepares your horse for situations where they will not be fed regularly such as handling by vets or taking your horse to a lesson where you can only feed occasionally within breaks.

ENDING THE TRAINING SESSION

Horses quickly pick up on the end of a session, and when you're using Connection Training, they often don't want to stop. They may even try to prevent you from leaving the arena or refuse to leave themselves because they want the training to continue. This is a lovely expression that they're enjoying the training, but you want them to stop calmly and happily.

It's useful to have a routine that tells your horse it's the end of the session, so that you can end calmly and positively. Also, ending the session abruptly can feel unpleasant for your horse and you don't want to end on bad-feeling note. A lovely way to end your sessions gently is to give your horse a little 'jackpot' (couple of handfuls of feed) on the floor or in a bucket when you're ready to stop to working. This shifts your horse into grazing mode and changes the energy of the session as you stop working together. Allow your horse time to eat and then take your horse back to their field or stable. Before you leave them, spend a few minutes together scratching, exploring or simply hanging out with your horse until you have both settled from your training session and your horse is ready to return to his herd. If your horse is very reluctant to leave the training area, you can continue your session as you walk him back to his field or stable and give his jackpot there instead, to help associate positive feelings with session endings.

You can also include this end-of-session routine between mini sessions. This will help your horse to understand when you switch exercises or into casual connection time and it teaches him that end-of-sessions don't necessarily mean you're stopping completely. This reduces tension and helps your horse to feel relaxed about breaks and finishing training sessions.

TARGETING—THE MOST USEFUL TOOL IN THE BOX!

Once you've established standing and walking together with your horse over a few sessions, you're ready to introduce the next behaviour - targeting. Targeting has many uses, as you'll see throughout the book. However, it all starts here— introducing the target to your horse.

WHAT IS TARGETING?

Targeting is a training tool used to explain to your horse what behaviour you're looking for. As you shift to reward-based training, you need a way to guide your horse to the desired behaviour without using traditional means, such as waving a stick behind her and inducing the flight response. This is the role of the target.

A target is any object you want to train your horse to touch with a body part. For example, it could be a mat on the ground that the horse stands on, or a nose target on a wall to teach your horse to stand and be tied up, or a target on the end of a stick that your horse learns to follow so you can teach leading.

We teach nose targeting first, for a few reasons. First, it's another easy behaviour

for your horse to learn. One of the first things a baby foal does is nuzzle her mother as she searches for the teat. This is an innate behaviour. Horses explore the world with their muzzles all the time, using their whiskers too. Their brains are very used to muzzle touching leading to a reward—foals do it right before they drink milk, and adults do it before eating and grooming. That makes muzzle touching one of the most strongly reinforced natural behaviours.

Secondly, by teaching your horse to touch his nose to a target, you can guide movement in the rest of his body. For example, if you want your horse to move forward, simply hold the target out in front of him and he will go towards it. No FEAR system arousal is required. If you'd like him to stand still, just hold the target in one place and he will stay there for the reward.

Nose targeting is clear, precise, and can easily be used to explain to your horse what you'd like him to do, such as leading, lunging, loading, standing tied, and many more behaviours. Because this technique is so useful in so many situations, when we say 'targeting' we generally mean nose targeting unless otherwise specified.

Although 'targeting' is used to describe touching any body part to an object on cue, it usually refers to nose targeting unless specified otherwise.

VIDEO RESOURCE

WHY IS TARGETING THE MOST USEFUL TOOL IN THE BOX?

See targeting in action for a wide range of behaviors and situations.

www.connectiontraining.com/video-resources

WHAT TARGET SHOULD I USE?

Any object can become a target. For the greatest success, a nose target should be:

• *Easy to see and touch.* It needs to be large and distinctive enough for your horse to be able to see and touch. Targets that are too small make it more difficult for your horse and encourage chewing or biting the target, instead.

• *Robust.* If your horse does try to take a bite, you want it to be robust enough to safely withstand it without breaking or splintering.

• *Lightweight.* Eventually you could be holding the target for lengthy periods of time, such as when teaching a young horse to be calm while taking your horse out for a walk in-hand. You won't want to carry anything heavy then.

• *Recognisable and different.* It's best to use something that is only used as a target. This way it will be more powerful for your horse than an object she's used to seeing every day that is not always associated with rewards.

Examples of targets include balls, plastic bottles, and lengths of foam attached to the end of bamboo canes or old whips. If your horse has a fear of sticks, use a short target, such as a cone or a round feed tub lid. As your horse comes to know and love

the target (and they all do!), you can then attach it to a stick. This will help him overcome his fear of sticks as he learns to move towards it instead of running away from it. You will also use many different objects as targets throughout your training, so this is just to get you started. Once your horse has learned the concept of targeting, it's easy to turn any object into a target when necessary.

INTRODUCING THE TARGET

To teach the behaviour of targeting, begin by holding the target out in front of your horse. It is natural for horses to sniff and investigate a new object. As your horse stretches towards it, mark and reward that moment as the first step towards your horse touching the target.

The reward will encourage your horse to try again and the marker told your horse that this exercise has something to do with the target. Next time, wait until your horse's muzzle actually touches the target before marking. After a few tries, you should find that your horse is clearly and willingly touching the target with his nose. Now you have to ensure softness and relaxation is associated with targeting, too, so if your horse is bashing or biting it, just wait a few moments until he is softly touching it with his nose before you reward.

Hannah is introducing the target to Tino. When you first hold out the target for your horse to touch, he might explore your hand or the food instead. Just wait patiently for your horse to work out the correct answer. This is a good exercise to start teaching your horse to solve problems.

However, if your horse persists in looking to you or the treats instead of touching the target, just drop the target down to your side for a few moments before holding it out and showing it again. Your horse is likely to look at the target more closely when you hold it up again. If he even thinks about touching it, mark and reward. You can also make it easier for your horse to succeed by changing your position or holding the target closer to their nose as Hannah has done with Tino here.

For targeting to be most useful in the long run, you want to help your horse build a great emotional association with the target. So, make him highly successful at touching the target and give lots of reward for it.

With a little repetition, Tino clearly learned to touch the end of the target. This process took fewer than 10 minutes.

THE STATIONARY TARGET: TEACHING "STAY"

As well as using a handheld target to guide your horse, you can teach your horse to move to and stay at a stationary target. A stationary target is fixed in place, and the horse learns to keep his nose on it.

Standing at a stationary target develops into a 'Stay' behaviour. When your horse stands next to you and walks with you, that keeps you and the treats at your horse's head. It's important to teach your horse that it's okay for you and the treats to change position and move away from him. Again, you will start this in baby steps. Can your horse stand quietly at his target while you rub his withers? If you move towards his hindquarters? While you walk all the way around? Soon you will be able to ask your horse to stand and stay while you walk away.

You can use a stationary target in many different situations. For instance, you can place it inside the stable and send your horse to it while you enter so he doesn't crowd the door. You can place it inside the trailer and send your horse to it when loading. You can also use it to teach behaviours such as standing tied.

Heather stands at the cone, her stationary target, while Rachel grooms her.

Another reason teaching this behaviour is important at this stage of training is that it improves your horse's problem-solving skills. The more your horse learns to take responsibility in the training sessions and to work out what earns the marker and reward, the more aware and skilled at picking up new behaviours he'll become. He's learning to be a better learner.

Once your horse understands to stay at the stationary target, you can use your gesture or vocal "stay" cue and fade out the target.

BUILDING STRONG FOUNDATIONS

These early lessons are the foundation of all you wish to teach your horse. They are the building blocks to a great relationship of trust and two-way communication. The exercises are straightforward in themselves, but adapting the training to suit your horse and find the best emotional balance can be more complex. Take the time to understand the principles of the training so you know what you're aiming for with your horse. Learn all of the options available to you so you can set your horse up for success and move on smoothly and easily.

As you begin to train your horse, will everything go perfectly? Of course not! That's to be expected and nothing to worry about (learn more about enjoying the ups and downs in Chapter 6). However, there are many things you can do to help make the process easier for both of you. The biggest mistake we see people make is teaching these behaviours without fully understanding the emotional component and how to adapt the training to help the horse stay calm, focused, and keen. In the next Chapter, we look at tailoring the training to your horse and creating that sweet spot of emotional balance, whether he's fearless, fearful, high energy or low energy.

CHAPTER 4

TAILORING THE TRAINING TO YOUR HORSE

It would be nice if we could give you a recipe that would work for every horse, but they are all individuals, so we need to adapt the training to the horse we're working with. Because the success of your interactions all come down to how your horse feels, you will even need to make small adaptations from day to day with the same horse, depending on the mood they are in or other external factors influencing the situation. The underlying principles are always the same – to help your horse feel relaxed, motivated, confident and willing – but how you get there will vary. This Chapter gives you practical techniques you can use to adapt the training to your horse.

PROTECTED CONTACT

If a horse has a history of mugging for food, is aggressive around food, or is fearful of people, training in with your horse may not be safe. Instead, you can start the training in 'protected contact'. This means that you and the horse are separated by a barrier. It could be your field fence, the stable door, or a pen you have set up for the purpose. The advantage of protected contact is that you can step out of reach if you need to. This keeps you safe and allows your horse to learn how to be calm, relaxed, and thoughtful without being punished for her behaviour.

It's important to remember that horses become pushy or aggressive only through their past experiences. For example, if food is limited, a horse may show natural resource-guarding behaviour, such as pinning his ears, when a bucket of desirable food is brought into the stable. If the human isn't aware of this, she may well put the bucket down anyway. The horse

Protected contact allows you to work with a horse with a fence between you. This keeps everyone safe while the horse learns to be calm, confident and polite. Once you have these basics in place, you can begin to work in with your horse.

has just been rewarded for pinning his ears, and this behaviour can quickly escalate when food is delivered.

Horses can also become aggressive towards people when they feel a need to defend themselves. As we discussed in

Chapter 1, when horses feel afraid but cannot escape, their brains will shift from the FEAR system to the RAGE system. They will learn to fight, both to prevent being harmed and to escape similar situations. The trigger could be an unavoidable experience, such as needing veterinary treatment. Or it could stem from violent 'training' methods, such as beating a horse in the stable or chasing him with something scary, like a plastic bag on a stick, while he's confined by a rope or in a small space. Unfortunately, these situations are all too common. Many horses will learn to associate humans with these experiences and will learn to fight if they cannot flee.

Hannah speaks of this experience with one of her horses:

Hannah and Murphy

Murphy is a little rescue pony who came to me when his owners were going to have him euthanised, as he was too lame to continue jumping for their child. It turned out that he hadn't received any dentistry and had a missing molar, so his opposite tooth had grown into the gum where the missing tooth should have been. He also had severe back problems from ill-fitting

tack and nutritional issues from the wrong diet. All of this meant that he was in a lot of pain and was desperately trying to escape the situation.

When he arrived, we turned him out in the field. The next day, I went into the field to catch him. As soon as he spotted me with a head collar, he ran away in blind panic. I immediately stood still, but because his attention was so much on me, he didn't see the fence and somersaulted over the top of it. Needless to say, we stopped that approach and let Murphy find his own way into the yard by following the other horses. It was my first insight into how extreme his fear was.

Once he was in the yard and arena, he changed from trying to escape to using very aggressive behaviours. The yard and arena are a big space, but he still felt confined. If a person entered, even without attempting to approach him, he would charge aggressively, often rearing up and boxing with his front legs or spinning and trying to kick out. Punishing Murphy for this behaviour would only have made it worse by increasing his feelings of fear and rage (and previous punishment was a key factor in his behaviour escalating to this stage in the first place). Instead, he needed space to be able to relax, learn alternative behaviours, and change his emotional associations with people. Protected contact was invaluable for this process.

I'm pleased to say that Murphy became a calm, relaxed, happy pony. I re-backed him, rode out safely, and had great fun teaching him loads of tricks. It took a few years before he extended this trust to strangers, but eventually he greeted everybody in a polite, relaxed, and enthusiastic way.

VIDEO RESOURCE

TRIBUTE TO MURPHY

Learn more about Murphy's story and witness the bright, fun and happy pony he became.

www.connectiontraining.com/video-resources

When working with a pushy or aggressive horse, you can begin Connection Training in the same way as outlined in the previous Chapter, but with the safety of a barrier between you. For example, stand outside the stable door with your treats. This may elicit old behaviours in your horse, such as pinning his ears. Simply stay out of reach, reassure your horse, and when you see a moment of softening and relaxation, mark and put the reward into a bucket. If he comes back at you aggressively while you approach with the treat, just step back and wait again until he's a bit softer. He will soon learn that softness earns rewards, and you'll see his behaviour and emotions begin to change. Remember, your horse has only done what's worked for him in the past, so now you are switching it around so that calm, relaxed, and polite behaviours are the most likely to get him what he wants. As he begins to feel calmer, he will associate these emotions with you, which will begin to change your relationship and trust.

Fearful horses benefit from protected contact too. If your horse is wary of humans a barrier between you often gives your horse a feeling of security and enables her to be bolder and build trust more quickly. Again, feed in a bucket if you cannot get close enough to hand-feed. Since you're always looking to mark and reward what you want to see more of, with a frightened horse you will begin by marking at moments when the horse looks at you, takes a step towards you, and so on. You want to encourage exploration, engagement, and boldness. In fact, when you get to the stage where the horse is confident enough to try mugging for treats, you have done your job very well and can now begin to balance the scale by teaching her to also be polite and calm as well as enthusiastic and bold.

Protected contact can be used in a wide range of situations for the safety and happiness of horse and handler. This pony, Valiente, was rescued from horrific conditions in Spain which had left his feet extremely overgrown. Once rescued, he then needed intensive veterinary care to return him to health. This combined experience left Valiente highly fearful about touch, especially when having his feet handled, and he was quick to show RAGE-stimulated behaviours such as biting and kicking. He felt much safer with humans on the other side of a fence and didn't leave the session or aggress towards his handler with this barrier. Of course, it was also safer for the handler, too. Claire, Director, Positive Horse Training Spain, taught him to voluntarily have his feet trimmed at liberty all in protected contact - this has actually become one of Valiente's favourite behaviours!

VIDEO RESOURCE

HOOF TRIMMING WITH A FRIGHTENED AND AGGRESSIVE RESCUE PONY

See Valiente's training from being too frightened to be touched to hoof trimming becoming his favourite activity.

www.connectiontraining.com/video-resources

MOVEMENT IN PROTECTED CONTACT: AROUND A ROUND PEN

You can teach all of the initial exercises (Stand Together, Walk Together, Targeting and 'Stay') in protected contact as you teach your horse how to be polite and calm around you and the training. One effective way to create protected contact for movement exercises is our 'Around A Round Pen' technique (some of our students have also started calling it the 'reverse round pen'). Set up a round pen in enough space where your horse can stay *outside* the round pen and be free to go around it. You stand on the inside and allow your horse to stay with you or move away as he pleases. You can make the pen out of electric fencing (not switched on!), cones and ropes, jump poles and stands, or other suitable materials.

Rachel working with Selena Around A Round Pen.

It's a great tool to help horses relax as they can move freely in their own space and you can safely wait until you see them settle and connect with you before rewarding. Although you can help your horse to relax, you can't force them to feel a certain a way. However, as you help your horse to soften through your voice, touch, movement and so on, and then mark and reward the good decisions your horse makes towards more settled behaviour, you are actually teaching your horse how to calm themselves down. And, that it feels good when they do this. This is incredibly effective because it empowers your horse to be able to calm down when they need to and it transfers to many different situations.

You might be starting this work with a horse who gets very tense or angry, and working around a round pen gives you the ability to stay calm and be there for your horse as they struggle through these difficult emotions. Reward any tiny improvement or good decision and you will see your horse's emotions and behaviour change. Because this change has come *from* your horse, it will be more powerful and effective at changing those negative emotions for good.

Using protected contact is a means of training. Once your horse understands the behaviour and is calm, relaxed, and polite about it, you won't need the barrier any more.

CASE STUDY: IMPROVING LEADING SKILLS WITH THE ROUND PEN

1. Rachel's pony, Heather, could get over-excited and rush in front, cutting her off when leading.

2. Using 'Around-A-Round-Pen' stopped Heather being able to do this and Rachel could reward her when she was calmly walking in the correct position.

3. Once Heather understood where Rachel would like her to walk when leading and was able to calmly stay in place, they no longer needed protected contact.

VIDEO RESOURCE

AROUND A ROUND PEN

Watch the Around A Round Pen technique in action for many leading and lunging exercises.

www.connectiontraining.com/video-resources

WORKING WITH FRIGHTENED OR AGGRESSIVE HORSES

As well as using protected contact, if you are working with a horse who is frightened of people or the interactions, there are other steps you can take to help your horse build confidence. You want to become as non-threatening as possible, so crouch down to make yourself smaller, take deep slow breaths and keep your gaze soft rather than focused. Be consistent and predictable so that your horse learns to trust your movements and let your horse come to you. The most common mistake made in this situation is to ask for too much too soon, so that the horse is always on the edge of being fearful. This takes longer to establish trust because you, the training and the situation are all associated with those feelings of anxiety. Take it slowly and only move on once your horse is truly relaxed and confident. This feels like slow progress to start with, but will be much faster long-term as you establish true trust and joy, giving you a strong foundation to build upon.

Defensive horses are often labelled as 'aggressive', showing behaviours such as biting or kicking when people interact with them. This behaviour has usually been triggered by fear initially, but without being able to escape it, has escalated into aggression when the RAGE system was activated. If this happens repeatedly, horses begin to associate people with those emotions and increasingly show these behaviours. The fear is often triggered by pain and it's common to find an underlying physical issue that is causing these reactions, so this must be checked out first. Horses are peaceable by nature and are struggling if they are showing aggressive behaviours when approached, touched or handled, needing slow and consistent positive experiences to help them grow in confidence and calmness. We have worked with many horses labelled 'dangerous' due to these types of behaviours and with the right management and slow, steady training, they can become happy and well-mannered horses.

Hannah is working with rescued pony, Bernie, at Hope Pastures Rescue Centre. He is very wary about people. Hannah is rewarding him for approaching her. This is the opposite of training him to turn away but, because of his anxiety, he doesn't need that lesson. He does need to be reassured that he won't be frightened or punished if he approaches people, so this is what she's rewarding. Especially because Bernie is so small, Hannah stays kneeling on the ground and allows Bernie to come to her. As he builds confidence in people, she can stand up and begin to be less careful in her movements. He will also get confident enough to start mugging for treats - a great sign - and then he will need to learn to stand quietly.

Whatever the cause, if your horse is showing tension at being approached or touched, especially if food is currently another trigger to escalate these emotions, you can begin the training using advance and retreat. For example, if your horse lunges to bite you if you get too close, begin in protected contact over a fence or stable door and stop your approach when your horse is aware of you but not pinning his ears to bite. Wait there, taking deep slow breaths and talking reassuringly. When your horse shows any signs of relaxing, mark that moment and step back.

This will teach the horse that they can get what they want (you moving away) by relaxing instead of biting. This process is highly effective to begin to change the horse's emotions and behaviour, gradually building upon it until the horse is relaxed as you approach. Retreating is not exactly a reward, since it's a release of the pressure the horse feels at your presence. However, the training principles work just the same as you look for small tries, mark it and give the horse something he wants in that moment.

Communication between you will improve as you look for signs that your horse is happy to approach and he learns that he has choice and control in the situation. This empowers horses hugely and builds their confidence in you, reducing the fear or defensiveness and building trust.

CONNECTION IS A CHOICE

All horses experiencing negative associations with humans or training need to be given choice to interact or not. Your horse can only say a true, 'Yes' if they are allowed to say, 'No'. This is especially important if you're working with very frightened horses. However, you may have an experienced horse who can be handled, but is still quite anxious and wary. Many of these horses are keen at first, but then wonder, 'What's the catch? Whenever humans have been nice to me before, there's always a trap. I'm not falling for it this time.' Hannah experienced this when she gave a retirement home to her favourite riding school pony, Poppy:

When I started working with Poppy, I let her decide how long to interact with me. She would engage with me for a minute or two and then leave, often snorting with her distrust of the situation. But because I gave her that choice, she came to learn that there wasn't any catch and that being with

Poppy had been in a riding school for most of her thirty years. It was a good riding school, but she'd had many unpleasant experiences there and was highly suspicious of any new person or object. She was even more wary if there was food involved; I think treats had only been used to catch her, worm her, inject her, and do other tasks she hadn't enjoyed.

me was actually fun and enjoyable. She lived for another twelve years after she came to me, so she had plenty of time to learn new tricks and have plenty of fun, even though she was in her thirties.

Giving an anxious horse the choice and freedom to leave the session is vital to building his trust. Connection is a choice. You build up your horse's trust by looking for the tiniest sign of re-engagement, such as looking in your direction. Leave a big reward for him and walk away. You will see your horse's curiosity, enjoyment, and trust build over time.

HOW FAST TO MOVE ON?

Different horses need you to move on at different speeds, and getting this right has a big effect on the success of your training. Generally, as soon as your horse is getting the behaviour right about seven or eight times out of ten, you're ready to move on. Moving on could mean asking for longer duration of the same behaviour, asking for consecutive behaviours, or shaping and refining the behaviour you're working on.

A common problem is spending too long repeating the basics, trying to perfect the behaviours. The truth is that behaviours can always be refined and are never 'perfect'. They will fluctuate day to day depending on conditions and the aim is to have fun with your horse, the two of you relaxed and enjoying your time together. It's better to have a moment of confusion that you calmly figure out together than to repeat a behaviour over and over to get it perfect. This is because these are the skills you and your horse need to confidently tackle puzzles and problems that training and life throw at you.

Another problem with too much repetition is that you then create expectations in your horse, which are hard to move on from. For example, if you've consistently marked and rewarded your horse every 2 seconds for standing quietly next to you for too long, you will find that your horse is more likely to get anxious or frustrated if you try to ask for more because you have built up this string expectation.

Finally, drilling behaviours is boring for your horse and, if you're not moving on or training something new, your horse won't be problem-solving, just repeating the behaviour for the food. This can easily make it all about the food, rather than about the puzzle and the connection, leading to over-arousal issues.

Speed of learning and progression depends on many factors such as age, previous learning experience and emotional state.

As always, this is a balance and moving on too quickly can be detrimental to your horse, too, especially if they feel over-faced. Sometimes you need to go more slowly and repeat the behaviour many times. This is the case if you're overcoming an emotional difficulty. For example, a bright and confident young horse may learn to touch the target after only a few repetitions, at which point you can move on to holding the target in various positions, asking for a few touches before feeding, and so on. However, if you're introducing the target to an anxious rescue horse, he may get very worried by any changes you make. For this horse, you will certainly make better and faster progress if you go slowly and repeat the same exercise many times over to build his confidence.

As a rough guide, it should take you 3-6 weeks (3 sessions per week) to train your horse to stand together, walk together, touch a target and 'stay'. This includes building some duration in each behaviour and fading the marker and rewards to some extent (more on how to do that in Chapter 5). However, this can vary greatly depending on the horse, the experience of the trainer and many other factors.

CASE STUDY: DIFFERENCES IN HOW FAST TO MOVE ON

These differences are apparent in the case of two horses Hannah worked with during a live demonstration. Euraj and Chia are both owned and trained by the same person, Hanna, and are even related, they illustrate the extreme differences you can find in how quickly horses can progress through the training. They were trained over about two hours, with lots of very short sessions interspersed with breaks.

EURAJ

Euraj, a six-year-old gelding, was very quick to stand quietly next to his owner, Hanna, with his head forward, not asking for treats.

Hanna then introduced the target, which Euraj also understood right away.

Euraj picked up these first basic lessons quickly. He was solid with them and was calm and confident throughout. His owner told Hannah that Euraj gets bored easily, and you can see why—he's so bright and confident!

Because Euraj was ready to move on, Hannah decided to teach him something new: lowering his head on cue. His owner began by holding the target down low for him to touch.

He was soon lowering his head to touch the target on the ground.

His owner then removed the target and he remained confident to lower his head when asked, even without the target to prompt him.

Euraj shows just how quickly you can (and should!) move through these early lessons if your horse picks them up fast.

CHIA

Chia, a twelve-year-old mare and Euraj's dam, reacted quite differently. She was wary about this new set-up—she was away from home, there was an audience, a microphone, and a strange person, and the marking, feeding, and training were all new to her as well. Whereas these unfamiliar elements didn't faze Euraj, Chia was much more anxious.

However, Chia spent a lot of time either staring into space or standing still, almost going to sleep. This kind of processing often arises when horses are anxious about the situation. It's important not to rush them through it, but just wait patiently until they are ready to offer the behaviour again.

Chia did this a couple of times during the demonstration. Hannah respected her decision by going to work with Euraj instead and coming back again later. When Hannah and the owner returned, Chia was usually eager to start again. This was a great lesson for Chia. It helped her start to find her voice and feel able to express her opinions.

Because Chia was hanging back, reluctant to come over and engage with us at all, Hannah started with targeting rather than standing quietly. Touching the target was something clear and positive for Chia to do and repeat.

At first Chia was too anxious to be able to touch the target, so she was rewarded for just looking at it and showing interest.

It can be hard to see your horse expressing lack of interest and even anxiety around you, but it's simply part of the learning process. We take it as interesting information because the horse is telling us something important. It might simply be that you've gone on too long and your horse feels overwhelmed, or perhaps there was nothing you could have changed and it was a necessary process for the horse. The important thing is that Chia was allowed to express her choices and was listened to, so her trust and confidence started to build. Throughout the demo, she became more eager to engage with the game and more confident and consistent at touching the target, which was great progress for her and showed that the training was working well.

Gradually she gained confidence and began touching it

THE RIGHT CHALLENGE

Part of progressing at the right speed for your horse is getting the level of difficulty right. Some horses love to solve problems and are highly adept at it. They will appreciate more difficult challenges. Other horses will quickly feel overwhelmed and anxious if you make the training too hard. You want to give your horse enough guidance that he's likely to be successful, but enough freedom to be able to make choices. It's not always easy to get that balance right. If you make the training too easy, your horse will never learn how to solve problems calmly and effectively. If you make it too hard, he won't be successful and will end up more frustrated than before.

We usually tell people who are starting out to go slower, take smaller steps, and make the sessions easier for their horse. This helps the horse to be successful and create a good association and attitude about the training. However, once the foundations are in place and the horse is happy and confident with the training, that's the time to push on.

On the other hand, we often have to encourage people with more experienced or confident horses to challenge them more and to expect better responses and higher quality behaviour. Of course, this varies hugely with each individual, but paying attention to your horse's abilities to calmly solve problems and working to his level will help your horse to progress in the behaviours and enjoy the learning process. As your horse builds these skills, he'll be happy to take on more challenges, and you'll get better results because of it.

With the best training, the progress can look seamless. When a horse is just starting to learn a behaviour, an excellent trainer can spot the horse having a thought in the correct direction and mark that. This gives the horse confidence to try a bit more. That gets marked. Then the improvements get bigger and bigger as the horse gains skill and confidence. The skilled trainer will take the behaviour to the point where the horse is at the limit of improvement in that session, give the horse a jackpot, and then stop or move on to an easy and familiar behaviour.

This is one of the real 'art' parts of positive horse training. It's easy for us to make the training too easy, and it can also be hard to stop when the horse is being successful and ask for too much, overwhelming the horse after it was going so well. We call that 'greedy trainer syndrome', and we all do it sometimes! Luckily, with most horses, you have quite a lot of leeway. If the gist of the training is at the right level, your horse will be happy.

You can always 'ask' your horse if he's ready for the next step of a behaviour. In fact, we recommend that you do so to ensure you keep moving at the right pace and making progress. Often, your horse will be ready to move on or at least have a good go at it. If not, your horse will tell you through offering the 'wrong' response, reluctance or hesitancy, not responding at all or getting a little tense. This is all part of the two-way conversation and, of course, you'll listen to your horse and make the puzzle easier again. Because you've established a strong foundation of relaxation through casual connection time and standing and walking together, you can easily return to calm any time you need to by taking a deep breath and asking for some of these behaviours. This process is highly effective at teaching your horse confidence in 'having a go' and it helps both of you learn that a little confusion or challenge is no big deal. In fact, you can both learn to stay connected and relaxed through it! This is a great life lesson for your horse and builds up his emotional resilience in challenging situations. Once your horse is relaxed and connected again, you can have another go at the challenging exercise. As you work more with your horse, you'll discover what he finds most challenging, what frustrates him, and what calms and excites him, and you'll be able to tailor your training accordingly.

As humans, we tend to think about learning as a linear process; you perfect step 1 and then move onto step 2. This approach can be difficult for horses because it leads to drilling each stage aiming for perfection and then making a big leap to the next stage. Horses can find this confusing and can easily be over-faced. Instead, think about progressing like the tide. When the tide comes in, each wave doesn't come in a specific distance further than the previous one. Instead, some only come a little way and others come much further, but the overall tide line is always advancing. This is a great way to think about horse training; always advancing but sometimes asking for an easy attempt and sometimes asking for a bigger challenge. This way, you'll make continuous progress without any big 'jumps' in the training, leading to a smoother and steadier learning process for your horse.

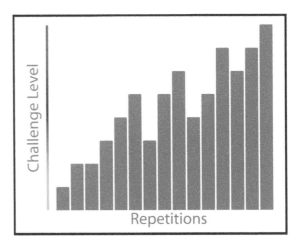

Make progress with your horse by moving forward like the tide coming in, rather than in continual steps forward. For example, if you were teaching an anxious horse to lift his hooves, you would begin just stroking his leg, where he can stay relaxed. The next stage is asking him to shift his weight off the leg you want to lift, which might cause some tension as it's a bigger challenge level for the horse. When you get this weight shift, reward him, and then return to simply stroking his leg to help him relax again. He'll realise that shifting his weight wasn't too bad after all as it didn't escalate to something he found really difficult and so he will be ready to do it again next time you ask. As you continue to progress - asking for the leg to be lifted fully, then take hold of the hoof, hold it up for longer and so on – keep returning to easier levels in that exercise regularly. You'll make smoother and faster progress this way because your horse will learn that big efforts are followed by easy exercises, which builds confidence, motivation, resilience and relaxation.

VIDEO RESOURCE

HOW TO MAKE STEADY PROGRESS WITH YOUR HORSE

Learn more about how to make steady progress with your horse by 'training like the tide'.

www.connectiontraining.com/video-resources

A horse who is both relaxed and motivated will be soft, calm and willing to work.

EMOTIONAL BALANCE

Essentially, the key to emotional balance is creating both relaxation *and* motivation in your horse. You can evaluate your horse's relaxation and motivation by knowing what to look for.

Relaxation is your horse's calmness and connection with you, along with freedom from fear, anxiety, and frustration. She will be relaxed about making decisions and solving problems. She knows she will not be punished for making a wrong choice. It also means she is relaxed about not getting a treat if she does make a different choice from the one you're marking, she'll just try something else. She remains calm and confident even when things don't happen quite as she expects – she is able to adapt and cope well with different situations.

A relaxed horse will have soft eyes, nose, and muzzle. Her ears will be forward with focus or flicking backwards and forward in concentration, not held back with tension. She will have relaxed muscles and movement, with no tense tail swishing, bit chomping, or head shaking. She will be prompt in her responses but won't rush through them.

A motivated horse will be focused on you and the behaviours you're asking her to do. She'll show obvious enjoyment of the sessions through things like wanting to go to the arena, being keen to do the things you're asking, and sometimes offering favourite behaviours.

FINDING THE BALANCE

In general, the more you work with your horse using rewards, the more expressive he becomes and the easier it will be to tell how he is feeling. Ideally, you want both relaxation and motivation together. But you'll probably need to work on one more than the other, especially at the beginning. If you have an anxious, tense, spooky, fizzy, or overexcited horse to start with, you will focus on creating and rewarding relaxation. If you have a horse who is distracted, disinterested, and disinclined to put much effort in, you'll begin by focusing on building motivation. You will constantly assess whether relaxation or motivation needs most of your focus and change the emphasis in your training accordingly, even on a day-to-day basis as your horse's mood differs.

Think about it as balancing scales. When the scales are out of balance, your horse will be inclined to feel or act in a certain way. For example, if your horse is spooky and distracted, that side of the scales has a lot of weight in. To balance it up, you want to reward your horse for every attempt to relax and tune in. You can help him to do this by choosing an appropriate exercise that will increase relaxation and reduce high arousal and then marking and rewarding moments when your horse takes a deep breath, lowers his head, looks to you etc. This will help to balance the scales until your horse is more relaxed.

In fact, what often happens next is that the scales go all the way to the other side. Now your previously whizzy and fidgety horse won't want to go forward. This is normal and brilliant—you have successfully changed your horse's feelings about stopping! And now it's easy to get back to balance by rewarding the 'whoa' a bit less and the 'go' a bit more.

In this scenario, the horse is very forward—he prefers to move rather than stand still, so that side of the scales is weighted more.

By keeping most of your rewards for behaviours on the 'whoa' side, such as downward transitions, slower rhythm, standing still, and so on, you will bring more weight to that side of the scales.

After your horse has had many positive experiences and emotions associated with slowing down, you will find that the scales balance out in time.

The process is ongoing; balancing the scales once doesn't mean they will forever be even. Instead, you will have to make changes all the time depending on your horse's mood, what you've been rewarding recently, and external factors your horse is responding to. For example, on a hot, sunny day, when your horse is likely to be relaxed and disinclined to go forward, you may need to reward forward movement to strengthen motivation. On a cold, windy day, when your horse is excitable and energised, you may need to reward a few 'whoas' at the start of your ride to strengthen relaxed behaviour.

No matter what you're teaching your horse, keep the emotional balance scales in mind to work out which behaviours and responses you need to reward more highly in that moment.

ACCOMMODATE YOUR HORSE'S PREFERENCES

Horses differ in personality and which behaviours they naturally love to do. We all know that some horses love to go and others prefer to slow down, but there are further differences in which activities horses prefer. The more you work with your horse using Connection Training, the clearer it becomes which activities and exercises he prefers.

A common mistake when approaching this area of training is to ask *only* for the more difficult behaviour. Even if you're rewarding it highly, you are likely to get stuck if you don't also allow your horse to do the behaviours he naturally enjoys. These behaviours will help to bring in plenty of joy and relaxation into the session and will keep your horse happy, relaxed, and focused, leading to more success all round.

For example, suppose your horse is the forward type and you'd like him to relax and slow down. Asking him to stand still will cause frustration and tension, even if you're rewarding it highly, because your horse still has a drive to move and go forward. Instead, by working with his energy, you'll get the best results. You could begin the session with some lunging, allowing your horse to move. However, you will mark and reward moments when he softens, slows his rhythm, and transitions downward. He gets to move, but you're drawing attention to and emphasising relaxation and slowing down. This way, you both get your needs met, leading to much more relaxation, communication, and willingness during training.

With a horse like this, going forward is itself a reward as it feels good. So, if your horse gives you slow and relaxed steps, you can mark them and then reward him by letting him go forward freely. The timing of your switch from harder to easier behaviours is important. Switching to the easier behaviour is a strong reward, so look for a great moment while working on the more difficult behaviour, when your horse has really tried, and use it then.

Perhaps your horse is too excited and keeps offering behaviours you haven't asked for. Simply waiting for him to stand perfectly still is likely to increase frustration in both of you, since your horse will struggle to do it well. Instead, give him something to do, such as walking with you, backing up, moving over, or targeting. In between each movement, ask him to stand quietly, then reward only those moments. Again, you're meeting your horse's needs by giving him something enjoyable to do and think about, but you're emphasising the quiet moments in between. This will help him learn that standing quietly is the way to get to do the fun stuff, adding even more weight on the 'standing quietly' side of the scales.

Going to the other extreme, if you're working with a horse who is feeling unmotivated and uninterested, give him plenty of breaks and time to just stand and relax, interspersed with small exercises. Give most of your rewards when your horse responds to your cues and increases his energy and effort.

As well as changing from horse to horse, day to day, and session to session, emotional balance can also change within a session. You might start off with a horse who's excited to be working with you and has plenty of energy. Later in the session, he's expended that energy, settled into the training, and now has more 'whoa' than 'go'. You will need to work on different exercises and reward slightly different moments as your horse's needs change in this way.

By working with your horse's natural preferences and energy, you're respecting his natural desires and drives. This not only prevents conflict and frustration, but also creates better communication and improves your bond. You're setting your horse up for success, since he's more likely to respond well to your requests when you consider how he's feeling. This is a constant conversation between you and your horse. As you progress, you will get more skilled at reading what he needs and can do in each moment. You bring more value to the behaviours he finds more difficult, and the scales will become more balanced.

TECHNIQUES FOR BUILDING RELAXATION

As you work on finding emotional balance in your horse, you will most likely be working to build more relaxation or more motivation. We'll start with techniques for building relaxation. This approach is helpful for horses who are high in energy, which can lead to extra bounce, spookiness, or general overexcitement about the training or rewards. Since every horse is unique, you may have to try a few different approaches to find which ones work best for your horse, depending on your horse's history and personality as well as whether the tension arises from anxiety, overexcitement, boredom, or other causes.

LONGER SESSIONS

If your goal is to build relaxation, long sessions can work to your advantage. As your horse becomes tired in terms of learning and movement, you will often find he relaxes considerably.

With horses like this, it's a good idea to let them get over that initial excitement and energy by expending it in a controlled way just before or during the start of the training session. Preceding your session with the Enrichment Exercise calms down many horses and lets them settle. Alternatively, you might go out for a ride, walking in hand for twenty minutes, or starting the session on the lunge (if your horse knows and enjoys this). You can also begin your sessions Around a Round Pen to allow your horse to move safely with extra energy. When you go out on the road or trail, even in walk, there are so many sights, sounds, and smells that your horse will most likely be quieter and more relaxed when you return. Working on a circle or lunge is less stimulating mentally but gives excited or anxious horses an opportunity to satisfy their need to move. Sometimes just working horses for longer, even without the specific movement work, takes them past that point of over-excitement, and they will settle and relax into the session.

MOVEMENT

As well as incorporating lots of movement at the start of a session, you can also incorporate it throughout the session. As a rule, more movement—along with fewer high-value rewards (such as food)—equals more relaxation. By adding frequent movement through leading, lunging, in-hand work, groundwork, and riding, you can help keep your horse in emotional balance.

India is a forward horse who needs plenty of movement in her sessions to keep her calm and focused. Here, Hannah is lunging India and using a target to keep her focus inside the circle.

LOWER-VALUE REWARDS

Lots of high-value rewards in quick succession tend to ramp up excitement and energy levels. You can combat this by using lower-value rewards. This could mean changing a food reward from carrots to hay or adding in more non-food rewards such as scratches, breaks, and praise.

FEED LARGE AMOUNTS

When you do use food as a reward, make sure you feed enough to get your horse chewing. Some horses also find it easier to relax and focus when the trainer doesn't carry the food on them. Instead, you can have the food rewards at the edge of your training area, use non-food rewards throughout the session and then take your horse to the food store occasionally as an extra special reward. You can give him his food reward scattered on the ground or in a bucket, which will promote relaxation before continuing on with your session.

MOVE ON

Many horses get over-excited or frustrated in training because they know the behaviour well yet are being asked for it again and again. You can break this frustration by remembering this: **It's Connection Training, not perfection training!** As soon as your horse has got the gist of the behaviour, move on with it. You could work on generalising it by asking for the behaviour in various locations, or you could pick one aspect of the behaviour and refine it. For example, suppose you're teaching a horse to lift his hoof. Once he understands the initial concept of lifting his feet, in one session you could work on holding it up for gradually longer periods of time and in the next session on using tools on the hoof. As he gets more confident you can add both together: holding it up for extended duration as you use different tools on the hoof, for example. This will keep your horse interested and focused on you and what you're asking for, as opposed to going through the same behaviour by rote for treats.

SLOW DOWN

Horses who are tense, whether from anxiety or excitement, often rush through things. In this instance, make sure you're the one setting the pace of the session and not rushing along with your horse. After you reward your horse, pause, then make sure you're the one who decides when to move off again. Don't let your horse grab the treat and plough on regardless. Be slow in your movements and reward slower responses in your horse. Take deep breaths and be aware of yourself, your horse, and your surroundings—this can help to break the intensity such horses can bring to the sessions. Take it slow and reward slow responses, and you'll both have time to think. A useful mantra to say to yourself is "Stop. Breathe. Think."

There's never any loss in just stopping until you can proceed calmly.

INCLUDE EXTRA CASUAL CONNECTION TIME

Without the relaxation of the CARE emotional system, your horse can quickly get too excited, which can lead to flight behaviours (the FEAR system) or frustration (the RAGE system). Make sure you spend plenty of time, both within and outside of formal training sessions, working on strengthening your bond and activating the CARE system. You can do this by walking together, scratching your horse (mutual grooming), exploring together, sitting with your horse while he snoozes, just chilling out together—any activity where you're not specifically asking your horse to perform, but are both enjoying each other's company. A strong focus on positive emotions throughout your training will also promote that bond. Creating and rewarding relaxation and connection with you will strengthen those emotional pathways in your horse's brain, and your horse will associate those good emotions with you, the training, and the behaviour you're teaching.

VIDEO RESOURCE

HOW TO GET RELAXATION IN TRAINING

What to look for and how to prioritise relaxation in training.

www.connectiontraining.com/video-resources

TECHNIQUES FOR BUILDING MOTIVATION

Some horses have no problem with relaxation but need more motivation. As always, you may need to try different approaches to find the ones that work best for your horse. Here are some techniques we recommend for building motivation.

SHORT SESSIONS

Using short sessions takes advantage of that initial excitement you often get at the beginning of a session and allows you to end the session when that excitement is still high. Your horse will remember and associate that emotion with the training, so you should start to see more excitement and enthusiasm in future sessions.

Short sessions can be really short—as short as a single touch of the target and reward—but you can do lots of sessions throughout the day. For example, while you're mucking out the stable you could pause every few minutes to do a mini session.

Once your horse is showing more enthusiasm, you can start to increase the length of the sessions. The key is to always leave the sessions with your horse wanting more so he starts the next one keen to begin.

HIGHER-VALUE REWARDS

Sometimes adding a bit of extra incentive by bringing in special rewards can work wonders in increasing motivation. You might change all your food rewards to higher-value treats. Or you can use a mixture, giving the higher-value food rewards when your horse tries a difficult behaviour or makes a great burst of effort. The extra value of the reward will highlight those moments for your horse.

REPETITION AND PREDICTABILITY

Many horses lack enthusiasm due to anxiety and lack of confidence. Because of past experiences or personality, they withdraw into themselves when faced with something new, unexpected, or challenging. Making sessions predictable and repeating the same behaviours and rewards can help these horses build confidence in themselves and the learning. For horses like this, the key is not to move on too fast. If you always ask for more every time he 'gets' a behaviour, he will become anxious again. Training won't be a very enjoyable experience for your horse, and it will take much longer for his confidence and enthusiasm to grow. Instead, make it easy and reward highly for small attempts, and you will see him blossom into an eager, focused, and happy horse who loves learning.

If your horse lacks enthusiasm because she is bored, rather than anxious, this technique will have the opposite effect. If that's the case, you will most likely do better by making sessions as unpredictable and varied as possible to keep her interested in the training.

REWARD ONLY A BIG EFFORT

Some horses who lack motivation due to boredom or are naturally 'energy conservers' are not willing to put much effort into anything. In this case, it can be easy to get into the habit of rewarding any tiny effort, because at least he's doing something! But in fact, you want to be very precise about the effort you expect and will reward. If your horse doesn't give you a good enough response to your cue, simply pause for a few seconds and ask again. When you do get a better response, be lavish in your praise and reward so he knows it's worth it. Over time, you will see your horse become motivated and eager and ready to put plenty of effort into training sessions.

PLAY

Sometimes training can get a bit too serious, which can switch off your horse's enthusiasm and enjoyment. Adding in a bit of play can make a big difference.

If it suits you and if it's safe to do this with your horse, running around a bit and encouraging him to follow and run with you can be a great way to build your relationship and make it more fun for your horse. You can do this at the start of a session to wake him up, periodically during the session to keep energy up, or as a reward for some focused effort. If your horse is a playful type, this can greatly increase the amount of motivation you see in the rest of your training.

You can use your horse's favourite behaviours as play. For example, if he struggles with dressage but loves jumping, intersperse the flatwork by popping over a small jump. If he loves object work (and most horses do), add touching a target, standing on pedestals, or pushing a ball along with the more concentrated, 'serious' work.

On this note, teaching a just-for-fun behaviour is a great way to add something different and make the sessions more interesting for your horse. Plus, if it's something that makes you smile—and who doesn't smile when your horse 'smiles' himself or brings you his fetch toy? —then it'll lighten you up too, and you'll remember that horse training is fun!

When you're both having fun, motivation is high and all training goes better. Balance motivation with relaxation, and you'll have some amazing training results with a horse who is truly focused on and connected.

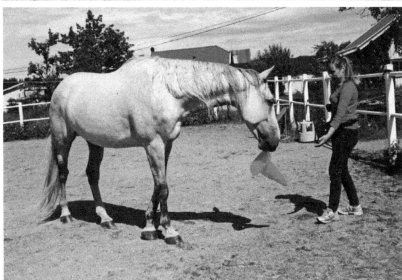

Intersperse more focused or challenging exercises with fun behaviours you both enjoy. Here, CT Coach Gesine Jimenez-Martinez works with Diesel, breaking up the focused lateral work with fun games like fetch.

EXPERIMENT AND ADAPT

As you can see, there are many elements of the training that you can adapt to suit your horse. You won't know for sure what will help your horse find that perfect place of relaxed enthusiasm, so you will have to experiment with different techniques to find out what works best. Don't be afraid to adapt the training in any way that helps your horse feel more relaxed, confident, connected and happier. There are many different ways you can apply these training principles in practice. Prioritise emotional balance for your horse and you will find you enjoy your time together and all of your training will become easier.

Chapter 5

TRAINING ESSENTIALS

This Chapter dives into some more principles around the training and aims to answer the many questions people have about putting CT into practice. For example, how often should you have training sessions? What's the best way to teach cues for each behaviour? How do you build behaviours from the horse's first try to a polished performance? How do you fade the marker so you won't be clicking and giving treats forever? How do you establish boundaries with CT? What about everything your horse knows already? This Chapter will address these questions and give you more insights into how you can incorporate CT into your horse's life.

CUE CLARITY

Let's begin by looking at cues, a cornerstone of communication with your horse. Cues explain to your horse which behaviour you want, when. If your horse isn't clear about when he's to stand calmly and when he's to walk with you, he may get confused or frustrated and you won't get the behaviour you're looking for. Consistent cues bring clarity to your training.

For example, in your first session, you began by standing next to your horse and rewarding him for standing calmly and politely next to you. Now when you stand next to your horse, it's a signal to him that the most rewarding thing he can do is to stand quietly. However, when you move away, he's got to know whether you wish him to stay where he his or come with you. To ask him to stay, you might put your hand up in a 'stop' position and say 'Stand' while you walk away. To ask him to come with you, you might gesture for him to follow and say 'Walk on'. If you're totally consistent with these cues when you teach and practice the behaviours, your horse will quickly learn which cue means what.

You need at least one cue for each behaviour, but you can have more than one. For example, you may eventually have several ways to ask your horse to walk on, such as saying 'Walk on', pointing your finger forward, or picking up the lead rope. This is fine. However, *each cue must mean only one behaviour*. If sometimes a pointing finger means walk on and other times it means stop, this will obviously be confusing for your horse.

Whatever your cues, you must use them consistently. Clear cues bring clarity, responsiveness, and relaxation to your training. Inconsistency in cues creates miscommunication between you and is one of the leading causes of frustration for horses. It's frustrating for you too, as you can't work out why your horse is not responding correctly. A useful way to check for consistency is to video your session. When you watch the video afterward, it may become evident that you've unconsciously changed something small and confused your horse, causing the behaviour to start breaking down. You can also get an expert to watch your video help you to see with more clarity.

When teaching cues, make sure they're really distinct and clear for your horse. CT Coach, Angelica Hesselius, has taught her pony to 'stay' when she holds both hands up.

When you want your horse to walk with you, ensure your cues for this are clear. Don't just march off away from them, but give your horse time to understand what you're asking and to come with you.

Your 'walk on' cues may involve a voice cue, lifting the lead rope or holding out the target for your horse to follow.

Through teaching Stand Together, your horse now knows to stand still next to you when you stand still with your energy low. This is your cue for standing relaxed.

This rescue pony, Hope, is blind so has been taught to come to a hand-clap cue.

USE NATURAL CUES

When you think about creating or choosing a cue for a behaviour, pick something that comes naturally to you. The cue should feel easy, straightforward, and memorable. Using the cues or aids you're already accustomed to is often a great way to go— they'll be clear for you, and often you'll just be refining them for your horse rather than having to teach everything from scratch. For example, teaching your horse to walk on when someone picks up the lead rope is a cue that will likely come easily to you so will be consistent and it is the cue that others will use if they lead your horse. This sets your horse up for success if and when he does get handled by other people.

GENERALISING YOUR CUES

In order for cues to be clear and consistent, you and your horse need to have the same understanding of what the cue actually is. For example, you may think your cue for backing up is the word 'back'. But when you say 'back', you unconsciously dip your head. Horses often pay more attention to visual cues than vocal cues, so your horse may actually be using the head dip as the cue to go back. You can then be surprised when your 'back' cue fails for no apparent reason. Because you changed position, your horse can no longer see the head movement and so has lost his cue.

Or maybe a behaviour that is solid in the arena is non-existent when you ask for it in the field. In this instance, the location itself has become part of the cue. To remedy this, you must spend time teaching cues in various locations and from different positions. This process is called 'generalising', and it is an important part of good training. The goal is to ensure your horse is responding to the cue as you want him to and not to other clues in the environment, such as a particular place or body position.

It's helpful to start generalising as soon as you begin to get the behaviour you want. Just move a few steps and ask again. Try outside the stable as well as inside, with the headcollar on and the headcollar off, and, where appropriate, from beside your horse as well as standing in front. These variations allow your horse to pinpoint the consistent cue and filter out all the extraneous elements.

CUE CONTROL

Cue control means your horse waits patiently for you to give her a cue and then performs the right behaviour when you ask. One of the hardest aspects of building and maintaining cue control is to resist the temptation to reward your horse if she offers the behaviour when you haven't asked for it. It can be hard not to reward your horse as you love her enthusiasm and appreciate her effort. But if you reward her when she tries behaviours you haven't asked for, you can create more tension and confusion in your horse. It won't be clear to her when a behaviour is important, so she'll throw behaviours at you in the hope of getting you to reward her. The horse becomes tense and anxious as she tries harder and harder to find something you'll reward her for. It's stressful and possibly dangerous for the handler, too. Both you and your horse will be happier and more relaxed when your horse is calm by default and clearly understands when you're asking for a specific behaviour.

The best way to build solid cue control is to always cue from, and return to, standing quietly together between each behaviour you ask for. Wait until your horse is relaxed by your side, then give her a cue for walking with you or touching the target, for example. After her reward or between behaviours, return to standing quietly and ensure that your horse is soft and patient before giving your next cue. Not only does this really help to clarify all your cues, it teaches your horse to wait quietly until you ask her for a behaviour. Standing quietly then becomes a go-to behaviour for your horse if she's ever confused about cues or eager to work.

Ensure your horse is standing quietly next to you before clearly giving your cue for the next behaviour.

Of course, there are exceptions to every rule and there are a few times when you will reward your horse for offering behaviours you haven't asked for. One is when you are teaching a new behaviour. If you're explaining a new exercise to your horse and he suddenly 'gets it' and offers the behaviour you're working on, this is a great time to reward because he's shown his understanding. You want him to know that that was what you were asking for and don't want to shut down his efforts at figuring out the answer.

Another time to reward your horse for spontaneously offering a behaviour is if he makes a good decision in a difficult situation. For example, if something startles your horse and he would usually spook and try to run away but instead stops himself and touches the target instead, you want to reward that great decision as you can then reconnect and continue on safely. However, once your horse has learned a behaviour and is quietly focused, you should only reward behaviours that you have asked for.

CUE TRANSFERRAL

Once your horse knows a behaviour on one cue, you can change the cue for the behaviour quite easily without having to train the behaviour again from scratch. Let's use the example of teaching your horse to bend the head to one side when asked with a rein cue. Once your horse has learned to touch the target, you can get him to turn his head by holding the target a to the side. At this point, the target is the cue. It gives your horse the idea to turn his head to touch it. But you don't want to be carrying targets forever. You will eventually want another cue that tells your horse to turn his head, such as lifting up the lead rope. To accomplish this, you need to transfer the training from the old cue to the new cue. The basic steps are:

- Practise the behaviour with a cue the horse already knows.

- Use your marker to tell the horse which part of the behaviour is important.

- Add a new cue to ask for that behaviour.

How does this work in practice? Let's continue with the example of teaching the horse a rein cue for a head flexion.

First, let your horse follow the target to establish confidence that turning is the correct answer.

Then start to gently lift the rope as you hold up the target. Mark and reward when your horse gives the smallest response. As you repeat this a few times, your horse begins to associate a gentle lifting of the lead rope with turning to touch the target.

Next, lift the rope without showing the target and pause for a couple of seconds. If the horse shows any sign of turning, mark and reward generously.

What if your horse doesn't turn when you lift the rope? In that case, simply present the target again to prompt the horse to turn his head. The old cue will remind him of what the new cue means. Just remember, as you continue to practice, to always use the new cue first and give the horse a chance to respond. Use the old cue as a backup prompt only when needed.

Soon your horse will start to flex as you gently lift the rope and you won't need the target at all. The cue has been transferred from the target to the rein.

It's a good idea to start cue transferral as soon as possible so the horse learns to pay attention to you rather than just the target. Horses love objects, and it's tempting to keep using them to get behaviours, but the aim of the target is usually to explain the behaviour you want and then to transfer it to a different cue. Cue transferral is a technique you'll use throughout your training, such as using the target to create behaviours, as well as in other situations such as transferring cues from the ground to the saddle.

VIDEO RESOURCE

TEACHING LEADING WITH A
TARGET AND ROPE

Watch this cue transferral process in action as a young cob learns how to lead on a rope, taught from following a target.

www.connectiontraining.com/video-resources

GETTING THE BEST FROM REWARDS

Rewarding wanted behaviours is core to Connection Training and, as we've seen, is inextricably linked to your horse's emotions. Understanding how rewards work to strengthen behaviours and the options you have available to you when training using a marker and rewards enable you to make the best training decisions for your horse.

VARIABILITY AND SECONDARY REINFORCERS

Many studies have shown that when it comes to using rewards most effectively, variability is far more powerful than predictability. Most horses are highly motivated by food and the addition of even predictable low-value rewards, such as chaff or hay cubes, will usually create enough interest and motivation without them getting overly excited or focused just on the treats. However, it's good to introduce different rewards for extra special moments, such as when you're working on a difficult behaviour or your horse has put in a great burst of effort. You can also highlight these moments by varying the amount of rewards you give, giving larger handfuls, or a few treats in a row, to mark the best moments from your horse. Using a variety of food rewards and amounts in your training, such as apples, carrots, mints, pony nuts etc., will often help to motivate horses who lack interest or enthusiasm.

You will also want to use non-food rewards and creating 'secondary reinforcers' increases your ability to vary your rewards. As well as strokes and scratches, these can include behaviours that your horse has already learned and loves to do. For

Pay attention to the exercises and reinforcers your horse loves. You can use them as rewards for more challenging behaviours. In these pictures, Hannah is working with three of her horses. Rowan adores standing on the pedestal, jumping is India's favourite thing to do and Toby has always loved a cuddle and a head rub.

example, if you have a horse who likes to go forward, you can reinforce a period of calm focus by walking on, or even asking her to pop over a jump. One horse might absolutely love backing up; another might love to do a trick behaviour, such as playing fetch or smiling; most of them love targeting. Some horses love to learn new behaviours, whereas others prefer to show-off well-known ones. These rewards are a combination of secondary reinforcers (things that have come to have positive meaning for your horse due to their experience with them) and innate preferences.

YOU'RE A REINFORCER, TOO!

The marker becomes a secondary reinforcer because it is consistently present at the time the horse receives primary reinforcers, such as food. Again, this comes down to emotional associations. Your horse felt good when he heard the click noise, so, in time, the click noise makes him feel good. However, the click is only a small part of this picture as there are many other things present in this situation that are also becoming associated with these positive feelings. As your horse experiences feeling relaxed, confident, joyful, interested and successful, he will begin to associate those feelings with the feeling of learning and problem-solving, the training location and the training tools. The entire training experience becomes rewarding. And, of course, you are present, too. You, too, become a secondary reinforcer. The more your horse feels good when in your company, the stronger your bond will be.

The more good things your horse associates you with, the stronger your bond will be.

This was shown really clearly with Ned, the difficult rescued donkey you met in Chapter 3. When Hannah started working with him, he didn't want to engage at all and chose to leave as soon as the food did. However, over a few weeks, he came to associate Hannah with food, yes, but also relaxation, interest, clarity and success. He began to choose to spend time with Hannah even when she wasn't training and, during their casual connection time, would stand with Hannah for cuddles or simply rest next to her.

This love of learning and joy in the training is clear to see in advanced horses as they often don't want to stop for food because they are simply enjoying the game. They love hearing their marker because it tells them they are doing well, but they will often carry on without wanting to stop for a treat.

Freckles was an active and willing participant as he learned to pick up the correct canter lead. He would whicker when he got it correct and often not stop for the treat. This meant he was being "intrinsically" rewarded. He didn't want to interrupt this by stopping for "extrinsic" rewards, such as food. This suggests his PLAY system had become aroused and he was simply finding it fun.

CUES AS REWARDS

When a behaviour has been taught with rewards, the horse wants to do it and therefore wants you to give the cue for these behaviours. Dopamine is the brain chemical that, among other things, signals pleasure or the anticipation of pleasure. Robert Sapolsky, author and professor of biology and neurology at Stanford University, has shown that dopamine is released in the brain not when the animal receives a reward, but when they get the cue for a behaviour they know. It's that feeling of 'Yes! I know how to do this!'

This means your cues are actually rewarding to your horse, which in turn means you have to be careful about when you cue your horse to do something. Let's use targeting as an example. Once your horse has learned to touch a target, he will want you to present one so he can perform this new behaviour and perhaps get an extra reward for it. If you consistently present the target to your horse when he's pushing forward into your space or has his ears pinned, you are rewarding that behaviour too. He will learn that the way to get you to hold the target out is to be pushy and aggressive, so this behaviour will most likely escalate. Instead, look for times when your horse is calm, relaxed, and polite before presenting the target.

This is the same process you have started by asking your horse to stand quietly between each cue. Since cues are rewarding to your horse, you are reinforcing him standing quietly by only giving your cue when he is waiting softly. This is true of any cue your horse understands and has good emotional associations with. As you can see, using cues as rewards will have a strong impact on the emotions and behaviour of your horse.

MARKING FOR INFORMATION: IT'S A CONVERSATION!

Good training relies on good communication between you and your horse. The marker helps this as a way of saying to your horse when you're happy with what he's doing. This means that, once your horse understands the marker

and it is becoming a secondary reinforcer, it isn't necessary to stop after every mark. You can also choose to mark and continue. This increases the opportunity for communication and helps to keep your horse relaxed.

In practice, this means marking a behaviour and asking your horse to keep going with the exercise, rather than stopping every time for an external reward. It helps with a) increasing duration of a behaviour, b) maintaining calm and focus and c) allowing horses to keep "in the zone" while they are working out a problem.

Let's say you want to increase duration asking your horse to hold his nose on the target for longer. How do you create that?

One approach is to allow the horse to stay at the target a millisecond longer, then click and treat. The next try, it's another millisecond longer, and so on until you've built up the duration. This can work very effectively. However, some horses interpret the delay in receiving the mark as a signal that they should try another behaviour, since, on other occasions, you have withheld the click when you want the horse to offer more or something slightly different. This can lead to confusion and frustration as the horse tries to work out what else you're asking for. We find that giving informative, or supportive, marks is more helpful in this situation as it tells the horse that she's doing the right thing and to keep doing it.

Rachel has a great example of this with her own mare, Roisin

When I was training Roisin to build duration on holding to the target, Roisin really struggled. She would hold for a few seconds, then try biting the target, nudging it, moving back from it—anything that might get a reward. When none of this

worked, she would get frustrated when she didn't get marked and zone out.

One day, I tried marking and re-cuing for her to continue without stopping for treats. Roisin touched the target; I marked. Roisin turned around for the treat and I simply cued the target again. She touched it straight away and so I marked and fed as usual.

After a few tries, Roisin realised that holding to the target was the desired behaviour since she was getting clicked for it. She didn't have time to try anything else, and holding to the target was getting marked. This told her she was doing the right thing, even if it wasn't always producing a food reward. Internally, she would have been receiving dopamine shots when I cued, when she touched the target and when I marked. The whole situation was rewarding for her. Doing it this way gave Roisin the information and reassurance she needed. It relieved her frustration at trying things and not being correct. To me, it functioned as a conversational tool and made our training sessions less mechanistic and more co-operative. The clarity it brought made her successful and thus, relaxed. After trying for months, Roisin finally understood what I wanted in just one session.

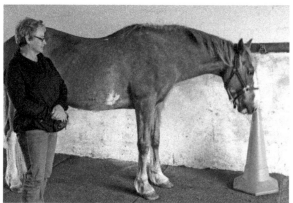

Roisin standing at her stationary target.

We are successful with this technique as we pay such close attention to the horse's emotional state, stimulating intrinsic rewards by being aware of their natural preferences and in simple recognition of their pleasure in achievement. To reward every click with food would disable our emotional connection and make it more of a business contract. In fact, many clicker trainers talk of 'being a vending machine' or 'paying your horse'. It's understandable, since this type of training was initially developed in laboratories, where there was a strict protocol of 'cue → behaviour → mark → reward' and often no interaction between animal and experimenter at all. However, since we're working one-to-one with our horses and wish to build a solid relationship based on fluid two-way communication, we prefer a more varied approach rather than this highly mechanised one.

This technique can be a key piece in getting the best emotional balance in your horse. Many owners come to us having started clicker training their horse elsewhere and are struggling with issues of over-arousal. They find this one change can really help their horses to relax during the training sessions, as well as boost the communication and relationship. Interestingly, as well as bringing more relaxation to the training, the variability of using click and continue also boosts motivation as you increase your horse's focus and interest. It also helps to make horses more resilient to variety and changes. As previously discussed, if you repeat a certain sequence, your horse will come to expect that any small deviations can cause a large amount of tension, anxiety and frustration. By marking and continuing where appropriate, we add in more variety and, although the horse isn't sure exactly what reward he'll get when, he knows that it's ALL good. This is a good lesson to teach horses for life.

Hannah has an interesting story about working with this technique with rescue horses:

When I first began working with the horses and staff at Hope Pastures Rescue Centre, I was a little concerned about ensuring consistency for the horses, since they are handled and trained by a range of different people. A lot of literature on clicker training strongly recommends to only have one person training each behaviour so that it is consistent for the animal, but this simply wasn't possible in the set-up at the centre.

When I began working with the staff and volunteers, I focused primarily on teaching them to create and reward the best emotional state in the ponies there. There were people training with different backgrounds and skill levels, who all interacted with the ponies slightly differently. This meant that the training had to be flexible enough to cater for everyone. One of the techniques I brought in was the use of click and continue, along with a variety of food and non-food rewards. Because of the variety of trainers and approaches, the ponies learned very quickly that they weren't sure what exactly was going to happen but that it was always good! The use of click and continue helped because we weren't setting the ponies up for a specific expectation each time and they were happy to receive a variety of rewards following the click, as well as to continue on with the exercise directly.

The emphasis was on relaxation and joy rather than precision and I quickly found that these were some of the most adaptable and resilient ponies I'd worked with. It almost seemed to give them a more optimistic view on life because they were expecting different but positive things. It certainly set them up to be confident being handled by different people and eventually rehomed successfully.

Like any training technique, this must be introduced to your horse in a clear and systematic way so that he understands it, especially if he's used to receiving a predictable reward every time you mark. Instantly changing any long-term habit is a sure-fire way to create confusion and frustration. If he doesn't get the expected reward, there will be a sharp fall in dopamine, which is punishing. This is likely to arouse his RAGE system and you'll see signs of frustration (as you do when you change anything abruptly with your horse and cause confusion). To prevent this, we mark and continue right from the start to prevent that expectation. In a horse who already expects food after every click, we introduce this gradually and with easy behaviours, giving plenty of big jackpots and soon change their expectations, so they stay calm and relaxed.

When you mark, it's important to know whether you are going to stop and reward your horse or whether you are going to ask him to continue what he was doing. If you're muddled, your horse will get confused too. For example, suppose you are training your horse to walk beside you in a certain position. If you want your horse to keep walking, you can click when the horse is in the right position and continue to walk; your horse will follow your lead and focus and will happily walk with you. After a few repetitions, you can click, cue a stop by simply stopping yourself, and give your horse a big reward. The horse will pay attention to the moment that was marked, but you still have time to cue a stop, and the reward will still be linked to the marker signal in the brain.

One thing you must make sure of is that the marker still has meaning for your horse. If you start marking everything, only rarely stopping to reward, you will find that your horse stops paying attention to the marker. This is because it has ceased to have meaning to him, as you're marking everything without distinction.

Your horse will also tell you if you get into a pattern. For example, if you get into the habit of giving a food reward after every third click, your horse will begin to pay more attention after you've clicked twice. This is known as being on a 'fixed schedule of reinforcement'. Knowing that no reward is coming for the first two tries, they will become mediocre and the horse will only put in extra effort on the third try, because he has learned that that is the

one which gets the food reward. Instead, use 'variable reinforcement'. Use a range of reinforcers and reward at various times —sometimes after every click, sometimes after a few. The important thing is that you are clear when you will mark and stop and when you will mark and continue on. Your cues, intent and body position will explain this clearly to your horse along with the marker. In fact, the marker is only one small piece of the training puzzle so focusing on all of the other elements will really help to keep your horse focused on you and strengthen the communication between you.

VIDEO RESOURCE

CLICK AND CONTINUE

You can see this in action in this video where Hannah is teaching Rowan how to collect in walk in-hand and using this technique to help build duration.

www.connectiontraining.com/video-resources

FADING OUT THE MARKER

Your precise marker is ideal for teaching new behaviours because of the clarity it brings. As you move on with a behaviour, you will begin to sometimes mark and continue as you build duration and refine it. Continuing with this conversation, the next stage is to fade out your marker completely from well-known behaviours since you no longer need the precision of the marker. We use vocal praise for this process because it is a natural part of the bonding process with our horses. This is mostly about the tone of your voice, rather than specific words, along with other signals your horse will easily pick up on, such as

your levels of relaxation, smiling, connection and joy. You will naturally praise your horse at feel-good times, such as when you're scratching or feeding him, and this will help your horse to associate a praising tone of voice with those times. Many horses already respond well to general praise because of this association. However, if your horse doesn't, then spend some time consciously praising your horse at moments of relaxation and joy throughout your interactions with him. You can then gradually fade the marker out of known behaviours and replace it with praise.

The difference between the mark and praise is the amount of precision. The marker says, 'That *exact* stride/head position/movement is what I want.' Praise says, 'Yes, that is all great. I love what you're doing right now.' The marker is precise for training; praise is for reassurance, encouragement, and acknowledgement of behaviours your horse already knows.

For example, let's say you're teaching your head-high horse to stretch down in trot. You will begin by marking every small try and stopping each time to reward those first efforts highly. As your horse begins to understand what you're asking for and offer it easily, you will start to mark and continue to build duration and refine the behaviour. Once you've trained a consistent relaxed stretch in the trot, you will gradually stop marking specific moments since your horse now knowns what to do, and, instead, will praise your horse to say, 'That whole circuit was lovely, thank you.' If you begin to mark the trot again at this stage, you might accidentally mark a moment when your horse is bent in a certain position or has changed his rhythm. He may then try to do all sorts of things to work out what you want. When you're training the trot in the first instance, this trial and error and clarity of the mark are exactly what you want to explain it to him; but as he progresses, you simply want to acknowledge and appreciate his good effort during the session as opposed to a specific movement. If you then want to go back and refine or improve the trot, you will bring the marker back in for that purpose.

Being able to work your horse for longer without stopping to give external rewards is part of the training process because, of course, you don't want to be stopping to feed every tiny thing for ever. How fast you can do this will depend on the emotions associated with that behaviour, not just whether your horse knows it well. For example, if your horse has trotted with his head high for a long time, it will likely be associated with feelings of discomfort in his body. It can take some time to change those emotions to joy and willingness, even after you've taught him how to move more comfortably. However, behaviours learned through reward, choice and joy will all become rewarding, at which point you can fade out the external rewards and your horse will continue to perform it happily.

Variably rewarding your horse now and again for behaviours he knows will keep each behaviour strong. Even if it's something you ask your horse to do every day and he does it easily and happily, occasionally adding an extra special reward will surprise him and keep up his motivation because he never knows when it might happen again.

HOW YOU EXPRESS YOUR EMOTIONS

The best use of rewards is always by understanding your horse's innate preferences and the communication and reinforcers you create through your time together. This is very much an individual process. Hannah has a great story to illustrate this:

With my own horses, I'm gushing in my praise. I frequently whoop when they do something spectacular. They know this means good things because it has been accompanied by other rewards over the years. So, a whoop from me often results in a little nicker from them, as they know they've done something great.

Once, I was teaching a long-term client with a bold, happy cob named Bobby. We were teaching Bobby to free jump. The first time he jumped, I whooped, just as I would have done with my horses. Well, unfortunately, Bobby's owner is much quieter than me in her praise, and the poor guy took my whoop as quite a strong punishment. It took us about fifteen minutes to build up his confidence to jump again—and yes, I stayed quiet this time!

How you feel and how you express yourself has a huge impact on your horse's emotional state. If you are appreciative, relaxed, and happy during your training sessions, your horse will relax and be joyful and enthusiastic, too. But as illustrated in the story above, your horse will become attuned to how you specifically express that joy. Social learning is so important to horses. They are highly social animals and it's vital to them that the herd is relaxed and happy. When training, the 'herd' is you and he will always follow your energy and intent, so this is another area to be aware of. If you're anxious, impatient, and critical, you'll find tension in your horse, no matter how many treats you give!

Recent research has shown that horses can read human expressions of happiness and anger and respond accordingly. When viewing angry faces, horses looked more with their left eye, a behaviour associated with perceiving negative stimuli. Their heart rate also increased more quickly, and they showed more stress-related behaviours. It's interesting to note that the horses had a

stronger reaction to photos with angry faces—a negative stimulus—than to the positive stimulus of happy faces. It appears, then, that the brain is more strongly aroused by threats. Therefore, make sure you have happy expressions and are genuinely enjoying yourself. It's easy to have a concentrating face that looks angry from the outside, and you don't want this strong stimulus to affect your training. Take time in your training to remember to breathe, smile, praise, and stroke your horse to ensure you're generally relaxed and so help your horse to be relaxed too.

Smile, breathe and laugh! Time with your horse should be fun and joyful for both of you.

ESTABLISHING CLEAR BOUNDARIES

Having clear, consistent boundaries applies to all aspects of your training and relationship with your horse. When we discuss boundaries, we don't mean you just get in there and tell your horse what to do or not do. Instead, you establish clear and consistent rules that both you and your horse understand, follow, and respect. This means you decide what behaviours you're happy with your horse performing around you and are consistent in your reactions to them. In addition, you understand and respect your horse's boundaries and limits.

This two-way communication means that you both stay safe and enjoy your time together.

Many problems arise in horses because of lack of clarity and consistency from humans. If you're happy for your horse to do something one day and tell him off for it the next, he will be confused and lose his trust in you, since trust is built through predictability. You must teach boundaries to your horse progressively, because he isn't born knowing what's acceptable and what's not in his particular human environment.

Building strong and clear boundaries incorporates many of the techniques discussed in this book. You must know what behaviour you want to see from your horse and what you're prepared to reinforce. You'll make this decision based on the horse in front of you—where he's at in his training and how he feels on that day. In this way, you will be able to set clear boundaries that you know he will be able to respond to and stay within.

Take the example of setting boundaries around food. You might initially control the environment by training in protected contact to set your horse up for success when establishing new behavioural expectations around food. That way, your horse can easily learn that only calm, polite behaviour will earn rewards without reverting to old behaviours like pushing or nipping that have to be prevented using punishers. He will learn to control his own behaviour because that is the way to success for him. In the process, he will also learn to feel calm and relaxed, since that is the emotional state associated with calm behaviour. Once the boundaries are established and understood in protected contact, you can start to remove the barrier and expect the same behaviour without it. You can also expand the boundaries by

building the behaviour into more challenging situations, such as during movement, at meal times, and during an event.

CRITERIA BOUNDARIES

Criteria boundaries are about building clear responses to your cues and ensuring that your horse keeps the quality of the behaviour high. For example, you want to know that when you ask your horse to lead with you, he'll walk calmly by your side, where you have trained him to be. It's natural, however, that horses will explore and test your boundaries. They wonder what will happen if they give you a different response to your cue. When you know what criteria you expect—in other words, what behaviour you're happy with and what you're not happy with—you will be able to respond consistently to your horse.

If you're not consistent with the behaviour you accept and reward you will encourage your horse to continue testing you and pushing the boundaries. Your consistency will build calm, strong boundaries in your horse's attitude and behaviour. Therefore, you need clarity in your criteria: I want your head straight; I want you to walk off with your shoulder moving away from me; I want you to halt with your head level with my shoulder, and so on. Being particular about these little things from the beginning, and associating them with calm emotions, will teach your horse that these behaviours are the only ones that get rewarded. He will do them consistently if you are consistent. We find that people who focus on polite and clear starting, leading, and halting right from the beginning create the most relaxed and polite horses.

Consistency in your training establishes consistency in your horse's response, but there will be times when your horse doesn't respond well to an established cue or is generally behaving differently in the session. If your horse is giving you less focus, energy or enthusiasm than normal, there is usually an underlying cause, such as confusion, anxiety, discomfort or distraction. This could be something within your training session such as a lack of clarity around a cue, or a change in environment, or it could be an external factor such as the weather, gut or hormonal discomfort. Even changes in your horse's herd life can have a profound effect on his emotional state and willingness to learn. For example if a new horse has been introduced to the herd, your horse will have been dealing with the social disruption in the field and that could be a contributing factor to a more distracted, anxious or tired horse when you work with him.

If you're not getting the response you expect from your horse, we recommend taking a holistic look at possible causes and addressing them where possible. This could include training in a different place, adapting your training plan to one more suitable for the day or even deciding that it will be best for your horse's well-being to not be trained on that today. If you do continue to train, focus on creating the best possible emotional states you can. This includes going back a few steps to make it easier and clearer for your horse and to spend a few minutes working on exercises that prioritise relaxation and the connection between you. This could be as simple as walking around together for a while, or spending some time grooming or cuddling your horse, or just having some fun with an easy exercise you both love. Once your horse has settled and you're back working as a team, try asking for the initial behaviour again and you will be highly likely to get a much better response.

WHAT NOT TO REWARD

Part of setting boundaries is also being aware of when not to reinforce your horse. If you begin to reward every little thing he does, the training will lose meaning because you won't be pinpointing specific behaviours and decisions he makes. If every behaviour is getting the same level of external reward, your horse will of course just want to do the easier or most enjoyable option. Moving on, expecting more, and rewarding only best tries will keep your horse clear on what level of behaviour will get rewarded.

This is relative, however, and it's important to be aware of all the factors contributing to the situation. For example, your horse may offer a certain level of behaviour easily at home, but will most likely find that much harder in a new situation. In this case, you will expect less from your horse and reward good attempts at easier behaviours.

One situation in which you should definitely not reward is if you feel that you're only rewarding to prevent your horse's tension escalating, such as the horse who gets tense and bites if they don't get fed regularly enough.

For example, Hannah has worked with two similar mares who learned that if they reared, their owners would immediately back down and reward them highly for easy behaviours. Both owners had full physical checks on the horses, and both were working on physically easy behaviours. In fact, both mares were simply being asked to walk on. They realised that if they even threatened to rear, they would get to stand still and be rewarded for targeting instead and so the behaviour was getting stronger (they were actually inadvertently being trained to rear!). This is a complicated situation because you don't want to push the horse over threshold, but you don't want to reward them for this behaviour either. The key is to get back to focusing on relaxation. With both mares, we worked them Around A Round Pen so that the owners were safe and could stay relaxed themselves. They asked the horses to walk on, talking softly and reassuringly to them. When they started to hit threshold and the mares showed signs of tension, they just stopped, breathed deeply and waited for the mares to settle, before walking on again. When they walked on quietly this second time, they both received big jackpots and a chance for some targeting. The mares began to learn that settling and continuing forwards led to rewards and feeling good. With some repetition, they both stopped rearing, became happy to go forwards and learned some valuable skills in how to calm down and reconnect when the tension increased.

This situation is only a problem if you see it consistently. There will be occasional times when your horse does get tense when the situation escalates and if rewarding your horse and asking for easy behaviours or feeding your horse helps them to calm down and stay safe, do it. However, if you begin to see it as a pattern, then it's a sign that the emotions are out of balance. Firstly, give your horse the benefit of the doubt, look at all possible causes and go back to basics and re-build the behaviour. You need to be sure that you're not over facing your horse but are asking them to do something they really can do. Then, take them to the edge of their threshold in that situation, help them to relax and connect with you and then try a step or two more, which you reward highly. Remember that your horse is struggling in this situation, they are not being 'bad', so we need to find a calm and compassionate way to teach them how to succeed at the challenge they are facing. This actually gives them great tools for life as they learn that staying tuned in with you and trying, even when it's hard, is very rewarding.

THE POWER OF CHOICE

Typically, domestic horses don't get much choice in their lives. Who they live with, what they eat, whether they're in or out—all this is decided for them. Likewise, in more conventional training, they are often not given much choice and are labelled 'naughty', 'lazy', or even 'defiant' if they show that they'd rather be doing something else.

In Connection Training, we want to give our horses as much choice as possible. When horses are given choice and support for their decisions, it can have a big effect on their attitude. When they know they won't be coerced or forced into doing something, they will become more confident. By letting them decide to take the next step or try harder, you will also build their joy in the training. It's a wonderful thing to see horses change from disinterest and resignation to full-on enthusiasm and joy when they realise they have control and their choices will be respected.

For your horse to have choice in the training, the most obvious route is to work your horse at liberty. That way he knows that he can leave at any time. For this reason, working at liberty is something we use and advocate a lot. However, you can give a choice in all situations, whether at liberty or not, by paying attention to your horse's emotional state and communication. If he doesn't respond immediately and promptly to a cue he knows well, he's showing that, for some reason, he's not overly keen to perform that behaviour. He may be tired, bored, anxious, confused, or frustrated. It is up to you, as the trainer, to listen to this reluctance and respond in a suitable manner. How you respond depends on the situation. Maybe you leave it and try again later, or perhaps you go back a few steps and rebuild confidence and clarity in the behaviour. What is important is that your horse knows he can 'voice' his reluctance and that he will be listened to. In this way, he will have choice in the training and therefore will feel empowered and confident.

For example, when Hannah was teaching India to free jump, India had to wait on her mat until Hannah called her over the jump from across the arena. After India went over the jump, Hannah would mark and reward India when she got to her. In one free jumping session, Hannah made the jump a little higher than India was used to and called her over it. India cantered up to the jump but, as she approached, realised she had set herself up incorrectly, so she chose to scoot quietly around it instead. Even though India didn't make the jump, Hannah rewarded her because India made a good decision in the circumstances. She didn't panic and go over threshold, as she had often done in the past when asked to do something that seemed too challenging. She just calmly told Hannah that it was a little difficult for her. Hannah lowered the height to make it easier, and India popped the jump nicely. Then Hannah put it back up to the original height. This time India was prepared and confident, and she jumped it eagerly. Hannah gave her a huge reward for her effort and ended the session there.

India free jumping with Hannah.

For many people, the concept of letting the horse run out, let alone rewarding her for it, is counter to everything they have been taught. However, this experience showed India that she always has a choice and that her decisions will be listened to. It also built her confidence in jumping and actually increased the likelihood that in future she'll be able to jump difficult fences the first time around. Had Hannah pushed her to jump no matter what or punished her for not making the attempt, India would have associated that anxiety and fear with jumping, making her more tense and less keen to jump from then on.

VIDEO RESOURCE

THE POWER OF CHOICE

Rachel explains and demonstrates the power of choice in this video.

www.connectiontraining.com/video-resources

HOW MUCH CHOICE IS TOO MUCH?

We know choice is important to give your horse a voice, but can you give your horse too much choice? Sometimes, giving choice is interpreted as giving little direction and leaving it open to your horse to decide what to do. Although a good exercise at times, this can often be overwhelming, confusing and frustrating for your horse

Or perhaps your horse chooses to pick up the fallen treats on the floor rather than work with you, or shortcuts straight to your treat bag. Can you say 'no' to your horse? Or do you just wait passively and hope that he decides to stop doing whatever he's doing and focuses again so you can reward it? Well, you can do that but there are more effective ways to get your horse back on track.

If you are in a training situation, your horse will still be under threshold, which means that although he's become a little distracted or pushy, he's still calm enough to connect and learn. In this instance, you want to redirect him to a more positive behaviour as calmly and quickly as possible. For example, let's say your horse

has got a little too focused on the treats, is pushing at your treat bag or pockets and is ignoring your cue to stand quietly next to you. You can gently use your arm to block his access to the rewards and then re-gain his attention by giving him a clear cue, such as to touch the target or walk on. When he's re-focused, he should be back to standing with you nicely. Or, perhaps your horse has been distracted by some lush grass at the side of the training area. You can quietly re-gain their attention by asking them to target or walk on or gently lifting their head. If your horse continues to ignore you, a little perseverance may help – don't increase the pressure but keep on asking your horse to pay attention to you. Your horse will follow your focus and you can reward them for coming back to you, again quickly diverting their attention to another exercise. Another technique that can be very useful if your horse is lacking attention is to simply walk a small circle then ask again. They are nearly always more connected and successful the second time around as they missed an opportunity for reward. Use the environmental set-up to limit your horse's choices, too. For example, if you're working on loading your horse, you can help set your horse up for success by parking the horsebox in a situation without distractions such as lush grass or busy activity. You won't force the horse into the horse box, but they won't have the option to simply graze lush grass instead of working on the challenging behaviour, either.

Because you're paying attention to your horse' emotions, you won't be asking them to do anything that they are too confused, anxious or excited to do. So, you can quietly bring them back to you and re-focus on the training. Again, consistency will help you to establish these training boundaries, too.

All of these techniques will work if your horse is still under threshold, but what do you do if your horse is over threshold and you still have to insist on certain behaviour? There will likely be the odd situation when your horse is too frightened, excited or anxious to be able to stay think and respond well. At this time, you are in a *management* situation, not a training one. Therefore, you simply have to manage the situation as quietly, calmly and positively as you can in way that keeps everyone safe. This might be a split moment, such as your horse diving across the road for grass, where you have to use more pressure than you'd like to prevent them, or it might be a longer time period such as when receiving emergency veterinary treatment and you have to restrain your horse for it. Horses, like all mammals, are designed to deal with some negative experiences and are emotionally resilient. They usually bounce back from these events very well. However, the problem may highlight some areas that need extra training and you might need to spend some time re-establishing good emotions and responses in those

situations. Dealing with horses over threshold, 'bad' days and resilience training are covered in more depth later in the book.

FITTING CONNECTION TRAINING INTO REAL LIFE

So far, we've discussed training techniques, but where does that fit into real life? What do you do about things your horse already knows? How often should you train? How do you handle your horse outside of training sessions?

HOW OFTEN SHOULD YOU TRAIN?

Unsurprisingly, regular and consistent training gets the best results, so training your horse 3-6 days per week will help you to see progress. One other benefit of training regularly is that horses love learning in this way, so the training can get very exciting, which is one contributing factor to over-arousal issues. Making the training more regular and routine can help horses be more relaxed about it. However, if you can't train that often, you will still see great benefits from the training.

PREVIOUSLY LEARNED BEHAVIOURS

You don't need to stop doing all the things you already do with your horse when you begin training this way. You and your horse will already have a good relationship and many behaviours that you both know and are comfortable with. Changing all of your training and handling approaches abruptly can be stressful for both of you and leave you feeling like you've lost a lot of your existing communication. Begin to add your CT session into your current regime, perhaps training this way after you ride or as part of your daily care routine.

Once your horse understands what the marker means and is calm and polite around the training, you can also begin to use it to improve and refine existing behaviours. Start by occasionally rewarding behaviours your horse knows already, such as standing calmly for grooming and leading nicely. Since these are behaviours your horse already knows, you can simply praise and reward it. Or, if you want to refine it or improve a specific aspect of it, you can use your marker for extra precision.

Even if you didn't initially train this behaviour with positive reinforcement, you can still reinforce it to draw your horse's attention to his best efforts. It will also help to bring more positive emotional associations to certain situations, too, such as when lifting feet or being bathed.

Observe your horse throughout these existing behaviours, too, so you can identify areas where your horse is anxious or resistant. You can then use Connection Training techniques to help him feel more joyful and confident in this area. There will also be certain existing behaviours and exercises that your horse is already happy to do and enjoys. You don't need to re-train these, so be confident to continue with them with your horse.

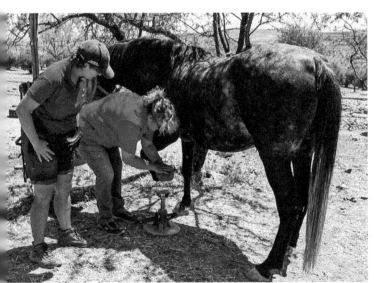

You don't need to re-train behaviours your horse is already happy to do.

VARYING THE SESSIONS

Varying the content of your sessions will also help your horse succeed as it will keep your training rewarding and interesting. While there's a time and place to use repetition and patterns for training, people have a tendency to unintentionally create patterns out of habit. Mix things up to keep it fresh for your horse. Do things in a different order, ask for different behaviours, do sessions in different areas, have other people do sessions, do long sessions, short sessions, on the ground, in the saddle. . . the possibilities are endless. A good way to incorporate plenty of variety into your training while still making progress is to have 'themed' sessions and rotate through them each time you train. For example, you might have 'daily handling' sessions where you work on grooming or hoof lifting, 'out and about' sessions where you work your horse outside of the arena, 'movement' sessions where you work on groundwork and lunging and 'ridden' sessions. You'll get more information on how to train in these areas throughout the book. These variations will keep your horse more interested in you and more focused and enthusiastic about training.

OUTSIDE OF TRAINING SESSIONS

Everything we've discussed so far has been about setting up your training sessions for the best success. However, it's important to remember that all the time you spend with your horse—both during and outside of formal training sessions—will affect your relationship. To build your bond with each other, it's just as important to spend time with your horse when you're not asking anything of him. This could be time spent grooming, walking together and letting your horse graze in hand, or just relaxing with your horse in his stable, field, or arena. You can do this as part of, or separate from, your training sessions. This time together helps activate the CARE system to build your connection, and it also ensures your horse doesn't just expect to 'do' things all the time you're present. Building the connection between you will make your trust stronger, your communication clearer, and your training more effective.

Remember to include non-food sessions in your training, occasional food outside of training and use as many different rewards as you can. The more you mix it up, the more your horse will stay focused on you and realise that all the work you do together is important, not just certain behaviours or in specific situations. You don't want to your horse to think there's no point in trying when he's not in a formal training session. Nor do you want him to think that training sessions are the only rewarding and exciting time, causing him to get over-aroused during training sessions. The golden rule is to reward only when your horse is as soft, relaxed, and polite as possible, whether in or out of training sessions. That behaviour and emotional state will then become your horse's default.

The time you spend with your horse outside of training sessions is important to build your bond together. It will help your training, too, as your horse is relaxed in your presence and doesn't associate you only with training. Think about the time your horse spends with his herd mates and emulate that through exploring together, grooming your horse and just sitting with him while he eats or 'hanging out' with him. You can also incorporate these moments within the breaks in your training sessions, too. This will activate the CARE system for both of you and promote relaxation and relationship-building.

CHAPTER 6
THE CONNECTED TRAINER

When you're working with a horse, it's important to remember that there are two of you in the partnership. It's time now to look at your role in the relationship and what you bring to the training sessions.

Horses are sensitive social mammals. They have evolved to survive in a herd, responding and reacting to each other's tiny movements for survival. When you're working with your horse, you tap into those herd instincts. We have talked about how their breathing, heart rate, and focus often match that of their handler. The energy, focus, and nuances you bring to the session will have a profound impact on the horse you're working with and the success of the training. And, how you treat yourself as a trainer will affect your own enjoyment and commitment, too.

JOYFUL TRAINING

Much traditional horse training is based on correcting the horse, which naturally means that the trainer's focus is mostly on what the horse is doing wrong. However, using a marker signal means that you are always looking for what your horse does *right*. This alone is a huge shift in perspective. Every time you click, praise and reward, it's a big sign to both of you that you did something well and will keep you smiling as well as your horse. Taking the time to appreciate all these small successes will keep you confident and joyful, which in turn makes you a better trainer and person for your horse. Hannah says that her training sessions are full of praise and you will hear her revel in all the small achievements. If you listen in, you'll hear comments like, "good decision!", "that was amazing," and "what a superstar horse!" Our aim is that both you and your horse 'smile' for much of your time together.

Focus on the positive aspects of your training session and smile! The joy and positivity you bring will relax your horse and improve your training.

CONNECTION TRAINING, NOT PERFECTION TRAINING

Perfectionism tends to dampen joy. When approaching horse training, it's easy to have an idea in your head of how it should go or what it should look like. You can then get stymied by your quest for perfection if you expect every step to be clear and to progress in neat, uniform stages. But, here's the secret: it's never perfect! Much of your training will be a bit messy as you and your horse muddle through and work it out together. This is completely normal (and part of the interest and fun!) so, instead, we focus on maintaining the connection, rather than aiming for perfection.

When you introduce new exercises to your horse, or try to take them to the next level, there is often a bit of confusion as you work out the best way to explain it to your horse and your horse does his best to work out what you're asking. This can lead to doubts that you're doing it right, but these conversations are often necessary as part of the learning process. This is why we constantly come back to connection; the aim is that you and your horse remain relaxed and willing as both figure it out *together*. Keeping the focus on connection, rather than perfection, means you both stay confident throughout the training 'wobbles' or plateaus, which in turn both keeps the sessions fun, improves your communication *and* means you'll be able to continue working on it until you figure it out.

This process is the same whether you're teaching basics like standing and leading, refining lateral work, overcoming problem behaviours or working on ridden exercises. There is often some confusion (the horse isn't sure what you're asking for) or lack of coordination (the horse knows what you're asking for but isn't sure how to do it) that takes trial and error to find the answer. This is the same for us, too. For example, if you're learning a new pose in yoga, you won't get it perfect right away, but you'll get the gist of it and can then refine it each time you practice. It's just the same when training your horse so have faith in the process, be confident to move on as long as your horse has a basic understanding of what you're asking for. Focusing on prioritising positive emotions will keep your horse feeling successful and confident, meaning he'll be willing to return to the exercise and refine it in future sessions.

Hannah is working on teaching Rowan haunches-in. Rowan knows to move her hindquarters towards Hannah at halt from a hand cue, but now Hannah asks for it in movement. This first attempt doesn't look anything like a haunches-in because Rowan has bent away from Hannah. However, she is moving her quarters towards Hannah, which is the important piece they were working on. So, Hannah clicks it and rewards Rowan. She repeats it a few more times to make sure Rowan understands the concept of moving her hindquarters towards Hannah while moving.

Then, Hannah switches her attention back to Rowan's bend, using the target to help explain what she wants her to do. This time, the movement is much more accurate for a haunches-in and is a great step towards it. Because Hannah kept it relaxed and rewarding, even when Rowan lost the bend or offered the 'wrong' behaviour, they were both able to stay connected and figure it out together.

This approach, as opposed to a perfectionist one, will also help your horse enjoy the learning process and remain relaxed when she doesn't know the answer or when something unexpected happens.

In contrast, some reward-based trainers teach that animals must be trained in such a way that they never feel unsure or make mistakes. Horses trained in this way are relaxed as long as everything follows their expectations, but as soon as something unexpected or confusing happens, such as the trainer clicking at the wrong time or getting distracted, the horse is quick to get tense and frustrated. The focus is on perfect behaviour, rather than positive emotions.

This approach also puts a lot of pressure on *you* to get it right all the time. We don't expect trainers to be perfect, either! Instead, we focus on staying connected and relaxed, comfortable in the knowledge that you will get there in the end. If your horse doesn't know the answer, that's OK. Or if your training gets interrupted by another horse escaping and causing mayhem on the yard, that's fine. If you mark the wrong thing, or fumble or make a mistake, that's all fine, too. If something goes wrong or is unexpected, get back to connection with your horse as fast as possible by simply standing or walking together and maybe giving your horse a nice scratch. Then when you are both relaxed again, carry on. This focus on connection, rather than perfection, builds general relaxation and emotional resilience in horses for both training sessions and the real world. You're teaching them that when life doesn't pan out as they expect, if they stay calm and tuned into you, it generally works out okay.

In our experience, the best sessions aren't always when you achieve some amazing behaviour. They're when you and your horse just feel like you're in perfect harmony and there's nowhere you'd rather be. Connection will lead to you and your horse being relaxed, having fun, and being in "flow" together.

If your session goes awry, take a moment to smile, breathe and re-connect, ready to get back on track.

GET CURIOUS

Just as you want your horse to feel relaxed and confident through the learning process, the same is true for you as a trainer. Whether you're training a behaviour for the first time or your horse is responding differently to how you expected, training is a constant learning curve of new experiences for you, too. The best way to keep anxieties and doubts at bay is to get curious.

Curiosity prevents judgemental thinking. Instead of thinking, "that went badly" or "I did that wrong" or "I don't know what to do", get curious and ask questions; "Why did my horse think I would mark that?', "What else could I try?" and "What would happen if I did *this*?" These will help you to assess the situation and come up with new solutions to try. Starting each question with, "That's interesting!" will help even more.

For example, say you ask your horse to trot on the lunge and he gets too excited, bouncing off into a buck and a canter. Instead of immediately blaming either yourself or your horse think, "That's interesting, I wasn't expecting him to do that! I wonder why he did? Perhaps he's feeling more excitable than usual because the spring grass is coming through. So, what else could I try? Well, let's see what happens if we just try for a fast walk first."

This approach improves you as a trainer because it enables you to stay confident and positive as well as coming up with solutions to your problem.

CUES, CLARITY AND CONNECTION

Communication is fundamental to good connection with your horse. As discussed in Chapter 5, clear cues are a vital piece of communication. We've looked at what makes a good cue. Now we're going to take that deeper and look at *how* you cue as we delve further into the subtle communication between you and your horse.

INTERNAL AND EXTERNAL CUES

Your horse is always responding to two sets of cues, which we call external and internal cues. External cues are the ones you consciously choose and teach to your horse, such as a squeeze on a rein to tell your horse to turn, putting your hand on his side to ask him to move over or saying 'walk on' to ask him to move forward. Internal cues are ones your horse follows instinctively, such as your breathing, focus, and energy.

These two areas combine in every cue so, as well as having a distinct cue, *how* you give it can make a difference in how your horse responds. For example, when you lead your horse, if you walk with purpose and energy, your horse will too. If you just mosey along, totally relaxed and enjoying the view, your horse will relax along with you. Technically, it's the same external cue, but your internal state shapes your horse's attitude and behaviour.

Another example would be the tension you hold when you give a cue. For example, when you're holding a lead rope, do you grip it tightly or have a soft, sensitive hand? The external cue of taking a feel on the lead rope to ask your horse to walk on is the same, but the tension you hold will change the way your horse responds. Other areas to be aware of when giving cues are the speed you move, the pitch of your voice or the intensity of your gaze.

Get curious and experiment with your horse giving known cues in different ways to see how he responds. It's very interesting!

How you give your cue will affect how your horse responds to it. Here, you can see how both horse and handler are relaxed, the feel on the rope is soft and open and they are staying mentally and emotionally connected as they walk together.

AND BREATHE...

Becoming aware of your breath is one of the most important changes you can make to improve your communication. Many of us are not aware that we breathe high, fast, and shallow, which brings tension to our movements and to our horses. Here's an exercise from Rachel to improve your awareness and control of your breath:

Wear a treat pouch or belt around your waist. Have it fairly tight. We're going to use it for bio-feedback. In other words, you'll want to feel the strap as we do the exercise.

Stand relaxed, with your feet straight and your knees relaxed. Put a hand on your chest and breathe into it. You will see your hand rise and fall as you breathe in and out.

Then take your other hand and place it on your midriff. Now focus on breathing into this hand. You will see it move in and out and the movement in your top hand will be less.

Finally, take your top hand from your chest and place it on your stomach, around the belly button. Focus on bringing the breath down to this hand. Feel your stomach move in and out with the in and out breaths.

Now, as you breathe there, be aware of the feeling from your belt. Is your stomach pushing into the front of it? Can you feel the back of the belt in your back? That's the one to focus on. If you can't feel much in your back, engage your core by gently using the muscles you need to draw the pelvic bone upwards. Now you will feel the back of your belt much more strongly. You will feel your back rounding and opening out.

This is the most grounded breathing you can do and is exactly what we want to be able to create easily when we're riding or handling horses, particularly if they are anxious. Any time you feel anxious you can start with the hand on the chest (or simply mental awareness if your hands are full) and work your way down as your tension dissipates.

Practice this exercise often. Decide to do it as you arrive at the yard, as you first greet your horse, as you tack up, just before you go into the arena, or when you stand on the mounting block. Practicing does two things: it helps your breathing to be deeper generally, and it teaches you to become more aware of yourself.

In addition to awareness of your breath, being aware and in control of your movements will also affect your horse enormously. People who rush around quickly, get distracted, or aren't aware of their movements tend to increase tension, anxiety, and confusion in the horses they work with. Increasing your body awareness while away from your horse will help you in your training sessions. We recommend tai chi, yoga, and Pilates for increasing your awareness, strength, and control of your body. When you're working with your horse, focus on exactly what you're doing and how you're moving to become more deliberate, calm, and effective.

This mind-body connection is important for both of you. Mental relaxation and focus go hand in hand with physical relaxation and focus; as you improve one, you improve the other. Focusing on this area within yourself will help your horse achieve the emotional balance we've discussed previously in the book.

VIDEO RESOURCE

BREATHE YOUR WAY TO A BETTER CONNECTION

Watch this video on using your breath to help your horse relax and connect with you.

www.connectiontraining.com/video-resources

SOFT CLARITY

Combining breath and awareness work with clear cues, gives you soft clarity. Humans typically find this difficult: we're good at hard clarity and soft fuzziness! Hard clarity is when you know exactly what you want from your horse but there are either unpleasant consequences if the horse doesn't respond well immediately, or the way the behaviour is cued is abrupt, pressured or insensitive. This is quite common in many types of horse training. Soft fuzziness is more common in positive horse trainers and goes to the other extreme. Everything is very gentle but there is little focus or guidance for the horse. Although this can be pleasant for the horse, you will struggle to make any progress and many horses experience confusion, frustration or anxiety at the lack of clarity.

Soft clarity means that you know exactly what you're asking of your horse, but the way that you ask is sensitive and gentle. It requires a combination of clear external cues and awareness of your internal cues, along with you staying calm, focused and positive. Even if your horse gives you an unexpected response or becomes tense or distracted, soft clarity will help you get reconnected quickly. In this situation, you will quietly and consistently re-direct your horse to a more suitable behaviour, such as targeting or walking a circle, while staying compassionate and clear.

Being able to maintain soft clarity, especially in difficult situations, will take practice and time, but it's a useful concept to remind you to give your horse clarity while promoting relaxation and trust through soft handling. You will open more of a two-way conversation as you watch your horse's responses and adapt your cues accordingly. You will find, with practice, that you can give a clear cue with a lot of energy and still stay soft—for example, if you're asking your horse to pick up into a canter. This subtlety allows for much more variation and communication between you and your horse.

ACHIEVING GOALS WITH A TRAINING PLAN

In order to be able to give your horse clarity, you need to know where you're going and the steps to get there. This is where goals and training plans will help you.

The goals you have for your horse might range from easier daily handling to dreams such as cantering confidently on the beach or improving your competition scores. Goals are great motivators. Keeping them clear in your mind's eye, or even creating a vision board, will help you stay focused and progress with your training.

To achieve your goals, it helps to work on a training plan for each of them. A training plan is a list of all the steps from where you are now to where you'd like to be. This involves breaking each behaviour down into smaller, achievable steps for you to work through progressively with your horse. This process enables you to dissect big (and perhaps seemingly unachievable) goals into bite-sized chunks you feel confident to work on.

TRAINING PLAN EXAMPLE: STANDING QUIETLY FOR THE FARRIER

This rescue pony is being prepared for the farrier. Here, he is getting used to the feel of the rasp on his hooves.

Here's an example of a training plan. First, we'll assume that this horse is happy to be caught and touched but does not pick up and hold up his feet when asked.

Goal:

The horse must be able to stand quietly for the farrier.

Behaviours needed:

- Pick up feet for a long duration.

- Be comfortable with a hoof stand, rasp, and being tapped on the hoof.

- Be relaxed when different people work on the hooves.

Behaviour breakdown:

- Horse shifts weight onto opposite leg.

- Horse picks up foot briefly

- Horse picks up foot and places hoof into my hand.

- Horse holds leg up for longer and longer each time until I can count to twenty.

- Horse holds own weight and lets me move foot up and down, back and forth.

- Horse holds own weight while I clean out the foot.

- Horse holds own weight while I tap with rasp.

- Horse allows me to place hoof on stand.

- Horse builds duration of keeping foot on stand.

- Horse is relaxed and stays in balance while I tap foot while it's on hoof stand.

- Horse allows someone else to ask for the foot and place it on hoof stand.

- Horse allow the other person to tap with a rasp while holding foot still on stand.

- Horse allows trimmer/farrier to pick up foot and place it on stand.

- Horse allows farrier/trimmer to start working on foot for a short duration.

- Horse increases the amount of time farrier/trimmer can work on foot while staying in balance with hoof on stand.

As you can see, you've now got smaller challenges you can work on with your horse in just a few minutes. You can fit these short bursts in and around your regular training sessions. For example, you could pick up the feet before and after a lunging session or while on a break from more forward work. You can also interrupt your yard chores by asking for a quick foot-lifting practice as you're mucking out the stall or after the horse has had his bucket. You know clearly what you're aiming for and the steps you need to train to get there.

BE FLEXIBLE!

Training plans are a useful tool, but they can cause problems if you get too fixed on them. What can look very straightforward on paper can feel very messy when you try it in real life. It's common to go out with a plan of exactly what to work on in your session and find that your horse has come in high as a kite and is struggling to focus on anything. Or perhaps you've been working on one step of your training plan for ages and your horse is just not making progress. Or maybe you find that after processing the work from your last session, he's jumped ahead several steps and you haven't planned that far ahead yet.

Use your training plans as a guide, but you must be prepared to be flexible. This means adapting your session depending on what your horse is like in *that* moment. If you planned to work on something stationary and calm, like hoof lifting, and your horse is full of energy, you might need to work on movement and relaxation instead. If you find that after several tries you're not making progress on a certain step in your plan, you'll need to try something else. This might mean

explaining that step to your horse in a different way, changing your rewards, or mixing up the other behaviours in the session to help create the best emotional state for learning.

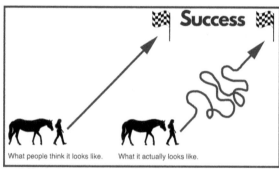

Life is less predictable than the steps on a training plan. Prepare to adapt and respond to different challenges along the way.

It's normal for behaviours to fluctuate and horses to vary. Keep your goal in mind, but always adapt your training to the horse you have on that day. When you put the connection and emotional balance first, you will be more likely to have a successful session. The behaviour *will* improve over time as you move towards your goal.

A BAD DAY IS JUST A BAD DAY

Unfortunately, bad days will happen. You'll have some sessions with your horse that feel utterly wonderful and leave you floating on Cloud Nine. You'll also have sessions where you felt everything went wrong and you were totally disconnected.

Bad days happen for all sorts of reasons. Perhaps you arrived stressed from work, tired from the kids, or distracted as you waited for a call from the garage that's fixing your broken-down car. You might be in a rush or feel under scrutiny because someone from the barn is watching your session. Maybe your horse is in season, the herd is upset due to a new horse arriving or an old one leaving, or there was a falling out in the field. Perhaps your horse is feeling spooky due to the wind, annoyed by the flies, or has a bit of discomfort somewhere. Maybe everything started off great, and then something happened that put your horse way over threshold and everything fell apart.

Whatever the reason, bad days will happen. But they really are just that—a bad day, not a failure or catastrophe. When something goes wrong, it is easy to dwell on it, but there's no need to. Keeping a training journal can help you see what's happening. Looking back over all your sessions will help you see that the bad day is just a blip and you are progressing well overall.

Keep in mind that different people can have very different perspectives on what constitutes a 'bad day'. For example, if one person takes her horse out for a ride and he's a little spooky, she can get anxious and despairing about his behaviour. However, another person could experience the same behaviour as nothing to worry about. You need to be sensitive to your horse's emotions, but don't panic if your horse throws up some unwanted behaviours now and again. It's worth remembering that he still is, and always will be, a horse. This means you will still see

behaviours such as spooking, pawing, rushing, barging, and planting from time to time. Connection Training can improve your horse's behaviour and emotions hugely, but don't expect him to behave perfectly at all times!

On days where your horse is tense or disconnected, you will need to adjust your training plan to make it easier and set your horse up for success. On this day, Selena was very anxious about a tractor working the fields close to the arena. We had to spend over half of the session working on walking together, targeting and other easy behaviours until she had relaxed and we could only work on more challenging exercises away from the side with the tractor. The next day, she was calm and confident again, even with the tractor, and she focused brilliantly throughout the session.

This is something we see with some people who train their horses in this way: an expectation of perfection and a lot of worry and anxiety if their horse shows anything less. We're here to tell you not to worry about it! Of course, you want to help your horse be as relaxed and happy as possible, but there will be days when he's feeling a little off or has different priorities from you. This is completely normal. When problem behaviours crop up, it's best to calmly deal with them as well as you can in each moment and continue with your training. Keep perspective on your progress and move on to tomorrow.

As you and your horse progress, you will start to find that your bad days aren't as bad as they used to be and your good days just keep getting better. Although there will probably always be some variation in the quality of your sessions, you will find that they generally improve overall until nearly all of your sessions are fun, connected, and joyful for both of you

BAD DAY, GOOD TRAINER

It's easy to be relaxed, clear, and happy when everything is going well, but it's even more important to stay this way when it's not. Many people get worried or despairing when they have a bad session, leading them to disconnect, tense up, or get cross with their horse. Needless to say, this doesn't improve the situation!

Bad days happen to everyone. Here, Freckles is shown getting over-excited and disconnecting from Hannah as he takes off bucking instead of lunging quietly. By staying calm and re-directing Freckles back to more suitable behaviours such as walking and trotting, they were quickly able to re-connect and continue on successfully.

You need to be at your best when your horse is at his worst. That's when he needs your guidance, clarity, and reassurance the most. Focus on your breathing and internal cues to help you stay grounded, confident and present for your horse. If you do find yourself in a situation that is getting out of hand, try focusing on *one thing* you want your horse to do, such as touching the target or taking a step back. Calmly keep your focus on that, softly repeating the cue and rewarding him when you can. Stay with that one behaviour until you are both

feeling calmer and more connected. Your horse will appreciate and respond to your clarity and focus, and you are much more likely to create a positive outcome.

INCORRECT OR UNWANTED BEHAVIOUR CHECKLIST

Bad days or moments happen for all sorts of reasons. Getting curious and asking questions will give you more understanding of both the cause and solution. Going through this checklist will help you address the problem in the right way for your horse.

1. Does your horse understand what you're asking? If you're consistently getting an incorrect response to a cue, take a few moments to check whether your horse actually understands what you're asking for. Make it a bit easier, check whether your cue is consistent, and make sure he truly understands it. It's very helpful to video what is happening and then review it to check your clarity, consistency and your horse's responses.

2. How is your horse feeling? Is your horse lacking motivation or relaxation? Review the tips in Chapter 4 to bring your horse's emotions back into balance.

3. Have you asked for too much? Have you worked your horse to the point of boredom or brain-fry (when he's learned too much to take in any more information)? Or, have you expected too much of your horse and he's lost confidence in the behaviour? It's your job to keep the sessions interesting and at the right challenge level for your horse, so taking a break or making it easier may help.

4. Is there something physically wrong? Maybe your horse isn't performing the behaviour because he has a foot abscess brewing. Perhaps your mare is in season and is suffering from cramps. Is your horse hungry or recently moved to a new pasture or feed? Any recent nutritional changes or medication can affect your horse. If a behaviour changes suddenly when your horse has been happy to do it for ages, it's nearly always due to physical pain or discomfort. It's sometimes hard to know if there's something brewing under the surface, but do check it out, with professional help if necessary.

5. What else is happening in your horse's life? New paddocks, new companions, mares in season, and other changes in herd life affect your horse's ability to concentrate on what you're asking for. He's with his herd twenty-three hours a day, so upsets and changes in the herd will have a significant impact on him. Other external factors such as the weather or events on your yard can also affect him. It doesn't mean you must abandon your training. Just adapt it slightly to be sensitive to his needs and help him relax and focus on the job in hand.

6. How are you feeling? Is the tension coming from you? Are you stressed, in a rush, concerned you're being watched or focused on work or family life? This is a partnership, so your emotions will affect your horse, too.

If you go through the checklist and find a likely cause of the problem, you have two choices. You can change your training to accommodate the issue and help your horse be successful, or you can leave the training for another day when things might go better. If nothing on the checklist seems to be the problem, it may be that there is an underlying cause you can't perceive, or your horse is simply having a difficult day. Let's face it, we all do sometimes! Whatever the cause, try and make it a positive interaction. Maybe you simply go out for a walk in-hand or spend time grooming your horse instead of training, or decide to train something easy and fun you

both enjoy. Boosting the positive emotions will have a constructive long-term impact on your relationship and training.

BE KIND TO YOURSELF

Traditionally, when horses act up, they get labelled 'naughty', 'stubborn', or 'silly'. As you change perspective and start to explore how they're feeling, what's causing it, and how you can change it, you may feel that all the responsibility for your horse's behaviour is now on your shoulders. As a trainer, it is up to you to decide what to ask of your horse and how to respond to his behaviour in a way you believe is fair and ethical. However, this doesn't mean that if you're having a bad session, it's your fault! Each horse will bring his own personality and history to the training, as well as his variability day to day. You cannot compare your training to that of someone else, because what might have been easy for one horse can be incredibly difficult for the next. Stay focused on the needs of your horse and use what works for him.

To find out what works might take some experimentation. This can be tricky too, as most of us would like a set list of tasks to do and rules to follow. We get asked for these tasks and rules quite frequently, but it is impossible to provide a one-size-fits-all solution, since every horse and human partnership is unique. You can learn to love trial and error learning and come to enjoy finding out what works best for your horse.

This means that, inevitably, you will try some things that don't work well. You will make some training decisions that, in hindsight, probably weren't the best. This is totally fine. It's okay for your horse to make mistakes, and it's okay for you to make them as well. You'll see in our videos in our online training courses that we make mistakes all the time. Often these aren't actual 'mistakes', but rather attempts that don't succeed—we don't know what will happen until we try them, so we give them a go and find they don't work. No problem! We just try something else instead. Sometimes they are actual mistakes, such as dropping the lunge line, clicking at the wrong time, or accidentally asking for a behaviour with the wrong cue. Again, these are not a problem—we just smile, help the horse to stay calm, and reward him for trying despite our mix-ups. This attitude keeps the connection and teaches your horse to be relaxed in a much wider range of situations.

Remember that you're learning too, so treat yourself as you're treating your horse. Give yourself small tasks, notice what you do well, and take note of these each session. Just as with your horse, ignore most of the unwanted behaviour in yourself, unless you can learn from it to improve next time. Keep the pressure off both of you to be perfect—remember, it's Connection Training, not perfection training!

CONSISTENCY AND PERSEVERANCE

Training horses well is a difficult skill combining many elements, from improving your own body awareness, observation skills, and timing to understanding your horse and the behaviours you're training. It takes consistency and perseverance to make great progress.

We often say that 'behaviours are fast, emotions are slow.' If you're teaching your previously highly strung, anxious horse to stay calm in new situations, this will take time. You'll have many relapses to old behaviour and emotions along the way, until those scales have tipped in favour of relaxation, connection, and confidence. If you're teaching your previously unmotivated and switched-off horse that

training and movement are fun, this will also take time.

Learning new skills takes time, and it's the practice that does indeed make perfect. Our students who make the most progress are the ones who learn as much as they can from books, videos, and live training and who practice with their horse every day or as often as they can. When you do this, it helps you to build your skills in training your horse and gives your horse more input in learning. In addition, the time spent together boosts your relationship and refines your connection. Sometimes you make great leaps of progress in a very short space of time. More often, the progress is so slow you're not even aware you're making it until you look back and see how far you've come.

If you commit to finding ways to make training work rather than reasons why it won't, you will see huge changes in your horse and your relationship together. However, Connection Training is not about quick fixes. We aim to address the root cause of the problem and bring the horse back into balance, inside and out. Being as patient and consistent as possible will allow you to make that change eventually, and although it can take a long period of time, it will be true and long-lasting.

ENJOY THE JOURNEY

It's common for the journey you embark on with your horse to change course along the way. As we step back and ask our horses how they feel about certain things, we often have some tough decisions to make. Often their needs lead us in new directions, and we must leave behind familiar approaches and even abandon our previous learning. It's likely this is happening to you as you read this book. Hannah discusses her own journey and how to enjoy your own:

Our horses are our true teachers. My horses are the ones who've pushed me to seek the necessary knowledge and skills I need to help them.

Years ago, I became determined to find a way to solve the many problems I was experiencing with Toby, which is what led me to clicker training in the first place. I also had a desire to help the difficult rescue horses I'd taken on which pushed me to improve and develop my skills. Eventually I began teaching what I'd learned which turned out to be the beginning of an unbelievably interesting and rewarding career. In the end, I was very successful with Toby and my rescue horses and they each became happy, easy riding horses (they're now all nearly 30 years old so are enjoying a mostly retired lifestyle these days), though it wasn't easy at the time.

Then I think back to my journey with India. She has challenged me so much as a horse owner and trainer as I seek solutions to her physical difficulties (metabolic problems such as chronic tying up and

repeating abscesses etc.) and her hormonal issues (seasonal pain and big behavioural outbursts and anxiety). I've had to really change my expectations of what she is capable of and have honed and improved my training to find a way which works for us.

Or Freckles, who made me find new solutions to bring more relaxation and enjoyment to the training. For him as a youngster, I challenged everything I thought I knew about reward-based training and experimented with new ideas to find out what worked.

Often, I work with people whose horse is perhaps not the best match for them. Maybe they love dressage but their horse really lights up when hacking out, or perhaps a high-energy horse makes their anxious owner more frightened. That may be the case, but it's often the place of the greatest development and learning when you're faced with a horse who challenges you so much. If you're committed to making it work, no matter what, you will find the answers you need and you will grow as a person and as a horse trainer.

In my own journey, it's been these tricky horses/stages/behaviours where I have learned the most about myself, about my horses and about the training. It's these situations where I've been forced to seek more knowledge and, more importantly, look at myself to see what I can change to help the situation. When you're in the middle of a learning curve like this, it can be tough! But, I can also tell you that these challenges have been the most rewarding and beneficial to me, my horses and my life. Looking back, they are also my proudest moments as I made the best decisions for my horses and we found joy and success together. The search for these solutions has given me a huge range of training skills, experience and adaptability that have made me the trainer I am today.

If you're working through some difficult challenges with your horse, remember that it is about your partnership only. You are on your own journey with your own horse and different things will come faster, slower, easier and harder than for other people and their horse. Everyone starts from a different place so don't compare where you are with someone else!

The second rule is to understand that all of this takes time. It takes time, practice and dedication to build competency in anything and training horses well is a complex skill that requires many different elements to work together. It won't be easy or perfect overnight but that's normal – stick with it and you'll grow together. If you have a horse or situation you find really challenging, that scares and frustrates you or has you despairing that you'll ever get

through it, stick with it! If you're committed to finding a way with your horse, you will. You will come out the other side proud to have done it your way, having strengthened your relationship and with new understanding of your horse, of yourself and your connection together.

Most of all, remember to enjoy the journey. It's a fascinating, fun and endlessly varied trip when training a horse. Find your inner pony-mad child and remember that you do this for fun and the love of these wonderful animals. If you and your horse have enjoyed each other's company, it's been a successful day! Appreciate the small things and enjoy each day's challenge. This is probably the most important thing that now makes every horsey day of ours feel successful. Even if it's blowing a gale and our horses are high as kites and we can't do anything we planned, we now happily adapt, come up with something we can do (even if it's a grooming session and some trick training in the barn) and enjoy all the small moments. It keeps us smiling, our horses happy and our connection strong.

CHAPTER 7

COOL, CALM AND CONNECTED: DE-SPOOKING FOR LIFE

"The innate reactions of domestic horses to anything they perceive as threatening, the legacy of their evolution as prey animals, are still our greatest problem with them." Lucy Rees, *Horses in Company*, 2017

Relaxation is at the core of Connection Training. However, horses are notoriously spooky and this anxiety prevents horses being able to relax and respond to you in many situations. Fear is the root of many behavioural problems horse owners face and helping our horses to become more confident is necessary for successful training. In this Chapter, we're going to look deeper into why fear-based problems are so prevalent in horses and what you can do to help your horse become more confident. This work will directly reduce your horse's level of fear arousal when encountering something spooky. It will help him to become generally much more relaxed and connected to you, no matter what.

WHY HORSES SPOOK

Horses are scared of only two things: things that move and things that stay still! Since horses are flight animals, they are always on the lookout for predators and ready to flee. This is fundamental to being a horse but humans can hardly understand it as our brains are set up differently. The brain's FEAR system in horses will be denser, neuronally, than that of a predator, such as a dog. It will also be highly sensitised, so it is easily activated. When something scares a horse—such as a loud noise, a gust of wind, or an object that brings up unpleasant memories—the FEAR system dominates the thinking brain. As explained in Chapter 1, arousal of the FEAR system triggers a 'freeze or flight' response. Most of us have experienced horses who froze when they encountered something frightening. They become immobile as they turn all their focus towards the scary object, making it difficult for the rider or handler to get their attention. They are making the 'Should I stay or should I go?' decision. With an increase in the fear stimulation, they will wheel and bolt, moving straight into the full flight response. As riders, we know that it's impossible to communicate with a bolting horse. Well-trained aids don't work, as the horse cannot process instructions when this brain system is fully aroused.

Behavioural signs that your horse is fearful include turning away from the stimulus in order to be able to run away; standing staring, with ears focused on the stimulus; showing the whites of his eyes; tensing the muscles in his face, especially clenching his lips and jaw; freezing; pacing; defecating; carrying a high tail; being unable to eat, and more extreme behaviours such as leaping away, rearing or bolting.

APPROACHES TO DE-SPOOKING

Many people view de-spooking a horse as a difficult challenge. But it can be done more easily than you may think. The key to success lies in choosing the right methods.

AVOID FEAR-BASED TRAINING

Traditional training systems typically provoke low levels of fear to create movement in a horse. For example, when teaching lunging, some trainers wave a long lunge whip behind the horse to get him to move forwards. This arouses the horse's FEAR system enough for him to move away from the whip. If he stops, the whip is waved again to keep him moving by re-activating the flight response. When he keeps moving, the whip is withdrawn. The brain remembers this aversive experience and tries to avoid it in the future. So, the next time the horse sees the whip held up, he takes it as a sign to move off before the situation becomes more aversive.

The problem with this approach is that the learned behaviour is forever associated with the bad feelings of the FEAR system. The horse may move away from the whip with alacrity, but inside the brain, the pathways being lit are the ones that feel bad. In some cases, this approach can actually over-sensitise the FEAR system, triggering the flight response as soon as horses are on the lunge or being ridden. Many gadgets have been designed to prevent horses from running when they feel this fear, but they always mask the symptom rather than address the cause. They give the handler more physical control, but they do not make the horse feel less fearful (in fact, they can increase fear levels as they remove the option of escape and introduce more pain or the fear of pain into the situation).

Not only does training in a way that routinely utilises the flight response increase general levels of anxiety in horses, it doesn't give you many options for teaching your horse to confidently approach a spooky situation. Let's say you're hacking out and there's a plastic bag in the hedge that is worrying your horse and he doesn't want to go past it. Typical responses to this situation include using more leg, or even the whip or raised voice to make the horse go forwards. The problem here is that the horse isn't learning that the plastic bag is not scary, he's simply learning that it's even more uncomfortable not to go past it. Since you're not helping your horse to feel more positive about plastic bags or unusual objects, the behaviour doesn't change, or it can even get worse as the horse experiences fear and discomfort every time he encounters that stimulus.

USE REWARD-BASED TRAINING

Luckily, there's another way to approach these situations; using rewards and building your relationship. We teach horses how to make safe and calm decisions in the face of a scary situation, so that they stay safe and connected to you. As you practice and generalise this concept, it transfers to all areas of your horse's life, helping them to become generally more relaxed, confident and curious.

With reward-based training, the pathways that are lit in the brain are the feel-good ones of CARE, SEEKING, and PLAY. In lunging, for instance, the horse starts by learning to follow a target. This behaviour is rewarded, and so the horse feels good about it and wants to repeat it. Soon the target is faded and a new cue, such as

'walk on', is transferred to the behaviour. The whole process feels good. For the rest of his life, when the horse hears the cue "walk on", these good-feeling pathways will be lit and the horse will actually enjoy (feel rewarded) simply by hearing that cue. This is the difference that makes the difference! With reward-based training, everything you do with your horse begins to feel rewarding and your horse is motivated to participate. He becomes more optimistic in general and far less anxious.

When faced with a scary object or situation, reward-based training dampens the FEAR system by arousing the SEEKING system. For example, a horse who is fearful of the plastic bag can play some fun games at a comfortable distance from it, such as targeting, to begin to relax in its vicinity. As you move closer to the plastic bag, he focuses on playing this safe, fun, rewarding game, until he's confident to explore the bag itself (and get highly rewarded for that). This creates a new pathway in the brain which feels good to the horse and he starts to experience positive emotions related to plastic bags. As long as you don't revert to forcing him past his Connection Zone again, the old fear-based pathway will start to disappear. It's like a footpath that stops getting used. It gets grown over and in a couple of years it's hard to see there ever was a footpath there. Beside it, we have created a brand-new footpath, the following a target behaviour. As this gets used again and again, its trace gets more and more prominent, meaning that your horse is increasingly likely to feel curiosity or confidence when faced with an unexpected plastic bag, rather than fear.

CONNECTION CREATES CONFIDENCE

Helping reduce fear is another reason we focus so much on building the bond between the horse and the human. When the horse is alarmed, this bond helps her stay at a lower level of arousal (freeze rather than flight) so she can still communicate and take instructions. This is because the arousal of the CARE system helps to reduce the arousal of the FEAR system. It's the feeling of relaxation and confidence you have when you're with someone you trust, compared to facing the same scary situation alone or with a strange or untrustworthy companion.

When your horse gets worried, we want her to turn to you and ask, 'Should I be worried about this? What should I do now?' We reward this decision to pause and connect highly, as it shows the horse is looking for a better answer than simply bolting. She is using her cognitive brain and not simply reacting from fear arousal. We want to increase the time between the worry and the potential bolt so that we can act to keep us both safe. We teach our horses that our decisions are trustworthy and that if they check in with us, they will be okay. This creates the safest horse possible.

But this only works if *we* are able to make the best decisions in the moment. Often, when our horses get tense, we get worried as well, which causes us to tighten up and lose clarity and softness, preventing us from connecting and guiding our horse well through the difficult situation. When you tense up, one of the first things to go is sensitivity through the hands. This causes your horse to feel blocked, like you've cut off that conversation between you, which can cause him to feel more anxiety. Staying soft when your horse is tense is a tough thing to do, but it makes a big difference. Even if you have to grab the rope or rein for a moment, as soon as you can, take some deep breaths, relax your shoulders, and soften your hands. Your horse will appreciate and follow this softness and begin to tune in and relax.

Keeping your focus is also important to guide your horse back to calm. If something spooks your horse, it's common for your attention to get drawn to that spooky stimulus too. This tells your horse that it really is something to be aware of and worried about. Instead, stay focused on what you want your horse to *do* rather than what you want him to ignore. Calmly and softly repeat your request until your horse softens and follows your cue.

If your horse gets tense and disconnects, keep your focus and stay calm. Give him something positive to do, such as touching a target or walking a small circle, to bring his attention back to you and help to settle him down.

For example, if you're leading your horse past a field of galloping horses, he might tense up and stare into the distance. Do not stare at the horses too! First breathe, then think of something you do want your horse to do. A good option here is to ask him to target. Calmly repeat your cue. As soon as he turns to you a little, mark. He may be too tense to take a treat, but just ask again. The key is for *you* to stay clear and focused on what your horse can do to be successful in this situation. Stay there and repeat until your horse is truly calm and connected, not just coping. Then you can go back to leading him safely past the field.

Fearfulness disconnects horses from us and so, along with this increasing relaxation we get softer horses. They want to be with us, and they enjoy their interactions as well as the training and rewards. By following a systematic approach to help your horse to overcome fears and become braver generally, you learn how to be calmer and more confident in scary situations too. So that when your horse is struggling, you can be at your best to help him.

KEEP YOUR HORSE UNDER THRESHOLD

A key component in teaching your horse to be less fearful and more confident in specific situations is understanding your horse's emotional threshold. As explained in Chapter 1, the emotional threshold is the horse's stress limit. When your horse is below this threshold—in what we call the Connection Zone—he can still learn. When he is too worried or excited, he goes over threshold and becomes unable to process information and make good decisions. He's been tipped into flight mode and reacts by trying to escape the situation.

Understanding and being sensitive to your horse's level of emotional arousal will make or break your training. For your training to be successful, you must keep your horse under threshold as much as possible.

The first step is recognising the signs of tension in your horse. Many people think their horse is over threshold when she's rearing or bolting—and she is, but she's *way* over it. Your horse is approaching threshold when she becomes *aware* of something in her environment that alarms her. You'll see her lift her head, focus on

the object or stimulus, tense her muscles a little, and tighten her eyes and mouth. The horse may not even have moved at this point, but she's beginning to show signs of anxiety.

This is the point at which you need to work. For example, you might be ten feet away with the saddle when your horse shows these signs of worry. Before you move on any further, you need to help your horse become relaxed.

Real life will cause your horse to go over threshold occasionally—you can't avoid it. A car backfiring, another horse touching an electric fence and bolting in the field, or something blowing across the arena can cause your horse to startle or even panic. Do whatever you need to do to keep everyone safe, then use your training skills to help your horse calm down and focus again. The more you do this, the quicker your horse will relax and connect back to you. Over time, his Connection Zone will expand because he has learned that it's all worked out okay in the past.

By monitoring your horse's body language, you will soon be able to pick up on those early signs of tension and react accordingly, keeping your horse under threshold and in a state of being much more relaxed, happy, and able to learn.

TEACH IMPULSE CONTROL

Impulse control is a vital exercise for de-spooking but applies to many other situations as well. It means that you teach your horse to control her natural impulses and think through situations instead of immediately reacting to them. This is a great tool to help your horse become more emotionally balanced so she is able to stay connected and safe in novel or unusual situations.

Teaching impulse control actually begins as soon as you start using reward-based training. As you begin to mark and reward your horse for turning away from the food rather than grabbing it, you have begun to teach impulse control. Your horse's impulse is to push and grab for the food; instead, he has to learn to control that impulse and offer an alternative behaviour instead. When this behaviour gets rewarded, it strengthens his ability to control his impulses. There are many other times when your horse needs to use impulse control: for example, by slowing down when he'd prefer to speed up or by walking with you past that lush grass or strange horses he'd like to say hello to, and so on.

Horses are expected to just have this impulse control innately across all types of horse training and handling. In fact, they need to learn it. By teaching your horse how to control his impulses in a positive and progressive manner, you'll teach him the tools to regulate his emotions himself and offer the best behaviour in each circumstance.

The key to being successful with impulse control training is to notice and mark good *decisions*. In a spooky situation, this might be when your horse is feeling anxious and would usually spin away, but instead, he stops and looks to you. He may still be tense and it may only be a pause, but this is a great decision as he controlled his initial impulse to flee immediately and looked for an alternative solution instead. Reward these decisions highly and you will establish strong impulse control, where your horse pauses and turns to you in difficult situations.

It's important to work on impulse control at the right threshold level for your horse. If your horse is scared of novel objects and his instinct is to turn and run, begin by approaching a novel object that's a long distance away, so that your horse is aware

of it but still under threshold. At that point, ask him to turn to you or touch a target, reward him highly, and then turn away from the scary object. In this way, you're beginning to teach your horse to tune in to you when faced with the unexpected rather than to instantly panic and spin away. As he learns that responding to your cues is rewarding and fun, he will build confidence in you and in approaching new objects. From then on, he'll be far more likely to stop and think and respond to your requests.

Reward your horse for making good decisions in challenging situations. The tractor was worrying Freckles and his impulse was to run away. Hannah dismounted to give him confidence and keep him under threshold. She rewarded him for standing still and connecting with her, instead. This gave Freckles a positive experience with the tractor, building his confidence in future and further reinforcing that standing still and staying with Hannah was a good decision.

As you can see, an understanding of threshold is vital for impulse control training to be successful. Once your horse is over threshold, he won't be able to offer anything other than an impulsive reaction. Instead, while working on impulse control, take your horse to the edge of his threshold and give him an alternative behaviour to do. When he responds well to your cue, reward him highly, and then take him away from the situation so he relaxes again. Next time you take him to that point of threshold in that situation, he'll be better able to respond well to your cue because it worked so well for him last time. In this way, you can slowly and positively teach your horse to listen to you and respond well in challenging situations.

Some horses find learning impulse control much easier than others. Young horses tend to find it very difficult. Begin by asking for tiny amounts of impulse control in very short sessions so they are successful and rewarded highly for their efforts. As they grow older, with practice and natural brain development, impulse control will steadily improve.

Some horses find impulse control difficult due to a combination of personality and past history. For example, a naturally 'hot' horse who has never been given the chance to learn how to learn and take an active role in changing his behaviour will likely find impulse control challenging. Older horses who have had very little handling, especially if they have been kept without other horses, are also likely to struggle. Just like with the youngsters, the key is to set up easy challenges where the horses will be successful. This approach allows them to build a strong history of being rewarded for even tiny attempts to listen to you rather than react impulsively. With patience and practice, you will see a big improvement.

DE-SPOOKING TRAINING TO BUILD CONFIDENCE AND CURIOSITY

Including de-spooking exercises into your training prepares you and your horse for scary situations you may meet in day-to-day life. You can control the environment in a training scenario to allow you and your horse to practice your skills in overcoming spooks while staying safe and not over-facing your horse. Through these exercises, your horse will also learn that, in general, new objects, sights, sounds and smells are rewarding and interesting. De-spooking training changes your horse's perception of the unknown from potentially frightening to potentially rewarding. As you can imagine, this has a profound effect on his general levels of curiosity, confidence, and calmness. De-spooking training exercises build on the Enrichment and Empowerment exercises in Chapter 2.

TURNING SPOOKY OBJECTS INTO TARGETS

A versatile and highly effective exercise is turning spooky objects into targets. Your horse should already know and love targeting, so when you hold out or point to an object and give the cue to target, he'll eagerly touch it with his nose. Asking your horse to target an object communicates that you'd like him to move towards it and touch it. It also turns this previously unknown item into a target, which is something your horse knows and understands, which increases his confidence. Often a horse will look at a novel object with his eyes on stalks, as if to say, 'What is that?' When you ask him to target it, you will likely see him relax and step forward as if to say, 'Oh, it's just a differently shaped target. I know what to do with that!'

The goal throughout is to help your horse have a positive emotional experience with new or unusual objects. This means you've got to progress at the right speed for your horse, beginning with easy objects such as grooming brushes and only progressing to more challenging objects, such as plastic bags, when your horse is ready. If at any stage, or with any particular item, your horse is showing signs of anxiety, such as snorting, stepping away, or being reluctant to move closer, then it is likely to be too much for your horse right now. Simply back off and either return to less frightening objects for a while or take her to a safe distance from the spooky item and try again. You'll have much more success if your horse looks calmly at the spooky object from ten steps away than if she gets within two steps and has high anxiety.

DE-SPOOKING THROUGH TARGETING: UMBRELLA

Watch your horse's body language for signs of tension to make appropriate training decisions. Here, Khalil is worried about the umbrella. His focus is on it, his face and mouth are tight, his muscles are tensed and he's positioned himself ready to flee. Khalil is still under threshold and in the Connection Zone, but only just. As a trainer, you would have to act quickly to reduce his fear and bring him to a confident place under threshold. Here, for example, you could walk away from him to take the umbrella further away.

For the purposes of capturing a photo, Hannah brought the umbrella closer to Khalil instead of moving it further away. This immediately sent him way over threshold and triggered the flight response.

To begin re-training Khalil's confidence around umbrellas, Hannah has crouched down and folded the umbrella to help Khalil build confidence and be successful. Khalil knows targeting well so comes up to target the umbrella when Hannah asks, although he is still showing low-level signs of tension in his posture.

As Khalil gains confidence, Hannah stands up and shakes the umbrella out a little. Khalil is showing that he is much more confident - he has stepped forwards towards the umbrella, is chewing his rewards happily and is now relaxed through his muscles and face.

As Khalil's confidence and relaxation grows, Hannah can open the umbrella out completely. Khalil remains calm and happy to target it, showing that Hannah is proceeding at the correct pace for him.

Khalil confidently targeting the umbrella held up high. He is really leaning towards it in his eagerness and confidence to touch it. Khalil's emotions regarding the umbrella changed from fear to fun in a 10-minute training session. It happened this quickly because he had only had one negative experience with the umbrella (when Hannah startled him with it at the beginning of the session), but has had years of positive experiences with targeting, training, Hannah and exploring novel objects. Generally, the longer and more extreme your horse's fear, the longer it will take to change his emotions to more positive ones. You may have to do many short sessions over a longer time period rather than make the change in only one session.

DE-SPOOKING EXERCISES WITH A TARP

Tarpaulins are a great tool for de-spooking exercises because they have many of the qualities that typically make horses anxious, such as unpredictable movement, they make a strange noise and are usually big. However, you can easily control it all and build up gradually as your horse increases in confidence.

Hannah is working with Khalil again. He was reluctant to approach the tarp initially, so Hannah worked on some easy targeting with him to build his confidence.

It didn't take long before he was feeling more confident and was able to follow the target down and begin to explore the tarp. Because he trusts Hannah, he also followed her as she stepped onto the tarp and crouched down to explore it, too.

Once Khalil had been confident enough to explore the tarp, he quickly realised there was nothing to worry about.

Holding the tarp is a different exercise as it's more likely to flap and blow towards the horse. If your horse is anxious, begin with cutting off a small section of tarp to build your horse's confidence. Khalil was very happy to target the full tarp when Hannah held it up.

The next stage is to begin to make it rustle and flap until you can wave it around and your horse stays calm.

Khalil began to get concerned about it when Hannah lifted it up to shoulder height, so she worked here until he was more relaxed. You can see that Hannah has positioned herself between Khalil and the tarp to give him confidence at this stage.

By keeping these challenging moments short, and rewarding Khalil for staying connected, he quickly built up his confidence with the tarp. In fact, it became one of his favourite exercises – a sure sign that Hannah did the training well!

The key to de-spooking success is to make the training fun. Khalil wasn't just at the stage of tolerating it; Hannah worked in his Connection Zone until he loved it. This is really when the emotions are truly changing to positive, so make the sessions interesting and rewarding until your horse is keen to work with the previously spooky object.

VIDEO RESOURCE

HOW TO DE-SPOOK YOUR HORSE POSITIVELY

Watch how to de-spook your horse gently by understanding your horse's emotional state.

www.connectiontraining.com/video-resources

USE A VARIETY OF DE-SPOOKING OBJECTS

Working with a wide variety of objects will help your horse to generalise that new things are fun and rewarding. As your horse continues to have positive experiences with an increasing number of spooky items, you will see that his confidence will generally increase in the face of something new. He will begin to view novel items with curiosity and will be much more likely to step forward and explore them calmly than to immediately want to turn tail and run.

Many horses are fearful about things behind them. To help your horse build confidence in this situation, you can introduce spooky objects into the 'stay' exercise from Chapter 3. Here, Hannah has asked Freckles to 'stay', while she walks around him with some balloons, building his confidence with unusual or moving objects behind him.

Crossing water is scary for many horses. Setting up a water challenge in your own arena is the best way to build your horse's water confidence slowly. Here, Hannah is working with India, who was initially wary of the new water obstacle but quickly became confident following Hannah's lead (this was Halloween-themed training, so please excuse the severed leg target! Though, it does prove that anything can be an effective target!).

Since you can't de-spook your horse with every potential object or scary situation, the aim of these exercises is to generalise the techniques and emotions so that you and your horse have tools to stay calm and connected no matter what situation your find yourself in. The more new things you introduce to your horse and the better his experiences are with them, the stronger this generalisation will be.

Standing near children on a trampoline is a challenging situation for many horses. Here, CT Member, Susanne Eichelberger, works with some easy targeting to help build positive associations with being near the children playing.

These exercises begin by rewarding your horse for being curious and exploring his surroundings confidently. It's invaluable to teach horses to see novel objects as potential toys rather than things to be scared of. It is also a fantastic tool to help horses become more confident about different jump fillers, flags, and dressage markers at competitions. However, in all these situations, you don't want your horse to be targeting them forever! Exploring these items is step one. Once your horse is calm, confident, and curious, you can begin to reward her for calmly walking past these items and ignoring them, staying connected to you instead. This process is highly effective. Officer David Patton of the Miami Police Mounted patrol says, "Connection Training methods have really helped me in preparing our police horses for work in the streets of Miami. Control, calmness, confidence!" If these exercises can help police horses remain calm when working on city streets, you can certainly use them to help your horse become more confident, too!

VIDEO RESOURCE

3 TOP TIPS TO DE-SPOOK YOUR HORSE

Get inspiration for a wide range of de-spooking objects and games, as well as top tips on despooking your horse.

www.connectiontraining.com/video-resources

TRAINING TO OVERCOME PAST FEAR

These object-based de-spooking exercises will help your horse to reduce anxiety when faced with novelty, but they are also effective if your horse has established fear around a specific object or situation. If your horse has a long-term fear, it will take longer to overcome it as you are taking them from negative to positive emotions, rather than neutral to positive. In these instances, there are some extra techniques that will make your training more effective.

SYSTEMATIC DESENSITISATION

The first technique is called 'systematic de-sensitisation'. This means progressively reducing your horse's fear and reactivity to a certain object or situation.

This technique is used frequently to help humans overcome fear. It is often called 'exposure therapy'. The principle is that you are exposed to the fearful stimulus, but at a low level of fear arousal. You stay exposed at that level until you begin to relax. This allows the brain to register the fearful stimulus but to experience it as being okay. The brain then stores the memory of being exposed to that stimulus at that level with little fear.

For example, imagine you are so terrified of spiders that you cannot even bear to look at one. The first level of exposure might be looking at a picture of a spider, which would cause a slight amount of tension but not trigger real fear. You would continue to look at the picture of the spider until you began to relax and experience a calm state. The next time you looked at the picture, it would cause less anxiety, and eventually it would not cause any fear arousal at all. Next, you would progress through increasingly fearful stimuli—perhaps different pictures of spiders, then a model of a spider, then a small spider in a tank, and so on. Each time, the exposure would be increased enough to create a small anxious response. That's necessary, because *you can't overcome fear without facing it*. It's all about retraining the brain by changing memories attached to the stimulus.

COUNTER-CONDITIONING

Along with systematic desensitisation, you can simultaneously use a second technique known as 'counter-conditioning'. Together, these two techniques are often shortened to 'SD and CC'. Counter-conditioning involves using rewards and other positive associations to change the emotion around the fearful object. The brain does not erase the old memory but makes a new pathway in association with the "fearful" object, but this time with positive feelings attached. The horse begins to associate positive feelings with the previously scary object.

One thing to note here is the significance of the brain forming a new pathway. The old negative pathway still exists and the objective is to never stimulate it again. In this way, it will slowly fade and the original behavioural response will not be triggered. This is known as "extinction". However, during the process of counter-conditioning you must try very hard not to stimulate this old pathway, or it will strengthen again. This can be difficult for us to do. Imagine you are counter-conditioning a horse who is afraid of injections. The training is going well but you haven't reached the stage of actually getting a vet in to practice with. Then your horse has an accident and needs veterinary treatment, including an injection. The new calm behaviour isn't strong enough yet for the horse to stand calmly and so you get the old flight response and the vet ends up twitching your horse to give the injection. As you can imagine, that will set your training back. So, if you are in the situation where the behaviour isn't strong enough for real life, see if you can use alternatives rather than trying to use your new approach before it's ready. For example, you could ask the vet for an oral sedative to use before the injection. In that way, you will keep your new pathway "clean" and not stimulate the old pathway either.

In order to counter-condition a fear response as effectively as possible, include as many things that induce positive feelings as you can, such as casual connection time, the marker, food rewards, and the target. Do not underestimate the power of the target! When horses have built up a strong positive history with it, these emotions will transfer to the more difficult stimulus, creating feelings of safety and success in the horse.

CASE STUDY: OVERCOMING FEAR OF THE SADDLE

Zulu, a rescued zebra-Arabian cross, had a bad history with saddles and would object strongly if anyone approached with one. He would run away if possible or pin his ears and bite or kick out at the person with the saddle. To change how he felt about saddles, we used systematic desensitisation and counter-conditioning.

Zulu already had this fear response when his owner, Rebecca Musselwhite of Jive Pony Equestrian Display Team, gave him a home. Because Zulu is a rescue. we are unsure of the history that caused this negative association with saddles and pads.

The first photo was taken during the initial assessment of the problem and the saddle pad was immediately removed after noting this response because we didn't want to push Zulu over threshold and create yet another unpleasant experience in relation to the saddle pad. Instead, we re-built the behaviour with positive emotions and Zulu's co-operation throughout.

Zulu displaying high level of FEAR and RAGE when he cannot escape the saddle being presented. If he was at liberty, he would run away.

Before we started the saddle re-training process, Rebecca ensured that Zulu was strong at touching his target. When the target (the traffic cone) was presented, Zulu immediately wanted to touch it because it brought him feelings of joy and relaxation.

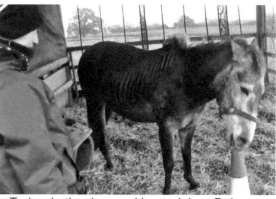

To begin the de-spooking training, Rebecca simply held the saddle while working on targeting. Even at this distance, the presence of the saddle pad caused Zulu to show increased signs of tension, such as pinning his ears, swishing his tail, grabbing the treats and being more reluctant to touch the target. You can see the tension in his face in this photo. Rebecca worked at that level until Zulu was totally relaxed.

From there, it was simply a case of gradually bringing the saddle pad closer to Zulu at a rate at which he was comfortable. Rebecca also used the exercise of turning spooky objects into a target to encourage Zulu to explore the saddle pad. If he turned away, walked away, pinned his ears, or couldn't relax and focus enough to touch his target, then the saddle pad was clearly too close to him. Rebecca simply went back a few training steps until he was calm and confident again.

This process ensured that Zulu was not pushed over threshold. He now had a way of telling Rebecca when he was struggling, with calmer body language, and she could respond immediately. He was able to choose to stay at his target or move away. He learned that if he moved away, Rebecca would back off. If he stayed and willingly engaged with the training, it showed he was relaxed and was happy to continue on.

This choice is important in overcoming fear. The horse will always feel braver when he knows that the way he deals with the scary object is his choice and he will not be forced to engage with it. It also creates excellent two-way communication between you and your equine. Horses are often trying to communicate with their owners. If they get listened to and get an understanding response, then they communicate more and more. If they get ignored, they shut down and communicate less. Targeting is a great way to help them communicate more clearly and for us to understand them better.

With the freedom to engage with the training and the use of so many rewards associated with the saddle pad, Zulu was able to be saddled at liberty, willingly coming over when he saw his saddle pad and standing calmly and relaxed as it was placed on his back.

VIDEO RESOURCE

OVERCOMING SADDLING FEAR

Watch Zulu's training in action as he learns to love his saddle pad.

www.connectiontraining.com/video-resources

FLOODING: THE WRONG WAY TO OVERCOME FEAR

Instead of systematic desensitisation and counter-conditioning, many trainers use a practice called 'flooding' when trying to overcome fear in horses. This means exposing the horse to a fearful stimulus in such a way that the horse cannot escape it. This is a common practice in traditional horse training, but one we never use at Connection Training. Since it's so common and may have been done to your horse at some time, we think it's important to discuss it here.

One example of flooding is teaching a horse to stand tied by simply tying him to a post and leaving him to fight until he realises he can't escape. Another example is continuing to apply a fearful aversive, such as throwing a tarp over him or chasing him with plastic bags, until the horse stops reacting. Yet another common example is strapping a saddle onto a horse for the first time and letting him 'buck it out'.

When these methods are used, it looks like the horse has accepted this new stimulus. But actually, the horse learns that all of his flight and fight behaviours haven't worked, and so he gives up. This is called 'learned helplessness'—the horse believes there is nothing he can do to change the situation for the better. The horse isn't any less nervous about what's happening; he's just stopped trying to escape. His SEEKING system has been reduced to a low level of arousal.

If you were afraid of spiders, the flooding equivalent would be for someone to shut you in a box with hundreds of spiders and ignore all your crying and panicking. At some stage, you would probably give up and go into a state of learned helplessness, too. The flooding technique *may* cure your fear of spiders, but it's equally likely to make you even more phobic about them. It certainly won't make you trust or enjoy the company of the person who did it to you!

For all these reasons, flooding is risky for horse training. Horses who have been subjected to flooding show a strongly raised heart rate in response to new objects, even if they don't show much of a behavioural reaction on the outside. If they don't go into learned helplessness, flooding will sensitise them instead. They'll get more fearful and reactive about the new objects and other stimuli. This fear will often increase until the horses are highly reactive to everything.

Many horses who are considered 'good' are, in fact, in a state of learned helplessness about everything that humans do to them. This is called being 'shut down'. It is actually a state of chronic depression and anxiety, where the SEEKING system is under-aroused. Horses who have experienced this treatment but have not become shut down tend to become highly aggressive, since their RAGE system is aroused as part of the depressive effect. The most seriously damaged horses tend to swing between fearful and aggressive behaviours, with no calm, relaxed state in between. This is very common with rescue horses.

To repeat, flooding is a practice we never advocate. However, we do spend a lot of time helping horses recover from previous flooding experiences.

TRIGGER STACKING

When you're training your horse to overcome fear, it's important to understand the concept of trigger stacking. Triggers are anything that your horse fears or dislikes, ranging from spooky objects and noises to hormonal changes, such as when a mare is in season, to attempting difficult movements or behaviours. When more than one trigger is present at one time, this is known as 'trigger stacking'. Each extra fear stimulus takes the horse closer and closer to the emotional threshold. Something minor can then tip the balance, and the horse goes into full fear arousal. Think of this as 'the straw that broke the camel's back'.

Trigger stacking often happens when riding out on the trail. For example, your horse might be okay if you meet someone carrying an umbrella, or if it's a windy day, or when a tractor passes. But if all three occur at the same time, trigger stacking can cause your horse to panic.

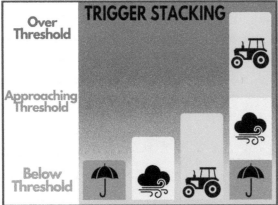

One example of trigger stacking could be when you're taking your horse out for a ride or walk. You meet someone carrying an umbrella which your horse is able to pass calmly. Or, it's a windy day which has caused your horse to be more alert and reactive than usual. Or, you meet a tractor, which worries your horse, though he is able to stand still while it passes slowly. Each of these stimuli trigger some anxiety in your horse at different levels, but he will generally be able to stay under threshold if you meet them individually. However, if you encounter them all together, or in quick succession, your horse's fear can easily stack up, or escalate, causing him to go over threshold.

Physiologically, trigger stacking has to do with adrenaline, a hormone that is released in times of stress. The first fear stimulus causes a release of adrenaline. If no other frightening things happened, the adrenaline level would eventually revert back to normal, and the horse would become calm again. But this takes time. While under the higher level of adrenaline, the horse is more likely to be frightened by objects that would normally be viewed as neutral. If another fearful stimulus happens before the horse is fully relaxed, the adrenaline spikes again. This escalating level of fear sensitivity can cause the horse to go over threshold and into full flight mode.

PREVENTING TRIGGER STACKING WITH A CHALLENGE SANDWICH

To keep your horse under threshold, successful, and enjoying the training, be aware of behaviours or situations he finds challenging. If you keep on asking your horse to do the challenging task again and again or to keep trying harder, you will find that his behaviour plateaus or deteriorates. This is because your horse's aversive emotional arousal levels are rising each time you ask for the challenging behaviour, and he's not getting much reward for his efforts—just a treat and then a request to do it again.

You will make much better progress if you sandwich the challenging behaviours in between two easy behaviours. This will prevent trigger stacking or pushing your horse over threshold in the challenging behaviour by putting him in a state of success and relaxation before asking for it. You can then reward him highly for his attempts at the challenging behaviour by giving him the opportunity to perform a favourite behaviour instead.

For example, let's say that your horse is scared of going past the wrapped haylage bales that have been newly stacked in the yard. Even if you keep rewarding him for each step he takes closer to the bales, he will likely be getting increasingly anxious. He might even stop taking the food rewards or refuse to go any closer. Every attempt from the horse to approach the scary object results only in being asked to give more and go even closer. Although you're adding food rewards in for approaching the bales, it's not a very rewarding situation as the horse's fear levels increase with each step closer.

If, instead, you start a comfortable distance away from the bales and ask him to touch his target, he will feel successful and confident in the presence of the new bales. He'll have that emotional state as you then ask him to step closer to the bales, rewarding him with food rewards each step of the way. After a few steps, when he's still feeling fairly confident about the bales, instead of going even closer, turn away, move back to a really safe distance from the bales and return to asking him to touch his target. Because you have now moved

further away and are working on an easy favourite behaviour, any anxiety your horse built up as he was approaching the bales will be dissipated.

Once he's relaxed and confident again, you're ready to turn back and move towards the bales again. This time, your horse has now had one positive experience of approaching the bales confidently without going over threshold and was rewarded by getting to play his favourite targeting game. On top of that, the targeting has brought his anxiety right back down, and he's once again approaching the bales with low adrenaline levels and positive emotions. This time you get much closer while your horse stays eager and confident. So, you reward him by retreating and working with the target again.

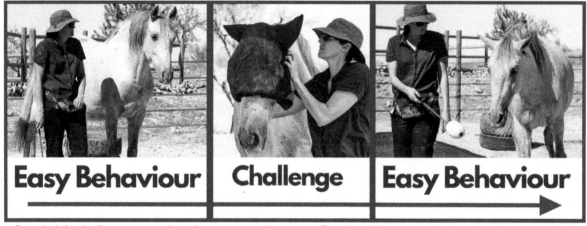

Sandwich challenge exercises between easier ones. Begin with an easy behaviour to ensure he's calm, relaxed and focused. Then, work on your challenging behaviour, keeping this session really short and highly rewarding. Then, return to an easy behaviour again. This will be an extra reward for your horse's efforts during the challenging phase and will also re-set his levels of relaxation, preparing him for success when you return to the challenging behaviour once again. In this example, the first easy, relaxing behaviour is Standing Together. The challenging behaviour is putting on the fly mask, and the final easy behaviour is some gentle and fun targeting.

You can see how this technique helps to both reward your horse for his efforts and set him up for success each time you ask him to work on a more challenging behaviour. This approach can be applied to any training situation, both on the ground and in the saddle. Take the time to

work out which behaviour your horse is finding difficult in some way, and then sandwich it between something else he finds easier.

It's best that the sandwiching behaviours help to create the best emotional state for the challenging behaviour. For example, your horse may love to pop over a jump, but that excitement may work against you if the challenging behaviour involves overcoming anxiety. Instead, you'll want the easier behaviour to be something that promotes relaxation rather than excitement.

You can also use this approach *within* the difficult behaviour. For example, let's say your horse is worried about lifting his feet. You begin with some targeting to set your horse up for success, then work on feet lifting, then return to the target—sandwiching the challenging behaviour in between an easy one. However, during the time you're working on hoof lifting, you can also sandwich the more challenging 'asks' in between easier ones. You might first reward just a weight shift off the leg you'd like to pick up, then wait for a full lift before giving a reward, then return to rewarding a weight shift again. This approach keeps your horse's confidence and enjoyment levels high.

Although it can feel slower in the moment, working with challenging behaviours or situations in this way is an effective and quick way to change your horse's emotions. It also builds confidence in his ability to tackle challenging behaviours generally and increases his trust in you that you will not over-face him. This technique works brilliantly with spooky challenges, but is just as effective with any kind of challenge such as when learning something new, finding an exercise difficult physically or when working on impulse control.

VIDEO RESOURCE

THE CHALLENGE SANDWICH

Learn how to set your horse up for success by using the Challenge Sandwich concept.

www.connectiontraining.com/video-resources

IF YOUR HORSE GOES OVER THRESHOLD

Despite your best intentions, sometimes you might ask too much of your horse, or circumstances outside of your control may result in your horse panicking. Sometimes horses can even go too far with an exercise and send themselves over threshold. For example, if you've been reinforcing your horse for touching scary objects, he might walk right up to something and touch it, then panic about it. If you see this coming, try to prevent it by rewarding your horse before he reaches the spooky item or by not letting him get too close.

If your horse does go over threshold for one reason or another, don't worry about it. Just manage the situation to keep both of you safe, then help your horse rebuild his calmness and confidence. You'll always build it much faster the second or even third time, and he'll soon be back to where he was. This is another valuable lesson in itself: your horse learns how to calm down and reconnect with you even if he does end up over threshold.

SEPARATION ANXIETY

Separation anxiety is another source of spooking. It can occur when you try to ride your horse out on his own, leave him behind while you take his companion, separate two stable mates at a competition, or transport your horse by himself. Again, the key is to build your horse's positive experiences in this situation. General de-spooking work will help to prepare him for this, since you've generally taught him to be calmer, more confident, and able to cope with difficult or unexpected situations.

However, separation anxiety differs from general de-spooking in that it activates not only the brain's FEAR system, but also the PANIC/GRIEF system. Signs of separation anxiety include shouting back to companions, trying to return to herd mates, baulking or planting, pacing, napping, sweating, and defecating. Horses have evolved as herd animals. Being caught on their own spells danger for wild horses, so it's something they will avoid at all costs. However, we often ask our horses to leave their herd, so take the time to teach your horse that this will be a good experience.

Start training your horse where he is comfortable and can have a positive experience. Is he resistant about leaving his herd mates when you try to take him out of the field? Then start there. Take him just out of the gate and play favourite and easy games with him, such as targeting or leading. Reward all those moments when he tunes in to you, rather than his herd mates, and responds well to your cues. Once you feel him relax, put him back in the field. This exercise begins to change the negative emotional associations with leaving the field into positive ones. Next time, he's likely to be more relaxed and more eager to come with you. You can slowly build from there until your horse will leave his herd mates willingly.

Learning to cope with separation anxiety is often easier for the horse who is leaving because he'll have you with him. Therefore, you need to train the horse who is being left behind too so that he remains calm and happy and has a positive experience with being left alone. This is usually a little trickier because this horse doesn't have you there.

Here's an example of how we used this process with a horse named Oscar. When his companion, Jet, was taken out for a ride or in the trailer, Oscar paced up and down the field calling for Jet. To begin the training, the owner gave Oscar his treat ball and then took Jet just outside the field gate. At this point, Oscar left the treat ball and came to the gate, worried about Jet leaving. The owner stood at the same place with Jet until Oscar relaxed and returned to his treats. To reward Oscar for his relaxation, the owner then returned Jet to the field. This was Oscar's first positive experience with being left behind by Jet. The owner than slowly built the time and distance that she took Jet away, while Oscar slowly learned to relax and enjoy his treats while they were gone. Within a few months she could take Jet out in the trailer while Oscar stayed happily at home.

Working through separation anxiety in this way is effective, but the key to success is to make it routine. The more often your horses are separated and have a positive experience with it, the easier separation will become for everyone. You can build this into your daily routine by feeding your horses their buckets out of sight of each other and building up the time spent apart, as well as focusing on it through training.

This helps to keep it a consistent and positive experience for the horses. The desired behaviour often deteriorates if it's not practiced for a while, probably because it is such an unnatural behaviour for horses to do. If there is a period of time when your horses are not separated, you may well find you have to repeat some of the early separation training to teach them to be calm about it once again.

Although training can reduce separation anxiety hugely in most horses, we have found that some horses cannot be taken out or left on their own no matter how much positive training they receive. This could be caused by an over-sensitised PANIC/GRIEF system from traumatic early weaning or another stressful separation, or it might simply be a personality trait. Difficulty coping with separation anxiety is often seen in horses who have lived in isolation at some point in their lives. Whatever the cause, you will need to find ways of ensuring that these horses always have a companion present to ensure their mental and physical well-bring.

CONNECTION CREATES CONFIDENCE

You can see from our discussion that our emphasis when working on fear and separation anxiety, is to focus on building connection. When your horse learns that she can trust your decisions to help her feel calm and secure, she will turn to you increasingly for help when she feels worried. In our view, there is no such thing as a "difficult" horse. Instead, we see a horse in difficulty. The reward for us is huge when we see our horses turn to us for help. It also creates a much safer horse to handle and ride.

It's usually much easier to work through separation anxiety with the horse you take out than the one you leave at home, because you are with her. However, you can train for relaxed separations with both parties, through consistent, systematic positive training.

CHAPTER 8

HANDLING AND HEALTHCARE

Everyone wants a horse who is easy to handle—not only on a daily basis, but in situations such as farrier visits and veterinary care. Difficulties with handling and healthcare procedures are stressful for both you and your horse, so addressing them is key to your relationship and your horse's physical and emotional well-being. In this Chapter, we'll look at the causes of handling problems and a range of training techniques, providing solutions for daily handling issues to working with rescue horses and what to do when your horse needs veterinary care.

CAUSES OF HANDLING PROBLEMS

Understanding why your horse is behaving in a certain way helps you to address issues systematically and compassionately.

Handling your horse includes a wide range of tasks—catching and leading him, tying him up, putting a rug (blanket) on him, grooming him, trimming his hooves, and so on. You want your horse to be calm and relaxed when being handled, but that's not always the case. He may pull and barge when you lead him in from the field, panic when you try to bathe him or bite or kick while the farrier or vet are trying to work on him.

It's important to understand that your horse doesn't kick the farrier or run away from you in the field because he's 'naughty' or 'dominant'. He does it because it works for

him. It's an expression of his emotion—he's trying to either gain something he wants or avoid something he doesn't want. When you understand why your horse is behaving as he is, you'll have more awareness and tools to help him change his behaviour.

Fear is the most common emotion behind any handling problems you'll have with your horse. He could fear clippers, rugs (blankets), lead ropes, the stable... the list just goes on. The source of his fear could be any of the problems below:

Pain and discomfort. A horse will try to avoid anything that causes physical pain or discomfort. This should always be the first thing to check if your horse's behaviour changes. Injury is one possible cause, and it may not be obvious. Internal injuries such as stiffness, misalignment, and strains are difficult to see but can cause a lot of pain and subsequent behaviour problems. Pain and discomfort can also come from poorly fitting tack, an unbalanced or heavy-handed rider, veterinary treatment, teeth problems, and more.

If your horse associates a certain situation with pain, he will avoid it if he can. He may shy away from being touched in a certain area of the body or move away from a painful object. If he can't leave the situation, he may resist, showing behaviour such as ear pinning and tail swishing.

Hormonal changes can also affect horses adversely, especially mares. You may find that your mare becomes more anxious and spooky and shows more signs of separation anxiety when she's in season. Hormonal changes can also lead to physical discomfort and pain. Your horse can't change this. You need to be sympathetic to your horse's physical state and change your training accordingly.

If you suspect pain is involved in any way in the problem, please consult with your vet. If your horse's behaviour changes suddenly, or you have tried to retrain the behaviour using reward-based training and the issue persists, it is most likely a health issue, and this must be addressed before the training can be successful.

Confusion. It's important to check that your horse knows what you're asking him to do. Often, horses aren't clear about the task in hand even when their handlers think they are. To ensure clarity and calmness, step back and check that your horse knows and understands your cues. For example, many horses are difficult to hoof trim simply because they have never learned to shift their balance on to the opposite foot. Instead, they lean on the lifted foot, causing problems for the trimmer. A systematic training programme will teach them all the stages in the process and make life much easier for everyone, including them.

Management issues. As we explored in Chapter 1, horses are social grazers with an innate need for freedom, friends, and forage. If these needs are not being met, your horse will show tension, both in and out of training sessions. It's important to establish good management practices before looking at the training.

If you suspect a management issue is part of the problem and need help in working out why, we recommend you consult with a qualified equine behaviourist. These professionals are trained to look at the whole life of your horse and to consider pain issues as well. They are often referred by a vet when pain is ruled out, and their fees may be claimable on your equine insurance policy.

History. The memories, and therefore anticipation, of distressful feelings or situations can be enough for the problem behaviour to continue for many years, even when the original cause has been fixed. In this case, you'll have to work to create new experiences and more positive associations instead.

Learned behaviour. Occasionally horses will learn certain behaviours from their companions. For example, if a mare runs away from humans entering the field, it is likely that her foal will learn this behaviour from her, along with the idea that unpleasant things happen when humans enter the field.

As you can see, all these causes of daily handling problems are associated with the unwanted emotional systems of FEAR, PANIC, and RAGE. As always, the crux of our training is to re-associate the situations with more positive emotions. If you can create strong positive associations with the behaviour, in place of the negative ones, your horse will be eager and willing to do whatever you need him to.

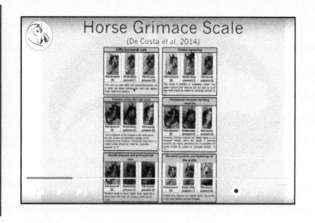
EMOTIONAL CUES

How do you know how your horse feels and which emotional system is being aroused with various tasks and situations? Each behaviour—and subsequently, each cue for the behaviour—will elicit an emotional response in your horse. When you're assessing how your horse feels about various tasks, look at his response to cues that signal it's about to happen. For example, when you approach him in the field with the head collar, does he come to you or run away? When you approach with the saddle, does he stand calmly or begin to fidget, pin his ears, and swish his tail?

These emotional responses are often linked to how the horse felt when first learning the cue. For example, perhaps you have a horse who was taught to back up through a pressure-based training system. He was asked to step back by being touched on the nose, and if he didn't, his trainer waved a heavy rope under his chin to make him uncomfortable and anxious. When the horse stepped back, the rope waving stopped. Eventually he learned to avoid the discomfort of the waving rope by stepping back when a hand was placed on his nose, but that cue became associated with the fear of the swinging rope. This tension may still be present, shown through pinned ears, or rushing the behaviour.

In contrast, if the behaviour was taught slowly to the horse, in a way that prioritises relaxation, confidence and joy, both the behaviour and the cue for it, will be associated with all those feel-good emotions of reward and success.

How the cue was trained isn't the only factor in how the horse feels about it now. For example, you may have a horse who, as a foal, had an unpleasant experience when taught to lead. In the years since, however, leading has meant going to his stable where there are always treats, going to the field to be turned out, or exploring the world out on walks. All these positive associations have now transferred to leading, and it is something the horse now enjoys and feels good about. Conversely, you may have a horse who was taught to lead through slow, positive, and calm training. Since then, the horse has had to undergo veterinary treatment and now associates the head collar and being led with uncomfortable and painful veterinary procedures. In this case, the horse now has negative associations with the head collar and lead rope.

The cues can look the same from the outside, but it is how your horse *feels* about them that determines whether the experience is positive or negative. A negative emotional response can vary from slight irritation to full-blown fear, and the time and input needed to change your horse's emotions to relaxation and joy will also vary accordingly.

How your horse responds when you give him a cue shows you how he feels about that behaviour. For example, does your horse come towards her headcollar or halter, showing that she enjoys the behaviour as well as the things that follow, or does she evade it, displaying more negative emotional associations with being caught?

TRAINING TECHNIQUES FOR DAILY HANDLING BEHAVIOURS

To create these positive emotions of relaxation and joy, you can use a range of training techniques. They are perfect for training a horse for the first time and for retraining behaviours that are now problematic for your horse.

While you're reading about these techniques, you'll probably think of lots of other situations in which you can use them. We can't cover every behaviour here, but the techniques and

Use these techniques to overcome problems or teach your horse positive handling and healthcare cooperation from the very start as CT Coach Claire Waldron shows here with mule foal, Maverick.

principles will work for all handling and healthcare lessons. The de-spooking lessons you learned in Chapter 7 are often applicable, too, since systematic desensitisation and counter-conditioning come into play when you're overcoming any kind of fear. The following techniques build on the basic de-spooking work.

GO SLOW AND STEADY

The most straightforward approach is to just progress with the behaviour slowly and steadily, always finding moments of relaxation that you can reward. If you're teaching your horse to be happy with being touched on their ears, for example, you'll begin stroking their neck where they're comfortable and rewarding them for keeping their head low and staying relaxed. Then, you'll slowly begin to move up the neck towards your horse's ears, steadily making progress until your horse is happy to have his ears handled. To be most successful in this process, watch your horse's body language for signs of anxiety so that you can keep him under threshold (refer back to Chapter 7 for more information on emotional threshold).

Example: Hind Feet Handling

India repeats this process, making slow and steady progress further down his leg, only progressing when he's comfortable with each stage and rewarding him for standing calmly.

This pony, Rafael, at Hope Pastures Rescue Centre was very afraid of people touching his hind feet, causing him to kick out. Staff trainer, India Evans, is working with him here. She has slowly progressed to being able to touch him down to his hocks and she's working on being able to go a little lower.

As she runs her hand down, she stays soft by breathing deeply and reassuring him with her voice. When she gets towards the edge of where Rafael is comfortable to be touched, she pauses a moment and then marks and rewards him for standing quietly.

She frequently breaks it up with scratches, cuddles and easy behaviours.

VIDEO RESOURCE

TEACH YOUR HORSE TO STAND QUIETLY FOR HOSING AND BATHING

See this technique in action in this video on helping a mare to overcome her fear of the hosepipe and water.

www.connectiontraining.com/video-resources

FIND THE CLARITY

If you're teaching something for the first time, you want a way to be able to explain to your horse what you want. If the behaviour is problematic, you want to be able to rule out confusion as a cause for your horse's resistance and anxiety. Both of these situations require more clarity to help the horse succeed.

As soon as your horse understands one behaviour, you can use it to train others. For example, once he knows how to follow a target, you can use it to teach him to lead. If he already follows a lead rope nicely, you can use it to place him in certain positions, such as teaching him to move his quarters over. If he knows how to step onto a board or low pedestal, you can use it to explain that he's to step up onto the ramp of a horsebox.

In all of these situations, you are using something your horse already knows to clearly explain the new behaviour. When you mark, you tell your horse which piece is important so that he learns the new behaviour. For example, if you're teaching him to move his quarters over, you'll ask him to walk a small circle following a target or with the lead rope, but you'll mark when he steps over with his hind feet. This explains to him that the important element now is the moving of the hind feet. With a few repetitions, he'll simply step over with the hindquarters when you ask, and you will no longer need the lead rope or target to guide him.

The timing of your mark gives your horse clarity, whether you're asking him to stand still or to do something specific. For example, if you're teaching your horse to pick up his feet, you can mark as he shifts his balance and takes his weight off that foot. This clarity can help eliminate confusion and is a huge piece in overcoming any unwanted behaviour.

Example: Leading

Leading problems can take many forms, such as barging, pulling, rearing, or planting feet and refusing to move. Again, you'll have to look at your individual situation to determine any reasons why your horse might be acting this way. Remember, at some time in the past your horse has used this behaviour to get what he needed or wanted. For example:

- Your horse has learned to plant his feet while coming in from the field because leaving his field mates triggers his PANIC/GRIEF system through separation anxiety.

- Your horse has learned that pulling or breaking free is an effective way to get to where he wants, such as to the grass verge, or avoid what he doesn't like, such as being shut in a stable.

- Your horse is confused and fearful about the feeling of the headcollar when being led and therefore wants to avoid it through any means he can.

This last one is surprisingly common. Leading is something many people think horses are born knowing and should just do. In fact, a horse's natural reaction to new pressure from a halter is to fight back against it. This fear and confusion can cause the horse to rear, pull, plant, or barge right from the start. These behaviours can become habitually ingrained and cause long-term problems for leading—especially when an extra trigger is added, such as a windy day, an unfamiliar environment, or a mare being in season.

Whatever the problem and the cause, and whatever stage your horse is in, you can train her to lead calmly and politely anytime you ask. You have already begun this training in the foundation work described in Chapter 3, when your horse has been walking and stopping with you and has been rewarded for staying in the right position and being relaxed about the whole thing.

A useful tool for teaching better leading is the target. By asking your horse to follow a target, you can use it to position him exactly where you'd like him to be for leading. This clearly explains to your horse what you *do* want.

Of course, you don't want to have to use a target to lead your horse forever. The target is a teaching tool to explain to the horse what you want. As covered in the cue transferral section of Chapter 4, once your horse understands the concept of leading to a target, you can easily transfer it to a rope cue so you no longer need the target.

This is a calm, stress-free, straightforward way to teach horses how to lead politely and softly. The target and rewards bring clarity and motivation, helping to change negative emotions to feelings of willingness and enjoyment, making your horse easy to lead.

Once your horse understands targeting, you can use it to position her and keep your horse focused when leading.

Targeting is an effective tool to bring clarity to a training situation because you can easily use it to explain to your horse what you'd like her to do. Other tools to make the solution clear to your horse can include everything from the way you use your own body position and cues to choosing to train that behaviour in a setting that helps your horse, such as teaching your horse to lead on a track rather than in an open space.

VIDEO RESOURCE

LEADING LESSONS

Review the lessons with Ned the donkey who pulled and barged, and Red the youngster who learned to lead following a target.

www.connectiontraining.com/video-resources

USE A STATIONARY TARGET

For exercises where the horse must stand calmly while something is done to him, such as being sprayed with fly spray or having a rug (blanket) put on him, using a stationary target works brilliantly. It gives the horse something clear to do and brings all the positive associations of the target into the situation.

It's a very simple technique: reward your horse for touching the target as you bring the fearful item into his presence. The target becomes a security blanket for your horse, but it also becomes another way for him to communicate with you. If he's not able to touch his target, you've gone too far. You can even train touching it as a cue for you: your horse tells you he's ready for the scary thing when he touches the target. That gives you permission to move in and do it. This empowers horses and reduces their fear because they have control in the situation. This technique works for many behaviours, such as touching, grooming, bathing, fly spray, putting on a rug (blanket), and lots more.

You can read more about this technique in the 'Counter-conditioning' section of Chapter 7.

RETRAIN WITH A DIFFERENT OBJECT

If your horse has a strong fear about a specific object, changing to a different object can help to make the training go much faster and more smoothly. The novel item doesn't have negative associations for your horse, so you can build up to performing the behaviour with that object first. Once your horse is confident with the new item, you can transfer the behaviour to the original stimulus.

For example, some horses associate saddles with fear or pain. To overcome the negative associations, start by putting lots of other items that aren't as scary, such as towels, jackets, and ropes, on your horse's back and reward your horse for staying calm. With enough repetition, your horse will love having things on his back because you've built up a strong positive history. At this stage, you can reintroduce a saddle, and all those new positive emotions will transfer over to it.

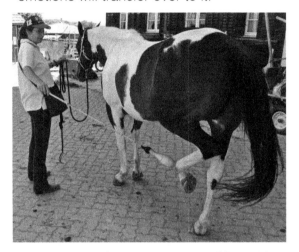

A good option for re-training leg lifting with horses who kick out or get anxious about having their legs handled is to use a target. You can teach your horse to calmly lift and hold their foot up until they touch the target with their foot as shown here by CT member, Susanne Eichelberger. This is safer for you and is a new, fun game for your horse that creates positive emotions about leg lifting. Once they're happy to do it with the target, you can ask with your hand.

Example: Head Shy Fear

Rachel's rescued mare, Roisin, arrived with severe fear about anything touching her ears. Here is her typical reaction to having the reins brought over her head. She would toss her head, spin, and pull away. It caused her a lot of distress.

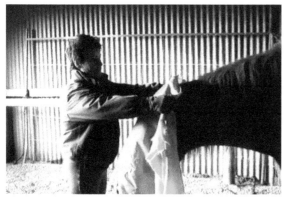

Because all ropes and reins triggered this fear in Roisin, Rachel retrained the behaviour with a neutral object—a green cloth. She began by rewarding Roisin for lowering her head down towards the cloth. Rachel had to begin in tiny steps because this was quite a challenge for Roisin at first. However, because the game was highly rewarding, and Rachel progressed at Roisin's pace, it soon became a favourite behaviour of hers. She loved to play with the green cloth and became so confident with it that she would duck her head right under it when Rachel held it out.

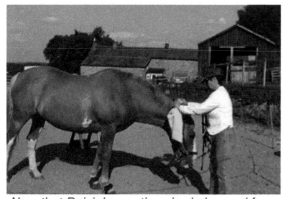

Now that Roisin's emotions had changed from fear to fun, it was time to reintroduce the old triggers, ropes, and reins. Rachel began by wrapping the reins in the green cloth to help transfer the positive association.

As the positive emotions associated with the green cloth were transferred over to the previously scary items such as reins and ropes, Rachel gradually faded out the green cloth completely.

Roisin became confident and relaxed about having ropes and reins put over her head and taken off, even when they dragged over or got caught around her ears.

These general positive associations transferred to anything put on Roisin's head. In this photo, Roisin was asking Rachel to put her fly mask on because she enjoyed the game so much!

VIDEO RESOURCE

OVERCOMING HEAD SHY FEAR

Watch Rachel train Roisin to overcome her headshy and bridle fears in this video.

www.connectiontraining.com/video-resources

TURN A FEARFUL STIMULUS INTO A CUE

Horses are frightened of things they don't understand, because they could be potentially dangerous. Turning something that the horse fears into a cue for another behaviour gives it meaning and clarity. For example, if your horse fears gunshots and there is a lot of shooting in your area, you could teach your horse that a gunshot means he should touch his target. You'd do this by having a recording of a gunshot you can play quietly. In a safe place, such as his stable, ask your horse to touch his target a few times. Then play the gunshot sound and ask your horse to touch his target. You'll play it quietly, so he doesn't go way over threshold and will follow the sound with your cue to touch the target, for which you'll reward him highly. With a little repetition, your horse will associate the gunshot sound with touching the target and will go to touch his target as soon as he hears it. You can then slowly increase the volume. When he hears actual gunshots, your horse will understand it means to go to his target instead of blindly panicking. You have given an unknown and frightening stimulus a meaning for your horse as well as plenty of positive associations. This process can also work well for training horses to be calm with fireworks going off.

Example: Fear of Arm Movements

Lily, a pony at Hope Pastures Rescue Centre, would bolt at any sudden movement anyone made, especially raising an arm. We taught her that a raised arm was a cue for her to touch her target on the floor. This changed the meaning of raised arms quickly and significantly until Lily was no longer fearful of this movement. It was a big step in building up her trust to be touched and handled.

VIDEO RESOURCE

BUILDING TRUST WITH A RESCUE PONY

Hear Lily's story and watch staff trainer, Sophie Kendrick, build Lily's trust in people at Hope Pastures Rescue Centre.

www.connectiontraining.com/video-resources

MAKE IT FUN

Activating the PLAY system in your horse's brain inhibits his FEAR system. Bringing joy and play into your training sessions will increase your horse's motivation and reduce his anxiety. You can mix small bursts of play and fun behaviours in among the more serious work. You can also directly reward difficult behaviours with fun ones. When you use games your horse enjoys as a reward, you create more positive emotions, which will change his behaviour.

Example: Reluctance to Be Caught

Charlie arrived at his new home unable to be caught in the field.

With patience, he came to trust the game and enjoy coming up to Helen to have some time together in the field.

His owner, Helen Gilbertson, tried to change this behaviour using many approaches, including food. But it was the inclusion of fun, using a behaviour Charlie enjoyed, that finally sorted the problem. She made a game of offering his target to touch for easy rewards.

From there, Helen played as many games as she could with Charlie in the field, until he was relaxed and eager to come up to her and be caught happily.

VIDEO RESOURCE

HOW TO CATCH YOUR HORSE

Watch as Helen helps Charlie to overcome his long-term aversion to being caught.

www.connectiontraining.com/video-resources

TRAIN AN INCOMPATIBLE BEHAVIOUR

If your horse persists in an unwanted behaviour for a long time, it becomes a habit. An effective way to change a habit for the better is to teach your horse a new behaviour that is incompatible with the old, unwanted one. For example, if your horse likes to kick the stable door, you can train him to keep his front feet on a mat. The two behaviours are incompatible because he can't do both at the same time. When you strongly reward the new behaviour, it will start to replace the old one.

You've begun to use this technique in your training already. Your horse can't mug you for treats and simultaneously stand quietly with his head turned away. You've replaced the mugging with the incompatible behaviour of keeping his head away from you.

Teaching your horse or donkey to stand quietly next to you is incompatible with mugging for treats or walking off.

Remember that it will take time for your horse to shift from the unwanted behaviour to the new one. Problem behaviours don't mean that your horse is being 'bad'—he is simply using behaviour that worked for him in the past. It either got him what he wanted or allowed him to avoid something he didn't want. Like all animals, he will always choose the behaviour which has worked best for him most often. Once the reinforcement history of the new behaviour outweighs the old behaviour, you shouldn't see the old behaviour any more.

TRAINING FOR HEALTHCARE PROCEDURES

Training for healthcare procedures is similar to training for handling, but often you need to consider that pain and discomfort may be inevitable in the procedures. The more preparation you do, the better your horse will cope in the event of an emergency or veterinary situation, even when some pain is involved.

PREPARATION AND PRACTICE

Including healthcare practice into your regular routine will prepare your horse for many different situations as it all becomes normalised. For example, when grooming your horse, be sure to touch her all over, including opening her eyes, manipulating her ears, touching all over her stomach, legs and teats (or sheath if it's male) and patting her as well as stroking her. You may need to train some of these slowly and positively at first to teach your horse to be relaxed with being handled all over, before including it into your grooming regime.

Begin doing this gently and sensitively, but as your horse becomes comfortable with it, start to focus directly on more challenging areas or handle your horse a bit more clumsily, rewarding your horse for calm cooperation as you do so. This teaches your horse to cope with the way a vet is more likely to approach her. It's also worth watching how your vet approaches and handles horses so you can mimic that behaviour.

Bringing other people in to handle your horse is also great preparation as it helps your horse get used to having things done to her in different ways by different people.

Depending on their past experiences, many horses are wary of men, people wearing farrier's chaps, or people smelling of veterinary chemicals. You can use your training to help your horse overcome these fears. Set it up as a training situation, and get your horse used to being approached and handled by as many different people as you can, always beginning where your horse is comfortable and building from there. Sometimes being handled by two or more people at once causes horses to get wary and anxious, so practice that, too.

If you keep your horse at livery, you can increase the positive experiences your horse has with the vet. Whenever the vet is called out to another horse, you can ask him or her to visit your horse and give him a treat. This will help your horse be more relaxed from the moment the vet arrives, which is more likely to lead to calm treatment.

Regular practice for procedures such as worming and injections will also prepare your horse for procedures, but keep it mostly fun and positive. For example, if you regularly practice worming your horse by putting apple sauce or soaked feed in the syringe, your horse will develop a strong positive emotional association with having syringes in his mouth. When you occasionally worm him with some disgusting-tasting paste, only a small percentage of his syringe experiences are bad, not all of them. If the positive association is strong enough, you won't get much deterioration in behaviour after the actual worming. He'll quickly be happy to accept the syringe again, and this time it tastes good like it did before, so he'll be willing to cooperate next time he needs wormer. Think of this like when you eat from a punnet of strawberries. Most of them are juicy and delicious but occasionally you'll pop a rotten one in your mouth that tastes disgusting! However, it doesn't put you off strawberries for life because only a tiny percentage of your strawberry-eating has been negative, so overall you still love to eat them.

This is the value of practising healthcare procedures regularly. Most of the time it's fun, rewarding, and painless for your horse, so he builds up good emotional associations and a good attitude. The odd moment of discomfort or pain won't have much weight in the training scales, so the behaviour will stay strong and your horse will stay calm and cooperative.

This pony at Hope Pastures Rescue Centre used to panic and refuse syringes in his mouth. Staff member and trainer, Sue Sunley, is shown working with him, targeting the syringe to encourage exploration and confidence, and teaching him to voluntarily hold still while his muzzle is held and a finger is inserted into the corner of his mouth. Regular practice will maintain this behaviour once it's been taught.

CAN YOU TRAIN THROUGH PAIN?

Many healthcare procedures, such as administering worming paste, giving injections, or cleaning wounds, can involve pain and discomfort. Can you really train a horse to willingly cooperate through these emotions? This is a great question, and the answer is absolutely yes! Using these techniques, you can teach your horse to accept a certain level of discomfort or pain and cooperate with you to get the job done. You might not get the usual high levels of joy and relaxation that you're looking for in the rest of your training, but you can certainly get stress-free cooperation that allows you keep your horse healthy without having to resort to force. This is better for your horse's physical and emotional well-being and is much less stressful and dangerous for you and your vet. Here are 3 examples of where Connection Training has enabled calm, happy and stress-free treatment:

Example: Hoof Soaking

Triana is a rescue mare working with Centre Director, Claire Waldron, at Positive Horse Training, Spain. When Hannah visited, Triana had a hoof abscess and needed her foot soaking. Although Claire had never done this directly with Triana before, Triana was relaxed with people and handling by then and knew targeting and standing on a board.

Despite being in pain, Triana cooperated beautifully as we explained where she needed to put her foot. It was clear to see that the pain increased as she soaked her foot, so we kept her highly rewarded with plenty of targeting and treats. If it got too sore, she quietly removed her foot from the bucket and we gave her a break before returning to it. This choice enabled her to stay calm and cooperate fully. Another person present had witnessed Triana with a hoof abscess in her previous home; despite everyone's best intentions, the process was scary for Triana and she fought several men trying to force her to soak her foot. It's testament to the power of choice, communication and rewards that this experience was so different for everyone involved.

Example: Wound Care

Hannah's horse, Khalil, sustained an injury to the side of his face which needed treating and dressing daily. This was unavoidably uncomfortable and painful. Hannah gave Khalil clarity and choice at each step of the procedure. He could choose whether or not to engage and hold his head still for the removal of the bandage or to have the wound cleaned. This might feel counter-intuitive, but giving Khalil this choice drastically reduced his fear of the situation, which in turn increased his levels of relaxation and confidence. He was then willing to cooperate for wound care.

Example: Injections

Hannah's mare, India, hated having injections and would fight anyone who tried to administer them. Hannah taught India to hold her nose on a target, then slowly began retraining injections. Now India goes to the target when she's ready for the injection and holds her nose there until it's done. The focus of the target and the good emotions associated with it help India to stay calm while having injections.

VIDEO RESOURCE

TREATING A WOUND WITHOUT FORCE

Watch Hannah train for co—operation from her horse, Khalil, as she tends to a wound on his face.

www.connectiontraining.com/video-resources

VIDEO RESOURCE

TRAINING FOR INJECTIONS

See Hannah train India for injections and discuss training for medical procedures in this video.

www.connectiontraining.com/video-resources

RESILIENCE TRAINING

There will come a time when you must insist on your horse's cooperation when he doesn't want to give it, such as when he needs the vet. It is highly unfair to your horse to give him full free choice until it comes to the point when you can't. If you always work your horse at liberty, but he's then made to stand for the vet to treat a wound, he's likely to feel stressed because suddenly all the rules he knows and understands have changed. Or you get ill and someone else at the yard must handle your horse, and they do things differently. Whatever the situation is, you need to teach your horse how to cope with it calmly for his emotional and physical well-being.

Resilience training helps to prepare your horse for the unexpected situations in life. It means teaching your horse to calmly respond to pressure from you or the environment. Just like anything else you teach, you must do this systematically and progressively.

Let's take leading as an example. You've been rewarding your horse for following you in your early sessions, then for following a target and transferring to a light rope cue. Along the way, you've been giving him plenty of choice and freedom. By doing all this early work, you have already associated plenty of positive emotions with leading. Your feel on the rope has been trained with rewards, so it's a cue that creates a rewarding response in the brain.

Now you need to teach your horse that sometimes he must follow the rope cue even if he'd rather go somewhere else. To do this, you want to set up your horse to resist you. This is going to be at a very low level—perhaps when you lead him to his field, you take him a step or two past the gate. Or you could put a feed bucket out and ask your horse to walk past it. In both scenarios, your horse will stop and resist going past where he wants to go. Now increase the pressure on the lead rope very slightly and wait. Do not keep increasing the pressure; just wait. When he makes the decision to come with you, mark! Reward him highly and then take him back to where he wants to go, to the field or the bucket. What's just happened is that your horse has resisted, and you've gently insisted. It's been a little uncomfortable but making the decision to follow your cue was highly rewarding. The next time you do this, you'll find your horse will follow your lead much faster because it worked out so well for him last time. Then if someone else leads him with more pressure than you normally use, he will understand that pressure as a cue and follow nicely. If you didn't train this, then in that situation the other handler is likely to increase the pressure when he doesn't respond. This will lead to, at least, an unpleasant situation for your horse.

RESTRICTION

Another common scenario is to prepare your horse for restriction. Someday she will have to stand still for a certain procedure or need to stay on box rest. You can help prepare her for situations like this in the same way—take her to the edge of threshold, ask for a little more, and reward her highly for staying calm and responsive. For example, you could keep your horse in her stable for a little longer after all her friends are turned out. Work with her over the stable door, such as asking her to back up and touch a target, until she settles down. Then you can take her out to her field.

Use resilience training in as many situations as you can, starting easy and making them progressively more difficult. You want your horse to experience some pressure and discomfort, because this is what he'll face in an emergency or during his physical care. You are teaching your horse that a little pressure is not the end of the world. The brain is set up to cope with many kinds of adversity in life, and training to cope with things that are unpleasant builds emotional resilience. Of course, this training is not his favourite thing either. But he'll learn to respond calmly, without panicking, which is such an important life skill for a healthy, happy horse.

The main caveat to resilience training is to ensure your horse is emotionally and physically capable of doing what you ask in that moment. This means he's still relaxed enough to think and respond. If your horse is really frightened and way over threshold, you first must help him calm down and focus. You can insist on your horse's cooperation only when he is capable of cooperating. Resilience training prepares your horse for understanding pressure and teaches him how to stay calm and do what you ask when he'd rather not, at low levels of anxiety or resistance.

Practice situations such as standing tied, staying in a stable and working with multiple people regularly, so that your horse is able to cope with restrictions or unusual situations or handling.

TRAINING DURING AN EMERGENCY

No matter how much preparation work you do, unexpected emergencies can take you by surprise. The techniques we've been discussing in this Chapter will set your horse up to be more successful in an emergency because you've taught him to be relaxed and cooperative for difficult behaviours. However, during an emergency you will often be under more time pressure and in a much more demanding situation than you have ever practiced. You must do whatever must be done in the moment to keep you and your horse safe.

If possible, use the tools you have available to you. Bring out the target, the marker, and some treats, if you can. Often, it's worth taking a few minutes to gain your horse's cooperation so the treatment will run more smoothly. This story from one of our students, Helen, illustrates this point beautifully:

I just wanted to tell you this story about my mare, Gertie. She came in from the field with a bad injury on her leg. When the vet arrived to see to it, she would NOT stand still—she kept fidgeting and pawing, no matter how much sedation they gave her. She was just getting increasingly wound up.

I finally insisted that we try to reward train her through the process instead. I began to bridge and reward her whenever her foot was on the floor and she was standing still. Slowly the vet started to approach and build up to treating the wound. Gertie then stood like a rock throughout. The vet was amazed and now thinks reward training is the best tool for gaining cooperation from horses for vet treatment!

Of course, it was all the preparatory work I had done with Gertie that helped her be able to stand calmly through this process, so thank you, guys!

I am using the techniques to change her dressings and tend to her wound in between vet visits, and it is easy and quick—without this I would have been dreading it every day! Her wound is healing well, thanks to being able to care for it properly.

USING SEDATIVES WITH TRAINING

If you do end up in a situation that is highly stressful for your horse, it can often be worth asking your vet to administer light sedation. As long as it's a sedative that calms the brain (effectively lowers arousal levels by acting on the amygdala) as well as the body, this can take the edge off the horse's fear and help him have a more positive experience. In turn, this means you won't have as big a setback in your training—things should get back on track more quickly, so you can continue to build your horse's trust and confidence for the future.

If you and your horse must go through any emergency, it's worth spending plenty of 'just-for-fun' time with your horse afterwards. Fun activities will help reduce tension and rebuild the trust, joy, and relationship between you.

SAFETY FIRST

No matter what you're training, safety always comes first. If something is going to harm you, your horse, or another person, you need to do whatever it takes in that moment to stop it.

Safety is especially pertinent when you are retraining a 'problem behaviour', since your horse will be bringing old, unwanted emotions to the training. The danger usually arises when either the training or an outside influence unintentionally triggers fear or excitement, causing your horse to

unexpectedly go over threshold. Do whatever you need to do to keep everyone safe but do it as calmly and gently as you can. When your horse is way over threshold, he isn't in a suitable emotional state to learn. *You are managing your horse, not training.* Try to ensure that everyone comes out of the situation unharmed. Once the immediate danger is over, regroup and decide how to progress for the best results.

WORKING WITH RESCUED OR UN-HANDLEABLE HORSES

Daily handling and healthcare procedures are the number one concern for highly fearful horses. Connection Training is so powerful for building trust with a frightened or un-handleable horse because it focuses on the relationship and relaxation without force or fear. Horses who have either been living wild or who have experienced abuse have highly aroused fear sensitivity towards humans and any increase in this pressure can quickly cause them to go way over threshold, making simple handling dangerous and stressful. The initial focus with highly fearful horses is to build their trust to a point that they are happy and relaxed with being handled daily and that any necessary healthcare procedures are as safe and stress-free as possible.

Working with frightened or rescued equines is a passion we both share. As well as working regularly with rescue centres, we have 7 rescue horses in our joint herd in the UK and Rachel has 8 more at her training centre in Spain. We have referenced many rescued horses and ponies so far and our techniques are effective at building trust and confidence. In this section, we're going to look deeper into working with fearful equines, including those who cannot be handled at all.

START WITH MANAGEMENT

For many rescues, whether they've lived wild and are now confined to a field, have lived alone and are now part of a herd or have lived with high levels of stress or fear for an extended time, there is a considerable adjustment period as they settle into their new life. Set up the management to support their transition as best as possible. This firstly returns to the three F's (see Chapter 1); freedom, friends and forage. Don't confine them in a small area until they are ready to do so happily. Help them settle into a herd with minimal disruptions. Ensure they have constant forage and, if they have been severely underweight, get advice from a vet or equine nutritionist to support their body back to health.

These two ponies, Valiente and Hope, were enclosed in a dark stable for the first years of their lives leading to many health issues such as blindness and terrible hoof problems. They were rescued by ARCH, an equine charity in Spain and fostered by Claire Waldron and Rachel. Their rehabilitation began by turning them out in a herd in a wide-open space, feeding them a healthy forage diet and beginning human interactions in a low-key way through daily presence and routine, before beginning with their more formal training.

Set up your daily routine so that you maximise casual interactions. For example, poo pick the field while the herd is in it, train your other horses near to the rescue or sit in the field while you take any phone calls or emails. This will help your new anxious horse get used to your presence gradually and naturally.

TRAINING TIPS FOR RESCUES

When you set up your training situation, make this as smooth as possible for your rescue. Perhaps you work in one corner of their field where they are already comfortable or work with a confident horse alongside to give them guidance and confidence.

When you first begin, all interactions with you are going to be a challenge because of the fear associated with humans and novelty. Spend more time in casual connection time than focused training to begin with, to help your horse become more relaxed in your presence. Sandwich short mini sessions of training in between stretches of just hanging out with your horse while he eats hay, or explores you in his own time. Incorporating the Enrichment and Empowerment Exercises from Chapter 2 regularly will also build your horse's confidence around new objects and situations to support the training.

With fearful horses, it's especially important to work on your own breathing and body awareness to help establish calm and trust. Keep your voice low and your movements slow and predictable while your horse builds confidence.

DAILY HANDLING ALTERNATIVES

While your horse is still fearful of being caught or touched, there are plenty of alternative ways you can achieve easy daily handling. For example, teach leading with a target so that you can move your horse when necessary without needing to use a headcollar before they are ready. While you're building confidence with hoof handling, see if you can set up a hard-standing area to work your horse or turn them out in daily to help with natural trimming until they are comfortable to have their feet handled. Use protected contact so that you both feel more comfortable with a barrier between you as you build confidence.

It will take time to build trust and overcome any negative associations with humans, so set your horse up for success in as many ways as possible to give you the time you need to make it a positive experience for your horse. This will build trust for life.

It's often a difficult decision to make between giving them the care they need while not breaking their newfound trust in people, especially when they need certain healthcare procedures before they are ready emotionally. Each situation needs to be assessed individually to decide the overall most positive outcome for the horse.

Hannah has a story to illustrate this dilemma:

A new pony, Joey, came into Hope Pastures Rescue Centre incredibly fearful of people but with a severe eye infection that needed treatment or could result in the loss of his eye. The staff had already begun to work with him, luring him into a cornered off area of the paddock with a favourite companion and beginning his training there. Joey was enjoying targeting a stationary target but was still highly fearful of being touched. They asked for my advice on treating the eye.

Since building up to positive and voluntary cooperation for eye treatment was not an option due to time constraints, my best advice was to sandwich the challenging eye treatment between as many positive experiences as possible. He came in for food, they relaxed together for a while, then did some training with exercises he loved and lots of rewards.

Then, to get the eye treated, 2 staff members closed in on him in a corner as slowly and gently as possible until one could grab the headcollar he was wearing and give him the medicine he needed. Although offered, he was too tense to take treats at this time. Immediately afterwards, the staff would go back to offering fun and rewarding exercises with plenty of choice.

It was far from an ideal situation. However, it enabled him to be treated twice per day as necessary and included as much positive time with the staff as possible. When I returned one month later, his eye was healed and he cantered over to the fence as soon as the staff approached, keen to interact. He now knew a few different behaviours and was very happy to be caught and touched.

The decision you make will depend on the severity of the fear and the urgency of the treatment. Make any situation as positive as possible, even if it's not ideal; discuss the use of sedatives with your vet, treat your horse where he feels most comfortable and add in as many rewards as possible. Even if you have a small set-back in trust, you will build it up again and they are very resilient animals. Frequent, consistent, positive interactions will keep the balance swayed in your favour.

BUILD CONFIDENCE THROUGH JUST-FOR-FUN TRAINING

When working with a horse who needs so many things training in order to provide even basic handling and healthcare, the inclination is to work on those as much as possible. However, all of these areas are difficult for your horse as you're working on overcoming fear. You will make faster progress by including plenty of behaviours in that are just for fun and don't cause your horse any conflict while working on them. This can include going to a stationary target, standing on a board or low pedestal or walking with you in protected contact. Pay attention to the behaviours your horse enjoys most and that help him to relax and include these into your training as much as possible. This will boost the positive emotions associated with both you and the training, growing his confidence more quickly.

Rescue pony, Valiente, learning to play fetch with CT Coach, Claire Waldron. This was a fun behaviour he enjoyed to support the challenging work on overcoming his fears.

VIDEO RESOURCE

TRAINING RESCUE PONIES FROM FEAR TO FUN
Follow the story of Valiente and Hope, two ponies rescued by CT Coach Claire Waldron and how she used many of these techcniques to help them change from fear to fun.

www.connectiontraining.com/video-resources

CASE STUDY: USING THESE TECHNIQUES WITH TWO UN-HANDLEABLE ZONKEYS

Zambi and Zee were two zebra-donkey crosses who couldn't be handled. Hannah's training of them shows how many of these techniques can be brought together to solve handling problems.

Zambi and Zee were both only a few years old when Hannah met them. They had already had several homes each, having to leave their herd mates every time. They came from different breeders, one in Europe and one in the United States, and had been flown across the world, with all the stress that entailed. Without being able to settle anywhere and build a relationship with specific people, they were overwhelmed and frightened by everything that had happened to them. On top of that, a well-meaning but misguided trainer had lassoed them to get their head collars on, which left them more frightened than ever. Hannah's task was to remove their head collars and build their confidence around being handled.

Hannah used many of the techniques described so far to adapt the training to each zonkey's individual needs. First, she chose to train them using protected contact because they were very anxious if Hannah was in with them. They always had the choice of whether to engage in the training or leave the barn to go into their paddock whenever they needed to. Giving them that choice was an important way to build their trust and keep them from feeling trapped. Hannah couldn't even hand-feed them to begin with, so she gave them food in buckets instead.

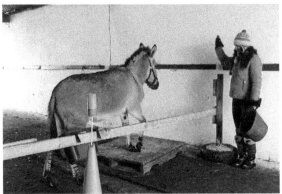

Both Zambi and Zee started their training in the same way: learning to touch a target and stand on a pedestal on cue. It was a big turning point when they realised Hannah's actions had real meaning they could understand. They started watching Hannah for cues rather than simply running away if she moved unexpectedly.

Zee

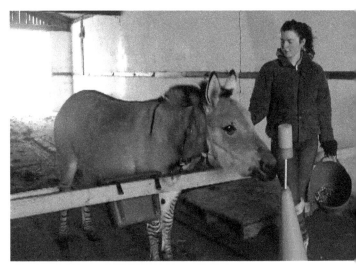

Zee was calm and relaxed with the training. She was happy to engage and happy to leave if Hannah asked too much of her—she'd simply return calmly, and they would take a step back and carry on. Hannah used the stationary target to guide Zee into position next to her, while she held her hand up towards her neck. Eventually, Zee was happy to bump into Hannah's hand as she reached to the stationary target. It really helped Zee's confidence that she was the one moving towards Hannah, rather than Hannah reaching towards her.

Very quickly Zee was moving her neck into Hannah's hand to be stroked and rewarded without the need of the target. From there, Hannah could take her head collar off easily. Success!

Zambi reacted totally differently to the training and it was soon apparent that she needed an alternative approach. Although she, like Zee, could touch a target and stand on a pedestal easily, she was doing these behaviours with considerable amounts of tension.

The next stage was to use the target to encourage Zambi to come towards Hannah's hand. Zambi understood what was being asked, but her fear of being touched created conflict, leading her to run away or get cross. She had so many negative emotions associated with being touched that Hannah realised it was going to take something more to weigh the scales in her favour.

Hannah used some of the relaxation techniques discussed in Chapter 7 to help Zambi soften. By slowing everything down, focusing on her own breathing, and reinforcing Zambi only for soft behaviours, Hannah was quickly able to help Zambi relax too.

So, time for a different approach: Hannah taught Zambi to play fetch. This was a brand-new behaviour for her, so she didn't have any previous fear about it. The game involved her coming towards Hannah with the fetch toy. It took a little while for her to pluck up the courage, but soon she was passing Hannah the toy happily. Her PLAY system was engaged, and this calmed her fear sufficiently to allow Hannah to hand-feed her calmly.

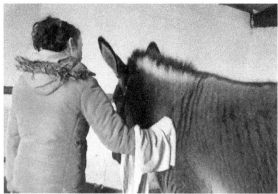

Next, Hannah tried working up to touching Zambi's shoulder. But this still caused Zambi to go way over threshold. So, Hannah taught her to touch her shoulder to a stationary target – she simply changed the nose target to a shoulder target by hanging a grey cloth over it to explain to Zambi when she was to touch it with her nose and when she was to touch it with her shoulder. She picked this up quickly and absolutely loved to do this behaviour. She would barge eagerly against the target with no signs of tension or anxiety which we were seeing before. Zambi remained keen and confident even when Hannah held the shoulder target.

In fact, if the hand was covered completely by the cloth, Zambi was relaxed about Hannah touching and stroking her and even removing her head collar. This shows the strength of emotional associations: human hands caused Zambi great fear that would take a lot of positive experiences to overcome, whereas grey cloths were an initially neutral stimulus that she'd subsequently only had good experiences with. This process enabled Hannah to build enough trust to remove Zambi's headcollar, too.

Although challenging at times, her work with these zonkeys highlights just how much two individuals can differ, even when they're being taught the same behaviour. Using a variety of techniques and focusing on building connection and a positive emotional state, as Hannah did, will pull you through every time.

Working with fearful horses and seeing them grow in confidence is one of the most rewarding aspects of our work. We love working with rescue horses and seeing them become relaxed, happy curious equines, sometimes for the first time in their lives. We support Registered Rescue Centres worldwide by offering them free access to the Connection Training Club, which includes all our Courses plus access to training help from us and our CT Coaches. We also have a subsidised place on our Connection Training Instructor Course for staff from registered charities, as we want to build a bank of experts in rehabilitating rescue horses and training staff working with them.

VIDEO RESOURCE

ZONKEY TRAINING – TOUCHING THE UN-HANDLEABLE EQUINE

Watch Hannah's work with Zambi and Zee as she built their trust and taught them new behaviours in different ways.

www.connectiontraining.com/video-resources

CHAPTER 9

LOADING AND TRAVELLING

You never know when you might have to load your horse. Even if you don't plan to travel to competitions every weekend, you may have to get your horse to the vet, escape wildfires or flooding, or move to a new home. Beyond that, travelling can be fun and enriching for your horse, as well as for you. When he's not fearful about it, travelling can satisfy your horse's natural urges to explore new environments. You can reduce his boredom, satisfy his curiosity, and give him fun experiences. Teaching your horse to be a happy loader means a safer and more enriched life and it's wise to make it part of your training goals.

WHY ARE THERE SO MANY LOADING PROBLEMS?

Unfortunately, many horses are frightened and stressed about loading and travelling. These horses are reluctant to load, and fear during travel causes them to paw, panic, rear, or sweat and arrive at the other end highly stressed and distracted.

It's not surprising that many horses feel this way. All animals are born with certain instructions or instincts that help them survive life in the wild. For horses, these include:

• Stay out in the open where you can run away from danger.

• Avoid enclosed spaces where you might get trapped.

- Stick with your herd.
- Stay on your home range.

Loading and travelling breaks all the internal equine rules. It makes you wonder why horses ever load at all, never mind enjoy the experience!

That's where training comes in. There are many components to creating a happy loader and traveller, and only when all these elements are addressed will your horse be truly relaxed and happy about loading. With the right training, you can teach your horse that loading is safe, and travelling is fun. She will learn that the horsebox or trailer is a safe space where she gets her favourite rewards and that going to new places is interesting. Your horse will become happy and excited to go somewhere new, and happy and content to return home. Getting your horse to feel relaxed and enthusiastic about loading and travelling involves understanding and training all the different elements involved.

Put simply, for your horse to be a good loader, you need to make the horsebox or trailer the place he prefers to be. Horses who don't like to load prefer to be outside the box; those who load calmly and happily prefer to be inside it. This place preference depends on the emotions your horse experiences and associates with loading and travelling. When your horse's positive emotional brain systems are activated by loading and travelling, he will display place preference. When the negative ones are activated, your horse will display place avoidance.

The FEAR, RAGE and PANIC/GRIEF systems are activated when horses don't load willingly. These systems create many behaviours commonly seen in unhappy loaders.

Place Preference — SEEKING CARE PLAY LUST — FEELS GOOD

Place Aversion — FEAR RAGE PANIC/GRIEF — FEELS BAD

When the FEAR system (freeze or flight response) is engaged around loading, your horse may get stuck at the bottom of the ramp. He may stare into the distance or even go to sleep (often a stress response when seen in training). If your horse is free to leave, he most likely will; if not, you might see him get fidgety as he moves from freeze to flight.

If you increase the pressure on your horse at this stage, he will most likely fight the head collar, pull back, try to escape, and possibly rear. Because your horse wants to flee but has been trapped, his RAGE system has been activated. This can also happen when a horse panics while trapped inside a horsebox or trailer, which is often when nasty accidents happen. Your horse is way over threshold emotionally by this time, so the SEEKING system is inhibited, and your horse can't think or solve problems.

If your horse suffers from separation anxiety, his PANIC/GRIEF system is being activated as he leaves the herd, leaves his home, and is isolated.

When these emotional systems are activated and associated with loading, your horse will display place avoidance. Clearly, he won't want to go up that ramp.

It's worth noting here that some training systems work on making the outside of the horsebox more uncomfortable than loading, so that the horse goes into the horsebox to escape that pressure. These systems are not creating place preference for being in the horsebox. What they are doing is creating a higher level of FEAR arousal outside the horsebox and a lower FEAR arousal level inside the horsebox. Given free choice, the horse will leave the area completely, expressing place aversion for the entire situation.

GOING INSIDE: TRAINING YOUR HORSE TO LOVE LOADING

So, how do you change your horse's emotions so that he wants to load? This process encompasses some of the techniques we have explored so far. Let's look at them in detail in relation to loading and travelling.

LOADING PREPARATION

There are many aspects relating to loading and travelling, such as standing tied, walking through, and standing in an enclosed space, stepping onto different surfaces, backing up and moving over calmly and being relaxed with the rattles and clunks a trailer can make. You can practice all of these elements away from the trailer in preparation for loading. This preparation will help you determine which aspects of loading your horse finds most difficult. For example, if your horse doesn't stand tied quietly in her home environment, she is likely to find it even harder with the extra challenges of travelling. Or, if your horse is terrified of walking through a narrow gap or standing on different surfaces, she will probably be worried about stepping on the ramp and into the enclosed space of a trailer.

Taking these lessons away from the trailer allows you to work on them separately and build your horse's clarity and confidence before they all need to come together at the horse box. Once your horse is solid in all these exercises, you will find the loading process at the trailer is much quicker and simpler.

Prepare your horse for loading by training all of the elements separately, such as leading, backing up and standing tied. You can also practice walking on strange surfaces and going through narrow gaps. Here, CT Coach Suzy Deurinck has set up a loading simulation to practice loading, perfect for safely and progressively helping horses to overcome fears associated with loading. It is also an effective way to practice loading if you do not have regular access to a vehicle.

Working through some de-spooking exercises, as explained in Chapter 7, can help to increase your horse's relaxation and confidence in the face of the strange sounds, movements, and experiences he will encounter when travelling. It is often the rattling of the trailer, lights from approaching vehicles or lorries thundering past that increase fear as you travel. Begin work away from the trailer teaching your horse that she has nothing to fear from these sounds by de-sensitising her to rattles, clatters and traffic noise. This will reduce the fear your horse may feel when confronted with these sounds when travelling.

VIDEO RESOURCE

LOADING SIMULATION AND PREPARATION

Watch this video for ideas on simulating the loading experience to train different aspects of loading.

www.connectiontraining.com/video-resources

FIND YOUR HORSE'S CONNECTION ZONE

The next step is to watch your horse closely and determine where his emotional threshold is regarding the horsebox or trailer itself. Some horses will get tense and anxious when they see the trailer hitched up or the ramp down, and they will leave the area if they have a choice. Other horses begin to freeze or defecate as they get closer to the ramp. Some appear to load fine but worry when the partition is closed on them.

Your first task is to assess your horse and find those first signs of tension to establish where you will begin your training. As always, start where your horse is comfortable. To create a positive association with the trailer or horsebox, you must begin at a level where your horse is relaxed enough to be able to listen to you, is choosing to stay with you and can respond well to your cues and rewards. Bear in mind that this could be across the yard from the trailer to begin with.

When you have determined where your horse's comfort zone is, where he is aware of the trailer but still relaxed enough to stay with you and respond calmly, you will begin using systematic de-sensitisation and counter conditioning to create a positive emotional association with the trailer. An easy way to begin to associate

feelings of relaxation and happy anticipation with the trailer is to feed your horse his daily bucket feed near the trailer. Begin at a distance where your horse will comfortably eat his feed and gradually move it closer each day. You can continue this on the ramp and into the box or trailer.

Feed your horse her bucket or scatter nuts near the trailer or on the ramp and quietly sit with your horse as she eats. You can build this into your daily feeding routine and it's a great way to establish calm and positive feelings with being near and, eventually, inside the trailer or horse box.

GO SLOWER, YOU'LL GET THERE FASTER

This is true for all areas where you are combating fear and is very important as you're working on overcoming your horse's loading anxieties. The temptation can be to continually ask for more from your horse as he achieves each stage. For example, as soon as he settles 30 steps away from the trailer, you immediately bring him several steps closer. However, this is where your

Challenge Sandwich (as discussed in Chapter 7) comes into play. You want your horse to feel relaxed and successful in proximity to the trailer. If you continually ask for more from your horse, he will likely feel pressured and his anxiety will rise. Next time you approach the trailer, that anxiety will still be associated with it so he probably won't be as keen to approach it again. However, if you work your horse where he is still under threshold and enjoying the session and then take him further away as he truly relaxes, he will associate only positive emotions with the trailer. He will then be eager to approach it again the next time.

For example, if your horse is anxious even approaching the ramp, begin by stopping your horse on the edge of his comfort zone. Then, reward him for coming forwards a step or 2 towards the ramp. Instead of asking him to then step even closer, turn him away, walk a circle and re-approach to the same point. This time, your horse will likely be keen to walk back to that same point because it was such a positive experience last time. Now, you can ask for a step or two even closer, stand there for a few moments, rewarding highly and circle away again. This process is the same for each stage of the loading process. Advancing and retreating in this way ensures your horse doesn't get over-faced and his enthusiasm and success rate remain high.

USE A TARGET

Use a target to guide your horse up the ramp. Since your horse now knows and loves targeting, this is a great way to bring the positive emotions associated with targeting to the trailer. Using a target also gives your horse clear guidance about where you want him to go as he will be stepping forwards towards it. It's crucial at this stage that you allow your horse to choose whether he can step forward to touch the target without pressuring him in other ways such as pulling on the rope. As he is overcoming his fear of loading, he must feel in control to remain confident. You will also gain a lot of insight into his emotional state by how willingly he moves forward to target, which will help you to keep the challenge at a suitable level for your horse and prevent him from going over threshold. Although the target is creating the guidance and forwards movement, use your marker to draw attention to any good decision your horse makes such as moving his feet, exploring the ramp and stepping forwards.

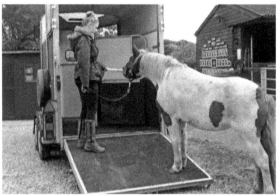

Staff member and trainer, India Evans, is working with rescue pony, Revel, at Hope Pastures rescue centre, teaching her to load using a target.

Stationary targets are also very helpful tools to help horses load confidently. You can place your horse's favourite stationary target inside the box or trailer to guide your horse inside. Since your horse already knows to stand at his stationary target, having it inside the trailer will also help him to stand quietly for longer periods of time once he's loading well. It gives your horse somewhere clear to go to and will help the box become a rewarding and comfortable place for your horse.

When you're loading your horse, watch out for him putting himself over threshold. Sometimes horses will be so keen to touch the target that they go further in than they feel ready for and then panic and blast back out again. Watch out for signs of tension or conflict in your horse and be ready to stop him going further in than he's comfortable with at each stage.

Once your horse knows to go to and 'stay' at a stationary target (as explained in Chapter 3, you can use it to give your horse confidence and guidance when loading. It also establishes standing still in the trailer and your horse can stand at the target leaving you free to move around them, which is great preparation for closing them in. You can begin with the stationary target at the ramp and move it further inside the trailer as your horse progresses.

VIDEO RESOURCE

TEACH YOUR HORSE TO LOAD POSITIVELY

Watch Revel learn to love loading by following a target into the trailer.

www.connectiontraining.com/video-resources

UNLOADING PRACTICE

Many horses have an issue with loading because they panic about unloading. It's just as important to train this step. You can train loading and unloading at the same time by asking for "one step forward, one step back". Make sure you give your horse time to work out the best position to be in to back off the ramp. You can use objects and poles to set up a guidance track if he tends to swing his quarters and come off the ramp at the side. Even if you have a walk-through trailer, it's worth training this for two reasons. Firstly, if you were ever in a situation where you couldn't open the front door. Secondly, because the exercise

itself helps the horse to relax more about loading. In fact, if you reward the backing off highly compared with going forward, the horse may learn to go on better purely so you can ask him to back off it. A little "reverse psychology" can go a long way sometimes!

Some horses also struggle with coming down a ramp forwards, especially steep ramps in big horseboxes. Practicing walking slowly down hills is a great way to practice this as you can choose progressively steeper slopes to lead down as your horse improves his balance, co-ordination and body awareness. You can also use your target to encourage your horse to step down the horse box ramp one small step at a time, until they are relaxed and confident about walking down it slowly.

MAKE LOADING FUN

This is a wonderful way to change your horse's attitude about loading. Include his favourite games and behaviours in and around the horsebox to bring the element of fun and joy into loading practice. This can relax the whole atmosphere around loading as you both enjoy the exercises and it's usually a brand-new approach to loading for your horse, which can help to reduce those old feelings of anxiety and resistance.

Here are some examples from Hannah of how she incorporated her horses' favourite games into loading practice:

All of these techniques will slowly change the way your horse feels about the trailer or horsebox until he *wants* to load.

Murphy loved to play fetch in and out of the horsebox.

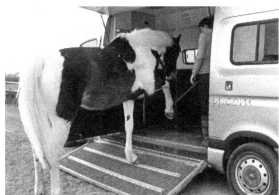

India preferred to "Spanish Walk" her way up the ramp.

VIDEO RESOURCE

LIBERTY LOADING FUN

As you can see from this video, Hannah's horses love to go in the box and don't want to unload (even the ones who started out with big loading issues)!

www.connectiontraining.com/video-resources

CLOSING THE DOORS

Most loading advice ends when the horse is happily going up the ramp. However, that's only the first part of creating a happy traveller. The next piece is ensuring that your horse is relaxed as you close the partition, ramp and doors. Many horses find this piece most challenging as it can make them feel trapped and claustrophobic, so plan to spend just as much, if not more, time at this stage as you did teaching your horse to be happy walking inside the horsebox.

Once your horse is happy going into and standing in an open trailer, you can begin to move partitions and rattle things around. When you begin, allow your horse to come out if he needs to, to prevent him feeling trapped and panicking. He will usually just load again and you can continue on with the training. If you do find that he's lost confidence, simply go back a few stages and repeat until he is confident and relaxed once again.

Practice this until you can bump him gently with the partition, rub the back bar over his quarters and begin to swing and rattle doors while your horse stays relaxed and chooses to stay in the horsebox at his target. Once he's at this stage, you can be confident that he'll remain relaxed as you tie him and shut the partition properly for the first time. You can make this extra rewarding by giving him favourite treats and giving him some easy, fun exercises to do such as touching a handheld target. As always, keep it short and successful and quickly release him to allow him to leave the trailer if he needs to. If he does, again, he should load himself again pretty quickly and be ready for another go.

Gradually increase the duration your horse can stand relaxed while closed in the trailer. You can give him a hay net with carrots hidden in or a bucket while he stands inside to make it even more rewarding for him. Ensure he's calm while you're at his head interacting with him and when you leave him to open and close doors, start the engine and so on. This will teach your horse to be relaxed after you load, to stand quietly if you get stuck in traffic or break down and wait patiently to be unloaded when you arrive at your destination.

Rachel is working with Rowan who was very anxious about being closed into the horse box. Here, Rowan is loose in the horsebox, eating from a bucket, while Rachel works on closing the partition. When she started this work, Rowan would stop eating and rush out as soon as Rachel began to move the partition. By working where Rowan was comfortable, Rachel taught her that the partition moving was nothing to worry about.

Rachel spent a long time at this stage until Rowan was truly confident about the partition closing in on her, even touching her, as well as Rachel moving around rattling the door catches, staring the engine and so on. Rowan is now very happy to be shut in completely and travels well.

When Hal's owner, Jackie Atkinson, moved back to the UK from abroad, Hal came, too. Having always been a confident loader prior to this, this shipping experience was long and challenging, involving time in quarantine and aeroplanes. Hal became terrified of being enclosed in a trailer or horsebox, despite a few years of gentle training approaches. He would plant his feet, defecate, run back and rear when asked to load.

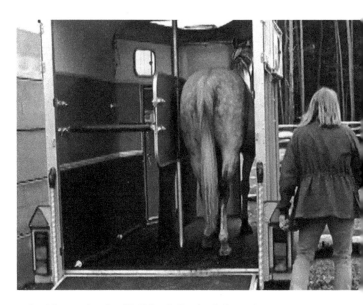

Jackie worked with this daily, building strong associations of success, joy and relaxation at the trailer. Hal began to see the trailer and pull towards it as his emotional associations changed and it became a place he preferred to be. Gradually, the target was moved further and further into the trailer, until he could load himself and stand quietly at his stationary target inside the trailer. He was not tied here but chose to stay in the trailer.

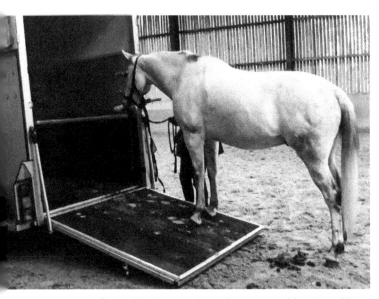

Once Hal learned the basics and had positive associations with the target and Connection Training, we put his well-loved stationary target at the top of his ramp. We looked for him to be able to relax while standing just with his front feet on the ramp and rewarded him highly. We kept these sessions really short, taking him for walks and a little lunging in between standing at his target on the ramp.

The next step was working on closing the partition, ramp and doors. In the past, it was being enclosed in the trailer that had really caused Hal to panic. However, now he was standing inside with positive emotions, his owner could begin to rattle and move the partitions and he was able to stay at his target. This built until she should close him in entirely and he stayed calm and relaxed throughout.

ON THE MOVE

Once your horse is happy to load and be closed in, you can begin to actually travel! Again, we begin in small steps, just moving a few metres before stopping the engine and returning to reward the horse and ensure he's calm.

As your horse gains confidence, you can go on longer journeys. It's best to simply return home at first as your horse gets used to the sensation and noises of travelling, without being over-faced by arriving somewhere new as well. The more you practice, the better your horse will become at balancing and the more confident she will feel with the sights, sounds and sensations of travelling.

If you have another horse who is a confident traveller and gets on well with your horse, travelling them together can help to boost your horse's confidence. Be careful when travelling two horses together, however, as being shut in close proximity with a strange horse or one they don't get on with can be a stressful experience, making travelling less enjoyable than travelling on their own.

If your horse is anxious about travelling because it involves leaving her herd mates, there are a few things you can do to help this transition. A simple, yet often effective, solution is to attach a stable mirror inside your trailer. Just as these work in stables to help horses feel they are not alone, they can have a powerful effect in a trailer or horse box, too. It is usually trickier to safely affix a stable mirror in this situation, so do ensure that you use a horse-safe mirror that is installed safely. Though it doesn't work in all cases, for some horses, having a mirror in which they can see their reflection eliminates all of their separation anxiety. Your horse is also more likely to relax if they can connect with

you. If possible, such as in a horse box, talk to your horse as you are driving and travelling.

As a driver, you must be aware that how you drive will strongly influence the quality of journey your horse has. Drive slowly, especially around corners, and brake and accelerate gently. If it's safe to do so, it's a good idea to ride in the back of your trailer to experience what it's like for your horse - it always feels much faster in the back and you will appreciate how hard your horse has to work to balance unless the driver is very careful. Horsebox cameras are now widely available and enable you to monitor your horse as he's travelling, helping you to make the experience as smooth and positive as possible.

THE DESTINATION EXPERIENCE

As you begin to take your horse on small journeys, ensure that the destination experience is a positive one. Take your horse to a friend's house where you can spend time reconnecting in an unfamiliar environment and helping your horse to relax. This is also a good place to practice loading away from home, which is often harder because of the context shift and heightened emotions in the horse or handler. Take as much time as needed to practice loading until your horse is calm enough to load easily and travel calmly back home.

So many people undo all their great training by rushing to close the horse in the trailer and move off quickly. Or they take their horse to high-stress environments such as competitions before the horse is ready. Both situations create fear and anxiety that cause the horse to go over threshold. These emotions are then associated with loading and travelling, so the horse is reluctant to load from then on. Instead, set your horse up for success by planning trips to quiet places where you will have time and space to help your horse relax and connect with you in the new environment and will be able to take your time re-loading. As your horse gains confidence and can remain calm and reload happily in new places, you can begin to take him to more challenging destinations.

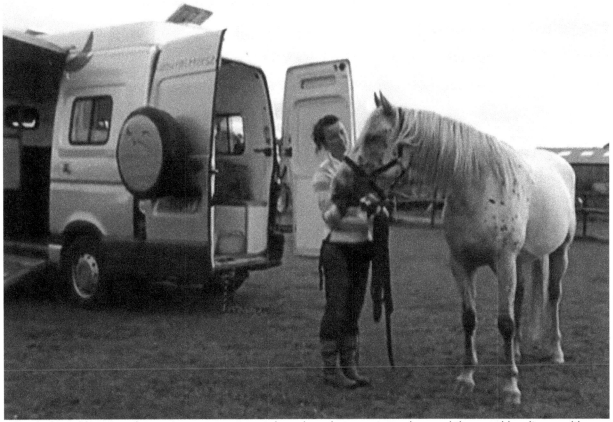

Begin by taking your horse to no-pressure, relaxed environments and spend time making it a positive experience for them. Firstly, work on helping them to relax and connect in a new place. Here, Hannah was introducing Freckles to travelling to new places and he was quite tense and excited at first. She worked with some gentle leading, lunging, targeting and trick training until he relaxed and was able to stay calm and focused on her. Practice loading in this new environment, which is likely to be more challenging for your horse. Load and unload your horse regularly throughout your trip so that your horse is truly relaxed when it is time to load and leave. Making this a positive experience will help your horse to anticipate positive things when you next travel, be ready to settle and focus when you unload at your destination and be happy to load in a variety of locations. This takes practice, so do it often at different locations until it is generalised for your horse.

PRACTICE REGULARLY

Now your horse is a happy, confident and willing loader! However, loading is one behaviour which can often deteriorate if you don't practice it. Regular practice and small trips will keep your horse confident and easy to load for when you need him to travel for emergency or fun.

CHAPTER 10

GYMNASTIC GROUNDWORK

Gymnastic groundwork is a holistic movement programme for your horse that is designed to increase your horse's overall fitness, strength and physical health. It's not about training high-level elite equine athletes for a specific discipline, but instead is about preparing your horse's body to cope easily with a wide range of movements, from cantering around in the field with his herd mates to being ridden happily and healthily in whatever discipline you choose. And, because it's Connection Training, all of this is trained in a way which is gentle, clear, and a positive, fun experience for both of you.

THE FOUR ELEMENTS OF CONNECTION TRAINING GYMNASTIC GROUNDWORK EXERCISES

In-hand work, including leading patterns and lateral work.

Poles and obstacle work to build body awareness and confidence in your horse.

Lunging, including how to teach your horse to move correctly on a circle, maintain connection at higher paces and work on-line and at liberty.

All Terrain Training using the natural environment to broaden your horse's confidence, balance and strength.

HOW DO HORSES MOVE NATURALLY AND HOW DOES GYMNASTIC GROUNDWORK HELP OUR DOMESTIC HORSES?

Horses in the wild move many miles a day, navigating different terrain such as banks, hills, ditches, rocks, rough ground, soft ground, woodland, narrow tracks and water. This constant movement and variety of physical challenges keeps their bodies strong, fit and healthy. Additionally, the sensory feedback they receive ensures they develop fantastic proprioception and control. Comparatively, our domestic horses have little opportunity to move freely in a natural environment and are often confined to flat, hazard-free paddocks and stables. They simply don't encounter the challenges of their feral counterparts which would naturally improve their body awareness, strength and fitness.

The best place to begin to improve this for your horse is by addressing his management and lifestyle which will improve his physical well-being as well as his emotional happiness. Ensuring your horse has plenty of turnout with herd mates will increase his movement. Feeding your horse on the floor or maximising grazing time will stretch the ligaments along his top-line, helping to support his back. A forage-based diet will keep his gut healthy and provide his muscles with the energy they need, and ensuring his healthcare needs are met will also keep him as comfortable as possible.

However, most domestic horses need some additional work to keep them in the best condition. This is clear to see in many grass-kept horses who still lack top-line and muscle tone. Despite being turned out, they don't get many physical challenges because they are well catered for and don't have to move much to get food, water, shelter or safety. The lack of variety in their movement causes horses to get stiffer, weaker and less sure of their bodies when faced with new challenges. This increases the risk of injury or anxiety. Additionally, we place extra and specific strain on our horse's bodies when we ride them or train them for a specific discipline.

Gymnastic groundwork is an all-over training programme that replaces the natural challenges faced by feral horse herds. The wide variety of exercises improves the general fitness of our domestic horses and enables them to be fitter, healthier, sounder and more comfortable on a daily basis. Whether your horse is big, small, old, young, ridden, or non-ridden, the aim of this work is to improve your horse's overall physical well-being from their individual condition at the start of this programme. It's a bit like yoga for horses. Although very few people will practice and excel in yoga to the level of a professional, everyone benefits from incorporating some of it in their lives and everyone in the yoga class works at the right level for them, making improvements in their own body, comfort and awareness. Some horses will be able to take this work to high levels, but it will improve the physical well-being of *all* horses at whatever level is right for them.

WHAT HEALTHY MOVEMENT LOOKS LIKE

In order to successfully train your horse to use his body better, it's important to know what it is you're actually looking for. This is explained in detail in the videos in our Gymnastic Groundwork Course on-line, and in many excellent books on equine anatomy and biomechanics. Here's an overview of some of the key elements:

STRAIGHTNESS AND SYMMETRY

A straight horse is one who is symmetrical. This means that they are equally supple to both sides, that their muscles are of an even size and strength, their strides are of even lengths and power and they have equal co-ordination on both sides or reins. Like humans, horses have a natural bias, preferring a specific canter lead or to go in a particular direction. This can also be exaggerated through training that is biased to one side, such as if the horse is usually led from the left side, as well as other factors such as injuries, or discomfort, such as from teeth, tack or hormonal issues. Asymmetrical horses will show stiffness, reluctance or anxiety when asked to do something that challenges them, such as to bend to their stiff side. Watch out for other signs as well, such as muscular imbalance, unevenness in their gait, holding their head or tail crooked and so on.

Working through the gymnastic exercises gradually retrains and balances up your horse's body. Our approach takes this slowly, gently and encourages with rewards. Our aim is for the horse to be confident and in control of their movements, so they remain relaxed throughout.

PROPRIOCEPTION

Proprioception is the awareness of the position and movement of the body. Horses who lack this are often labelled as "clumsy" or "don't know where their feet are". Poor proprioception can be a factor in horses who stumble and trip, knock into poles and jumps, barge into you or stand on your toes. Good proprioception leads to higher levels of body awareness and good coordination.

Horses naturally improve their proprioception by having to navigate banks, logs, streams and rocks but, again, many domestic horses don't interact with obstacles or objects in their home environment. You need to provide substitutes, using objects such as poles and pedestals. All terrain training is also brilliant for this as you encourage your horse to explore different surfaces, slopes and obstacles in the environment around you. You can also train specific movements that require co-ordination and awareness, such as backing up and lateral movements.

BALANCE, RHYTHM AND POWER

Focusing on balance, before asking for more impulsion or faster movement, allows your horse to maintain that healthy balanced movement in the faster paces, and keeps them confident, soft and relaxed. Often, horses are asked to go forwards too soon, causing them to become unbalanced and leading to behaviours such as rushing, tensing up, leaning on the reins, "motor biking" around turns, bucking and disconnecting. We break down the movement to focus on helping horses find their balance first, which means that they are moving evenly and in control of their own bodies and balance. As horses become more balanced they will relax, and as they feel more confident in their movement they will naturally find a good, even rhythm.

From here, we can then gradually ask for more power and the horse can happily offer more impulsion while maintaining balance and rhythm. Not only does this lead to healthy movement, it also keeps horses relaxed and confident.

POSTURAL ENGAGEMENT

Postural engagement is an umbrella term for horses moving in a way that allows their body to move freely and healthily, both on the ground and ridden, whether in collected, working or extended movement, on the straight or on a circle, and during hacking, dressage and jumping. The most common issues seen from a lack of good postural engagement include horses rushing, moving with too much weight on their forelegs leading to heavy, unbalanced steps, lifting the head high and contracting the back, causing it to drop. Consistent movement out of correct alignment leads to tension, pain and resistance. Instead, postural engagement means that the horse is in the correct alignment and balance for the movement he's performing and is able to maintain it himself (self-carriage). This requires both awareness and physical ability. It involves the horse engaging his core muscles to support and lift the back, and enabling the hind legs to step further under his body by tilting the pelvis, providing both power and support. This, in turn, enables the horse to carry more weight through the hind legs, lightening the forehand and allowing the shoulders to move freely. The horse's steps become lighter, they will stretch through their top-line, lifting at the base of the neck and rounding their poll.

Moving in this way is easy and efficient because the horse's body is working as a whole as it is designed to do, without tension or resistance through the muscles. The resulting movement is relaxed, soft and graceful and your horse will be able to quickly and easily change movement or access power while staying in balance. Postural engagement will feel good to your horse, though it can be hard work at first if your horse is not used to using his muscles in this way. For this reason, we teach it slowly and progressively and through a variety of exercises.

Postural engagement in horses is the equivalent to the correct postural spine alignment taught in yoga, Pilates, Tai Chi

and other movement practices. The easiest way to understand it is to feel it yourself, including both incorrect and correct alignment. Yoga teacher, Helen Gilbertson, shows you how:

1. Bend your knees and arch your back as much as possible.

This hollows your back and compresses your spine. This is common in horses and ones who do this consistently, through pain, weakness or lack of education, will move with a dropped back, head high and take short, stilted strides as their hind legs cannot step under in this position. It is uncomfortable to move much in this position and can develop into serious damage in the horse's back if they are trained or ridden in this way consistently.

2. Round your back as much as possible.

3. Stand straight and align your spine.

Now we've gone to the other extreme as you tuck your pelvis right underneath you and flatten out your lower back. In this position, you will feel that your abdominal muscles have engaged to create it and that you can easily lift your legs, though you will feel like you've hunched and collapsed forwards. This is less commonly seen in horses, though a braced, rounded back is indicative of misalignment and pain.

Relax your body then begin by bringing your navel towards your spine. Feel your abdominals engage gently as your tail bone drops slightly. Now take your awareness up through your spine, lengthening it out and becoming taller. Look ahead, lift your chin until the jawline is parallel to the floor and draw your jawline back until your head feels stacked on top of your neck. You should now feel balanced, light, uncompressed and your spine should feel supported and strong, yet free to move.

VIDEO RESOURCE

YOGA FOR HORSEMANSHIP

Join yoga teacher, rider and equestrian vaulter, Helen Gilbertson, to learn how yoga stretches and body awareness can help your horsemanship and riding.

www.connectiontraining.com/video-resources

Now, let's see what correct and incorrect postural alignment looks like in horses:

Contracted, tense, unsupported spine

Hollow, dipped back

Hindlegs trailing out behind, unable to step under fully

Bulging underneath neck

Abdominal muscles not engaged leading to 'saggy' belly

Leaning onto forehand, leading to heavy unbalanced steps

This picture shows a contracted position and, unfortunately, you will see many horses worked or ridden in this posture.

Spine aligned and supported from tail to poll

Back lifted and Moving Freely

Hindlegs stepping under to provide support and power

Neck is gently arched as the horse lifts through cervical spine

Abdominal Muscles Engaged (see abdominal line) allowing the pelvis to tuck slightly, the hind legs to step under and to lift the back.

Forehand lifted with light, balanced steps

This picture shows Rowan moving with engagement in self-carriage, including some clear points to look for in healthy equine movement.

Both your body and your horse's body are designed to move to both extremes of this position, between a hollowed and rounded back, depending on the movement being performed. Also, movement is dynamic and there will always be contraction and extension of different muscles at different stages of the stride. However, coming back to correct spine alignment as a default position allows your body to work healthily, just as it does with your horse. This is the core of postural engagement, though the exact frame will change slightly depending on conformation, exercise and level of work.

SYNCHRONY AND FEEL

The similarities and connection between your body and your horse's body go even further than simply understanding what you're asking your horse to do. Some fantastic studies by ethologist, Lucy Rees, show how important synchrony of movement is in feral horse herds. Lucy has shown that horses synchronise with each other; that there is no particular lead horse, but that they practise moving as one. This is vital for survival because, when threatened, the horses' response is to bunch together and then flee as a herd. This bunching makes it harder for predators to single out animals to attack. The herd must be able to move together, at speed, without colliding, in order for everyone to stay safe. It's part of the survival strategy for horses, so this behaviour is innately built into all horses and does not need to be learned. They practice synchronising their movements at all opportunities, from grazing next to each other, to mimicking the way they stand when they doze next to each other and following each other's gaze and focus. Horses who are more closely bonded will synchronise more often.

When we're working with our horses, we can tap into this natural synchrony to deepen our bond and refine our communication. Other studies have shown that horses even match their heart rate and breathing rate to their handlers, another example of just how deep and innate this synchronisation is. We call these body cues, 'internal cues'; cues that do not have to be taught and that your horse responds to naturally. These need to be in alignment with your 'external cues', the ones you have taught such as targeting, use of the rope and voice cues etc., so that your horse is not confused or conflicted in the training. You can also use your internal cues to bring more clarity to your training. For example, if you're walking together with your horse, you can slow your rhythm, deepen your breathing and soften your gaze to help your horse relax, or if you're asking for more energy, you can lift your focus and change your movement to help your horse respond in kind.

Bunching up with Mum is an innate behaviour born with foals. Even though Maverick is over a year old, he still likes to have close contact with Mum, Selena.

VIDEO RESOURCE

FOLLOW, MATCH, LEAD

You can see synchronisation in action as Rachel teaches the 'follow, match, lead exercise' to build connection in movement.

www.connectiontraining.com/video-resources

REHABILITATION

Gymnastic groundwork exercises are an important part of rehabilitation, such as recovery from injury as well as overcoming chronic pain, stiffness or unhealthy movement patterns. When horses have experienced pain or discomfort, it understandably can make them resistant, tense and anxious when being handled and trained. By prioritising emotional well-being as you build your horse's physical fitness, you will reduce tension and promote relaxation and joy through the training. As your horse understands what you're asking for and is offering that himself, it boosts confidence because he is in control of his own movements throughout the training, ensuring he's not pushed into painful positions. This, in turn, also builds motivation as it feels good in his body and is fun to do. We have helped many of our own and clients' horses to overcome long-term emotional and physical movement problems and become sound, strong, supple and joyful in movement through this programme.

PREPARATION FOR RIDING

Our gymnastic groundwork exercises are beneficial in preparing your horse for healthy, happy riding. They transfer directly from the ground to the saddle so, once you've taught a specific exercise, it's much easier to ask for it when on board. The extra strength, stability and awareness built from gymnastic groundwork also helps to prevent injury and is a key element in helping the horse to carry a rider comfortably. In our opinion, any riding horse needs to be trained in this way for riding to be ethical. It's only by moving correctly with a rider that a horse can stay sound and healthy for life.

CASE STUDY: SOPHIE AND LILY

Lily is an 8 year old Irish Draft horse who suffered a stifle injury as a 5 year old. Although she is now pasture sound, she was unable to stay sound in work, showing locking stifles and frequently dropping, or catching, her hindlegs. With her owner, Sophie Pickard, we first worked through the Foundation lessons, ensuring that Lily was relaxed, focused and understood the CT approach. Although very flexible, Lily lacked strength. Her weight was carried very much on her forehand, and she had big muscles through her shoulders and chest, compared to an under muscled back end.

We worked through a combination of in-hand, lunging and body awareness exercises, focusing on bringing Lily's awareness to her hind legs and teaching her to move with postural engagement, gradually strengthening her hindquarters to take more weight and lighten her shoulders. Sophie interspersed the groundwork with mini sessions of riding, of 2-5 minutes at a time, to build Lily's connection and enthusiasm in the saddle, too. This was all done in walk at this stage. After just 2 months, Lily was noticeably more muscled in her hindquarters and had stopped catching her stifles almost completely. She was more balanced, aware and in control of her movements. This made movement more comfortable and enjoyable for Lily and she is now very keen (sometimes too keen!) to go forwards. Through making her an active participant throughout the training, Lily was eager to participate fully in all the exercises and offered movement in self-carriage regularly of her own volition throughout. This really demonstrates the combination of physical health and emotional joy that are the cornerstones of our gymnastic groundwork. This improved movement, motivation and communication were necessary preparation for the ridden work and transferred well to the saddle and are the beginning of long-term soundness and a happy partnership both on the ground and under saddle.

IN-HAND WORK

We'll begin by discussing the practical aspect of gymnastic groundwork training by focussing on in-hand work. In this type of gymnastic groundwork, you teach the exercises while in a leading position next to your horse's shoulder, neck, or head, building on the leading lessons you have already begun with your horse.

LEADING WITH CONNECTION

In-hand work builds from the leading exercise of walking together from the foundation behaviours. A natural, relaxed walk is the foundation of healthy movement and, by connecting with your horse in walk, you'll be setting your horse up to be relaxed and responsive throughout your training. As you're doing this, focus on walking around the track or perimeter of

your training area. This gives you a focus on where you're leading your horse and sets up walking on the track as a default behaviour that your horse will return to between exercises, ensuring that simply walking straight is incorporated right from the start. It can be all too easy to get caught up in training 'stuff' and find that your horse can no longer walk in a straight line!

You can begin to shape your horse's movement during this exercise by introducing a stretch down in walk. The easiest way to create this is to use your target to explain to your horse to lower his head and stretch forward. You can put this onto a voice cue to transfer to different situations in future such as lunging and riding. Your horse will also naturally follow internal body cues here, too, so breathe deeply, slow your rhythm and lean forwards slightly – your horse will mimic your position and relax and stretch down, too.

Using the target to teach straight walking on the track and to encourage Selena to stretch down in movement.

ISOLATIONS FOR BODY AWARENESS

You can improve your horse's body awareness and control of their movements by isolating different parts of their body. Isolations like this are the foundation of more advanced movements such as bending and lateral work. Some examples of isolations would be lateral flexions (where your horse turns their head to each side, moving the quarters over and moving the shoulders over. All of these exercises are taught first from halt and require your horse to become aware of which part of their body you're isolating and asking them to move, and then how to move it. This can be surprisingly challenging for many horses if they haven't done this work before.

When you teach these exercises, the Connection Training approach differs from traditional methods. Traditionally, trainers will increase the pressure of the aids during in-hand work until they get the response they're looking for. For example, when asking a horse to step over with his hind legs, a traditional trainer may increase the pressure towards, or on, the flank with the whip until the horse takes a big enough step sideways. In this scenario, the horse's flight response is triggering the movement. Because his FEAR system is aroused and creating the behaviour, he will learn the behaviour with a feeling of fear. He will have tension in his body and experience the cue and the exercise as unpleasant. It will take longer for him to learn the cue and even longer for him to perform the movement softly and with relaxation.

Instead, we want the horse to have choice and awareness throughout, to be calm and relaxed and to offer movements which are slow and considered. This really shows your horse is understanding what you're asking and is creating the movement themselves (as opposed to, say, just moving away from a whip. Our favourite method is to lead the horse in a small circle following a target, and mark as he steps over with his hind leg. Already you've brought his awareness to his hind legs, and he hasn't been induced to run away from anything, so he is calm and relaxed throughout. The next time, you might use the target to bend his head towards you as he focuses on moving his hind legs. With

only a few repetitions, your horse now understands that you want him to move his hind legs over and will probably be delighted in his new-found skill, offering lovely big steps that you can reward (or refine) as necessary.

Using the target to teach Leo to move her quarters over. You can see how the target brings her towards her handler, and she's stepping under neatly with her right hind. In time, the target will be faded and Leo will respond only to the hand signal to move across with her hindquarters.

We begin by teaching horses to move their shoulders and quarters away from the handler first, since this is most often asked for in situations such as when grooming or loading. Once they've established this, however, you can also teach hip and shoulder targeting, where your horse moves his shoulder or hip towards you, instead of away from you. Here, CT Member, Carolien Hendrinkson, shows that her horse targets his shoulder to her hand.

You do this by first creating the movement by using a target to ask your horse to step towards you. Mark as your horse's shoulder touches your hand to draw attention to that moment. As your horse begins to understand the movement, fade out the target until he is moving his shoulder to your hand without it. An important element of this exercise is that you teach your horse to stop moving when their shoulder or hip touches your hand. This prevents horses knocking you over or swinging into you.

VIDEO RESOURCE

MOVING THE SHOULDERS OVER

You can see this process in action as Hannah teaches Rowan how to move her shoulders over.

www.connectiontraining.com/video-resources

VIDEO RESOURCE

VIDEO RESOURCE HOW TO TEACH HIP TARGETING

This video shows you a how you can teach your horse to target his hips towards you.

www.connectiontraining.com/video-resources

BENDING AND CIRCLING

Progressing from stretching in the walk and body isolations, you can work with your horse on teaching her to bend and stretch laterally in movement. Again, the target is a great tool for this as you can use it to guide your horse around you. Mark those moments as your horse begins to bend her body around the circle. To start with, you might only get a small tip to the inside with your horse's head - reward it! Your horse will be able to bend more easily through her body as you practise.

Some horses are very stiff in their bodies before they start this work and most of them will be one-sided. This exercise will clearly show you which side your horse

Using the target is a great way to initially teach your horse to bend around a circle.

finds it easier to bend to. If your horse is struggling to bend, you will find that she keeps her neck straight and falls into the circle with her shoulder instead. If this is the case, you can use your hand to support her shoulder as you ask for the bend. Since you will have taught this as a cue to move the shoulders away from you, it will be a clear cue for your horse as you incorporate it into this exercise. Reward any small try from your horse and you will see that she improves in suppleness and becomes more even on both sides over time.

Once your horse is bending, you can refine it further. For example, you can mark when she steps under with the inside hind or you can change the pace and balance of the walk, the size of the circle or move up into trot.

LATERAL EXERCISES

Lateral exercises are any movements that involve the horse going sideways such as leg-yield, shoulder-in, haunches-in and half-pass. They have been used for centuries because they improve balance, suppleness and strength in horses, supporting the horse's body to stay sound and carry a rider. Once you have taught the above exercises, they are fairly straightforward to train because you have taught all the necessary elements and it becomes a case of simply combining the cues.

Let's look at shoulder-in as an example. In shoulder-in, your horse moves parallel to the side of the arena, with his hindquarters carried closer to the wall than his shoulders and his body curved towards the centre. Essentially, this is a combination of several behaviours you have already taught: walk, lateral bending, moving the quarters and moving the shoulders. For many horses, you can begin the shoulder-in by simply asking for these behaviours together. Remember, you won't get a perfect response first time - reward any attempt from your horse at combining those cues. You can work it out together as you refine it.

If your horse is struggling, you can make it even easier by adding a barrier, such as Around a Round Pen which will prevent him from being able to walk in front of you as you teach it. Using objects in this way to explain exercises to your horse can be an effective way to bring clarity and fun to the sessions. For example, you could use poles to set up a channel and leg yield from one side to the other; you can have cones to mark out your haunches-in area and you can put poles across the diagonal as you begin to introduce half-pass.

VIDEO RESOURCE

HOW TO TEACH LEG YIELD IN-HAND

See how to combine your cues and use a target to teach your horse leg-yield in-hand. This is a great way to introduce lateral work to your horse.

Hannah asking Freckles for shoulder in at liberty

VIDEO RESOURCE

HOW TO TEACH SHOULDER-IN AND HAUNCHES-IN AT LIBERTY

See Hannah use isolations to teach shoulder-in and haunches-in. She shows them in-hand and then in the saddle, making the link from groundwork to ridden work clear.

www.connectiontraining.com/video-resources

TEACHING POSTURAL ENGAGEMENT

We now return to postural engagement and will look at how you can train your horse to move in self-carriage directly through work in-hand. Self-carriage encompasses both collected and lengthened movement. During collection, the engagement is maintained and the steps become higher and shorter. When lengthening, again engagement is maintained, but the horse stretches his frame to take longer strides. This is a continuum of engaged movement, with extreme collection, such as a passage, at one end and extreme extension, as shown in an extended trot, at the other. You will begin in the middle, finding the natural and comfortable pace for your horse. From here, you will vary the balance and stride length only slightly, asking for a hint of collection and lengthening out the strides gently, only asking for as much as your horse can offer without losing engagement. This middle range is required for sound, healthy movement. Once you've trained this, you can develop it further if you choose, gradually working towards each end of the spectrum, asking for more collection and extension as your horse improves ability.

This work will take time and is supported by the other gymnastic groundwork exercises. They will improve your horse's strength and suppleness; lateral exercises, such as shoulder-in, are specifically designed to encourage horses to carry more weight on their hindquarters. Training engaged movement builds directly from the leading exercises.

Once again, we turn to the target as the tool to explain to our horses what we'd like them to do. Beginning in halt, use your target under your horse's chin to encourage him to rock his weight back slightly without taking a step. This is the first step of teaching him to carry more weight on his hindquarters. Practise this a few times and then ask for it at walk, again placing your target under your horse's chin. As you're doing this, you also want him to raise his head slightly, so that he's not in the stretch-down position. You're looking for your horse to slow down and take higher, softer steps with his front legs as his shoulders lighten.

This is the very start of teaching postural engagement and you will only see tiny changes at first so, when you're teaching this, use "benefit of the doubt" marks, especially if you haven't done this sort of work before. You won't be sure what you're looking for, so reward your horse highly if you even *think* he changed his balance. This will keep him trying things out and it will become clearer as he makes bigger changes in the way he's moving and you can refine it together. Intersperse it with plenty of stretching down and other exercises as it will take time for your horse to build strength in the muscles required to maintain this position and you want him to enjoy the learning process without feeling too fatigued in his body.

Once your horse is beginning to collect his movement, you can then encourage him to lengthen his frame and stride, while maintaining engagement. This is a prime example of creating balance and rhythm first, then adding more forwards energy. Now your horse is more engaged at a slow pace, as you increase the pace he can maintain that self-carriage and, instead of losing his balance onto his forehand or becoming tense, hollow or rushing, you will find that your horse gives you longer, more powerful strides, extending the walk. If he does lose the engagement and balance, you have the tools in place to create it again – just come back to your slower engaged movement and try again.

1. The first step is to establish long, relaxed movement. As your horse relaxes, she will naturally stretch down, though you can encourage this further with a target if necessary.

2. Now, you can begin to teach engagement. First at halt, then in walk, begin to change your horse's balance towards more collected movement. Rowan still needs the target to explain and support this movement. You can see that her hindquarters are more rounded as she engages her core and steps under with her hind leg, her shoulders are lifted, creating light, high, delicate steps in front and there is a clear arch under her neck as she stretches through her topline. However, she is slightly over-bent here as her nose is just behind the vertical.

3. Once this is established, you can begin to extend the walk slightly, lengthening your horse's stride. Through this movement, your horse should remain engaged, meaning that she is light and balanced, creating long, powerful strides, rather than rushing and quickening the pace. You can see Rowan's core engagement in her abdominal muscles, lifted topline and freedom through her shoulders, as she stretches forwards and lengthens the walk.

Changing between these balances is a great exercise in body awareness and communication between you. As you begin, you're only asking for a hint towards collection or lengthened movement as your teach your horse the exercise and begin to work his body in this way. Being able to ask your horse to slow down and collect slightly is an effective way to rebalance your horse in a moment and develops beautifully into a half-halt. You can use this to regain lost balance as well as prepare your horse for transitions and other exercises. The aim is to keep the training soft, positive and successful for both of you so that you can enjoy refining it together.

VIDEO RESOURCE

TEACHING ENGAGEMENT WITH THE TARGET

Watch Hannah using the target to teach Rowan how to change her balance in walk, beginning steps of collecting and lengthening.

www.connectiontraining.com/video-resources

GYMNASTIC JOY

Conventionally, much of this type of in-hand work is practiced with total focus on the precision of the movements. Although it is important that your horse is performing them correctly for his physical health, it is just as important to prioritise his emotional joy. Don't get so focused on the perfection of the movements that you forget to foster the enjoyment of learning. This can mean that it can take a little longer to get the physical results, but is more than worth it as you'll have a horse who expresses the innate joy of these movements.

While your horse is learning these movements, they will be messy and crude as he works out how to move his body in that way. The first time you ask for a shoulder-in, the response will most likely not look much like a shoulder-in! That's okay—messy movement is a normal part of the learning process. If you stay relaxed and rewarding, your horse will be keen to refine the movements until he can do them to the best of his ability. In fact, since horses trained positively raise their own criteria in behaviours, you will find that your horse tries harder each time you practise it. You will be able to perfect the behaviour while making it a fun and enjoyable process for both of you.

See everything as an experiment—it's neither right nor wrong, it's simply interesting and leads you to the question, 'What will I do next?' If you try a new exercise and it goes wrong, it doesn't matter—just try it another way. If your horse simply isn't getting something and you both feel the frustration rising, go off and do something else—pop her over a jump on the lunge, play her favourite game, or ask her to follow you around the arena at liberty. It doesn't matter what it is, just do something different to keep you and your horse connected and joyful. When you come back to the exercise, it is almost guaranteed to be better. This way, you build your relationship and communication no matter what happens. There are so many ways to teach a skill that you will find a way that works for your horse, and you will improve as a horse trainer and communicator as you work that out.

AT LIBERTY OR ON A REIN?

As you can see from our photos and videos, we teach in-hand work both at liberty and on a rein. What should you choose and why?

Working your horse at liberty and with a target is a great way to ensure that your horse fully understands the exercises and is choosing to engage with the training. It leaves you free to focus on observing your

When taught positively and used sensitively, ropes and reins can enhance your communication with your horse. They are simply tactile cues, and not used to control or force the horse.

horse without handling ropes and reins and you can easily switch between exercises. However, teaching and practicing these behaviours using ropes and reins is necessary preparation for riding or taking your horse into situations where he can't be at liberty. As previously discussed, you can still give your horse full choice in the training, even when on a rope or rein, by observing his emotional state. He will tell you if he's relaxed and enjoying it or if he's feeling tense, and you can respond appropriately whether he's on or off a rein to ensure a positive training experience. Respecting your horse's feelings and giving him a voice and a choice is true liberty, anyway!

Ropes and reins can also bring more subtlety and clarity to the training. When you are working on specific balance and movement exercises, precision is important. It is difficult to train this precision at liberty, especially when you want a specific behaviour to be done in different ways at different times. For

example, you could teach your horse to bend his neck to the left when you tap on the left side of his neck, but sometimes you want just a tiny bend and other times you want much more. If you teach your horse to follow the rein cue, you can easily ask for a little flexion with the rein cue and stop there—your horse will flex a little and then keep his head at that point. If you want more flexion, you can ask again with the rein; when you get the amount you wish for, pause there and your horse will hold it. It's soft, clear, and easy for you to ask and your horse to understand.

When you are using ropes or reins, you must be sensitive with them and not use aversive levels of feel. They are there as a tactile cue for your horse to help bring clarity to the training. You still want your horse to be mentally engaged with the learning, so he must be free to try different things while you use the marker to explain exactly what you're looking for. Many horses don't have the most positive history with ropes and reins, so take the time to ensure your horse is comfortable and relaxed at each stage of the training.

However, if you have a good eye for lateral exercises and great timing, you can train them all at liberty. Even if you teach these exercises on a rope or rein most of the time, practicing them at liberty occasionally is also a great thing to do. This will build on all the other work you have done with your horse at liberty and will test that your horse fully understands the in-hand movements and can perform them on his own.

Hannah and India working on leg yield in a headcollar and lead rope.

Hannah and India working on shoulder-in using body and hand cues only.

Hannah and India working on haunches-in in a bridle.

Hannah and India working on half-pass using the target.

LUNGING

Lunging—sometimes spelled 'longeing'—is a valuable exercise for your horse. When we talk about lunging, we mean that the horse is moving in a circle around you. He might be on a lunge line, going Around a Round Pen, or following a target at liberty. Whichever method you use, lunging gives your horse space and freedom to move within training sessions. It also allows you to observe and improve your horse's movement without riding him, especially at higher paces such as trot and canter. Lunging is great for young horses because they need to learn how to expend energy safely. You can teach them how to stay calm and balanced while their energy is high, which is a great building block towards a calm, safe riding horse.

Working on bending your horse in-hand is great preparation for lunging. It's a smooth process as you gradually increase the distance between you and your horse into a lunging position, while maintaining the balance and inside bend you have established through the in-hand work.

Begin by asking your horse to follow the target while you are close to him. Gradually increase the distance until your horse is working on a bigger circle around you.

Ideally, during lunging the horse will be relaxed, focused, balanced, and responding to your cues. Unfortunately, lunging is often practiced by chasing the horse around with a lunge whip in unbalanced circles on the end of a line. This means many horses have had prior negative experiences with lunging. They may show tension, be reluctant to go forward, repeatedly turn in, anxiously rush around the circle, or—in extreme cases—rear or bolt. If your horse shows any of these behaviours, you can retrain your horse to lunge calmly and happily. As ever, if you're retraining rather than training for the first time, it will be a longer process, since you must counteract those negative emotions and make lunging a positive experience for your horse.

LUNGING THE CONNECTION TRAINING WAY

When teaching your horse to lunge, make sure he's moving *towards* something rather than away from something. Traditionally, horses are taught to go forward on the lunge by pressure from a lunge whip behind them, triggering the FEAR system and flight response. Instead, we prefer to engage their PLAY and SEEKING systems by asking them to follow a target or our lead. We reward them for moving forward, building progressively from one step to many circles.

This builds beautifully from the in-hand work as you've already taught your horse to bend around you. You can transition this into lunging by gradually increasing the size of the circle and the distance between you and your horse.

However, when lunging, we tend to stay closer to our horses than is traditionally taught. Because our horses are following our body position and movement, it is often easier to influence their balance and movement if you're moving as well, rather than standing in the middle of the circle as your horse goes around you. Think of it as you walking a smaller circle, say 10m in diameter and your horse is moving with you and around you on a larger circle, say 15m in diameter. You can then increase and decrease your speed, lengthen and shorten your stride to help your horse with transitions and balance changes as you both move together around the circle.

LUNGING AROUND A ROUND PEN

You can use the Around a Round Pen technique for teaching and improving lunge work with your horse. As you may recall from Chapter 4, this technique calls for you to stand inside a round pen while your horse goes around the outside. It's a great way to explain the exercise to your horse because it's clear that she follows the fence in a circle. Begin by taking a leading position close to your horse, then gradually move further into the centre of the circle into a lunging position. Your horse continues to do the same behaviour while you change your position, which prevents a lot of frustration when you're trying to tell the horse where to go.

Using Around A Round Pen is a clear and easy way to explain to your horse what to do when you're lunging.

As well as giving your horse clarity, the fence guides your horse's movement and helps her stay balanced. This is especially useful in faster movements such as trot and canter. Without the support of the fence, he might fall onto the inside shoulder, turn in, or spiral in ever-decreasing circles.

Another benefit of the Around a Round Pen technique is that it gives you protected contact. Some horses, especially young ones, get excited when you ask for faster movement, which can cause them to have a buck and a bounce. With the fence there, you are completely safe and can stay calm while you teach your horse relaxation and impulse control at faster paces.

Once your horse understands what you'd like him to do when you're asking him to lunge, you can fade the tools, asking your horse to work on a lunge line or at liberty without the need of a target or round pen.

This yearling was getting excited and playful when going forwards. The round pen gave him a clear guide of where to go, while keeping the handler, CT Coach Angelica Hesselius, safe and enabling her to stay soft and calm.

Angelica could then reassure Tiny and, when he relaxed and softened, mark and reward him.

This teaches impulse control as the horse learns to stay calm and focused during movement.

Just as with any behaviour, you don't want to ask your horse to work on endless circles on the lunge. Mentally, this will get boring; physically, especially with a young horse, it can put too much pressure on his body. Lunging calmly and in balance is a positive workout for your horse, but keep the sessions interspersed with plenty of other work to keep your horse mentally and physically happy.

BALANCE AND ENGAGEMENT ON THE LUNGE

You want your horse to find relaxed balance, rhythm and engagement when working on a circle and you can shape and improve your horse's movement on the lunge. To begin, you'll look for a relaxed walk with a good rhythm. If you have a horse who rushes, you want to shape slower movement or, if you have a horse who plods, you want to shape faster movement. There are different ways you can work on both getting the forwards energy *and* getting more relaxation; you can intersperse the forwards energy with plenty of slower, softer movement. Experiment with increasing your speed to encourage your horse to go forwards while, at the same time, breathing deeply and lowering your energy. Try waiting for your horse to overcome that initial excitement at going forwards and settle into it slightly before rewarding. With consistent practice, you will get whoa and go in balance with both horses, while they stay soft and connected with you.

You can also mark for better inside bend, increased hind leg action, more relaxation and steadiness, a better head position, engagement—whatever you're looking for your horse to do in movement.

In the following photographs, Hannah is liberty lunging her horse, Freckles, demonstrating bending, lengthening and collecting.

Hannah liberty lunging Freckles, demonstrating bending, lengthening and collecting.

'BUT I HAVE TO STOP ALL THE TIME!'

When using reward-based training to work on movement, both on the ground and in the saddle, a common complaint is that just when it's all going well, you must stop and reward your horse. This can be frustrating at first, but it's a crucial part of the learning process for your horse.

To understand this, think of a similar situation when you've been trying to learn a specific physical skill, such as the sitting trot. Suppose your instructor makes you work on it for lengthy periods of time. Sometimes you get it and it feels great; other times you're bouncing around like crazy. Your instructor tells you many different things to try. Eventually you have a break, but now you're tired and sore and the whole experience has blurred. You don't know exactly what worked and what didn't, and you'll struggle to replicate your successful moments.

Imagine instead that your instructor gives you one aspect of sitting trot to focus on, such as letting your lower back move in time with your horse's strides. You struggle for a few moments, and then you get it. At that moment, your instructor tells you that you did it right, and you come back to walk or go into rising trot. Pinpointing the exact moment and then having a break from it helps you remember the exact feeling and changes you made. It's an achievable goal, you were successful, and you'll be keen to give it another go. Your sitting trot will improve quickly because you fully understand each element and can replicate it easily.

Stopping and rewarding your horse after each successful moment has the same benefit. It makes what you're asking crystal clear, it's achievable, your horse is successful, and he'll be confident and keen to do it again.

This is another example of going slower to get there faster! When you follow this approach, your horse will understand what you're teaching him to do and will want to do it. Stopping and rewarding your horse as soon as he gives you the smallest step in the right direction is a temporary training tool. Once he understands what you want, you can start to ask for more duration and use variable reinforcement so you're no longer stopping him all the time. Because he's been an eager part of the learning process, and because moving in this way now has a strong reinforcement history attached to it, he'll be happy to progress and work for longer periods between breaks.

One thing to watch out for when you're stopping to reward them, is that many horses learn to stop dead when they hear you mark, which can be quite abrupt when stopping from a trot or a canter. This can cause unhealthy impact on their body as well as emotional tension. You can change it easily, simply by marking the best moments, then gradually slowing your movement. Since your horse is mimicking your body, they will slow down with you, making a more gentle and gradual transition to halt. This might mean that it takes half a circle between marking and rewarding your horse, but your horse will certainly understand what behaviour you marked as well as learning to transition down to a halt slowly and to stay tuned into you, instead of just slamming on the breaks. Teaching this on the lunge also establishes it for when you are riding as well.

Funnily enough, for many people one of the hardest things about using a lunge line is managing all that rope! Many traditional trainers insist you must never let it touch the floor for fear it trips you or spooks your horse. However, we prefer to ensure that the horse is totally relaxed with the rope so that if it does trail or tangle, your horse will remain calm.

MANAGING LUNGING EQUIPMENT

Hannah lunging India with a lunge line and target.

Before you even begin to lunge your horse on a line, it's important to do plenty of de-spooking work to teach him that the rope is nothing to worry about. Practice running it over his back, flicking it around his legs, and trailing it on the floor around and behind him. Throughout all this training, reward your horse for staying calm. He'll soon become blasé about the lunge line, no matter what kind of tangle you get into! This sets both of you up for success. Your horse will be relaxed and safe even if you make a mistake with the line, which gives you the freedom to practice until you feel confident coiling and uncoiling the rope as needed.

You can teach your horse to lunge without using a line at all. However, these tools are useful if you cannot lunge your horse at liberty as well as to ensure your horse stays calm and confident if someone does lunge him in the traditional manner, such as if he is tested for soundness at the vets. Many horses have had previous bad experiences with this equipment, so you might need to use the de-spooking techniques, such as systematic desensitisation and counter conditioning (see Chapter 7), to ensure that your horse is relaxed and confident in this situation.

The equipment you choose to use is up to you - as always, ensure your horse has freedom to express how he feels and be sensitive to his emotional state so that he is relaxed and willing on the lunge.

VIDEO RESOURCE

WHY AND HOW TO LUNGE YOUR HORSE

Watch this video to see more of the Connection Training approach to lunging in action.

www.connectiontraining.com/video-resources

BODY AWARENESS EXERCISES AND ALL TERRAIN TRAINING

The final elements to our gymnastic groundwork exercises are the use of objects and the natural environment to improve your horse's proprioception.

Using objects is an effective and fun way to teach your horse to place his feet with precision and gain more control of his own body movements. It is an intrinsic piece of teaching your horse to move well. The list of exercises you could use for this purpose is endless, so get creative! Here are a few we use regularly, of varying degrees of difficulty.

POLE EXERCISES

There are countless pole configurations and exercises you can use with your horse. These are some basic exercises to get you started.

One Foot at a Time

Halt your horse in front of the pole and ask her to step over one foot at a time. Mark as your horse lifts each foot and reward and pause in between so that each step is thoughtful and precise. Once your horse can do this going forwards, you can ask her to back up over it one foot at a time, too. Then raise the poles to increase the challenge. In this picture, CT Coach Claire is working on hind leg awareness with Triana. You can see they are both focused on Triana's left hind as she carefully lifts it over the pole.

Multiple Poles

When one pole is easy, gradually begin to add more. See if your horse can halt at any point as she's going through the poles. This is a great test of balance and body awareness. With a pole set up like this, you can also ask your horse to go between the poles (e.g. from right to left in this picture) instead of over them, halting and backing up through the corridors they create.

Circles and Fans

Set your poles up around a circle or in a fan so that you can ask your horse to bend and circle as she steps over the poles, rather than simply walking over them in a straight line.

PEDESTAL

A large, low pedestal is a fantastic tool to build your horse's confidence and body awareness - the horse has to clearly step up onto it and if he falls off or misplaces his foot, it's clear feedback but not dangerous. When you begin working on pedestal

exercises, you may find that your horse struggles to even step on it easily to begin with - just work with front feet first until he's confident stepping onto it and off it. Then you can progress to working on the hinds, too. The first time your horse does mis-step and fall off, he might need some reassurance to be able to step back up again. However, with a little repetition, we find all horses gain a lot of confidence and stop worrying at all if they fall off, stepping right back on again immediately. In fact, they all seem to love pedestal work and it quickly becomes a firm favourite for most horses.

Begin just asking your horse to step on and off with her front feet first.

The next stage is to ask her to walk forwards over it. Here, Rowan has halted with her hind feet still on the pedestal. Slow, precise movements will benefit your horse in these exercises, so keep it steady and reward your horse for deliberate and thoughtful steps. Once your horse is confident with this, you can also ask her to back onto the pedestal, too.

India has worked extensively with the pedestal and is confident standing squarely on it. She can even turn a full circle on this pedestal without stepping off - that's good body awareness and control!

ALL TERRAIN TRAINING

The natural world provides great opportunities to teach your horse how to confidently navigate different terrain. The variety adds extra interest and exploring the world together is a great way to boost your relationship. The opportunities you have available will vary greatly depending on the environment you're in, so use what you can find around you. Asking for exercises like back up or circles on different surfaces such as grass or gravel or a gentle slope will provide a different challenge and feedback for your horse. Keep your eyes open for banks, puddles, trees, branches, sand heaps, ditches, curbs, speedbumps or anything you can safely ask your horse to step on, over or through. As always, start easy making it progressively more challenging as your horse gains the skills and confidence.

Hannah asks India for shoulder-in going up a gentle slope. Even a shallow hill or uneven ground challenges your horse considerably more than performing these exercises on a flat surface.

This exploration should be fun for both of you, so look out for safe opportunities to play with your horse in your local area. Here are some examples from Hannah and her horses to give you some ideas.

Gymnastic training is an essential requirement to keep riding horses healthy and sound. It's also great for keeping non-ridden horses supple and sound into their old age. It doesn't have to consist of endless circles in an arena. In fact, the more variety you bring into it the better, by working in all four areas of gymnastic groundwork. We'll usually combine several exercises into each session, such as working on some lunging and then poles and object exercises, or going out for a walk, before returning to do some in-hand lateral work when our horse is warmed up. These exercises are all fun and contribute to suppleness, strength and straightness.

This picture perfectly illustrates how the natural environment influences how your horse moves. You can see both the gymnastic benefits and the proprioception needed for Freckles to step up the bank.

Taking your horse into water is a fun way to let him explore how he moves. Depending on the depth and the surface, he'll have to move differently and the resistance of water is a great way to build strength.

VIDEO RESOURCE

OBJECTS AND ALL TERRAIN TRAINING

See how to use objects and All Terrain Training to build your horse's co-ordination and confidence.

www.connectiontraining.com/video-resources

CHAPTER 11

RIDING WITH CONNECTION

Riding your horse can be a great way to enrich his life, as he gets to explore further afield, meet new horses, and experience different environments. It's an effective way to build fitness and provide some of the movement horses need and love. However, for riding to enhance your horse's life, it must be enjoyable, rewarding, and fun for him as well as you. Whether you're looking to improve your horse's way of going, or simply ensure that your horse enjoys riding as much as you do, Riding with Connection will help.

In this Chapter, we will cover the Connection Training approach to riding; why training your horse's body and mind are equally important; and how you can refine and improve your horse's responsiveness, relaxation and movement under saddle. The following Chapters then cover more detail on how you, as a rider, can connect more deeply with your horse, addressing common ridden problems such as napping and spooking and starting or re-starting your horse under saddle.

HOW DOES CONNECTION TRAINING WORK WHEN RIDING?

Connection Training principles are just the same when riding as they are on the ground. We focus on how you can communicate most effectively with your horse, how you can set up the lessons to be as clear and progressive as possible to help your horse to learn them and how you can reward good moments to bring clarity and motivation to your ridden training.

For example, if you're teaching your horse to respond well when you ask him to walk on, you will mark your horse when he responds to your aids and then reward him, giving him a treat from the saddle. Just like in the groundwork, the marker tells your horse which response you liked, in this instance, a forward walk. You can then stop your horse and reward that moment, but your horse will know from the marker that it was the improved walking response that earned the reward. Your variety of rewards from the saddle are just as varied

as on the ground so you can also use scratches, favourite behaviours and praise, especially when you're in the process of fading the marker and food out of learned ridden behaviours.

Your horse will have personal preferences in regards to their favourite behaviours. For example, Hannah's mare India loves poles and jumping but finds lateral work more challenging. Hannah asks for a small amount of shoulder-in or leg-yield and, when India responds well, rewards her by jumping some fences. Hannah's gelding, Freckles, is the other way around: he adores flat work and struggles with jumping. After popping a small jump on Freckles, Hannah often asks for some collected trot or lateral work, which he loves to do. The more challenging behaviours are still fun and only asked for in small amounts, but by breaking up the more difficult exercises with easy, fun ones, you will keep your horse's enjoyment and motivation as high as possible. These rewards will depend on the individual horse and will vary from day to day. They are used in amongst other rewards such as food, jumping off and doing some groundwork, easy exercises like targeting, scratches, breaks, praise etc.

As riding becomes an interesting and rewarding experience for your horse, you'll see his levels of relaxation and motivation rise. He'll be keen to be ridden and you will deepen your connection through your ridden partnership.

or a bit of everything, your horse needs to be physically healthy and emotionally happy. Our riding work builds directly on our gymnastic groundwork exercises as we teach our horses to be supple, strong and body-aware in a way that is clear, progressive, fun and builds your connection together.

For your horse to be happy when ridden, he must be comfortable and confident in his movement. To build his physical

HEALTHY MOVEMENT, HAPPY HORSE

In order to create the most positive emotions around being ridden, we need to look at the situation holistically. Whether you ride dressage, jumping, Western,

abilities, he must be relaxed and willing throughout his education. Neither element is more important. For example, if you teach your horse a technically correct shoulder-in, but he's anxious or unwilling as he learns it, this tension will carry in his muscles as well as triggering negative emotional states such as FEAR and RAGE.

Equally, you will certainly create tension and conflict if your horse does not have the strength, fitness, or flexibility to perform the movement you're asking of him or if the movement is detrimental to his health. In Connection Training, we address both the emotional and physical elements of training simultaneously, building horses' strength, suppleness and balance through training which is clear, fun and joyful. Throughout, we also focus on the relationship between horse and handler, creating strong communication and connection as you move from the ground to the saddle.

Let's firstly look at the physical element; why the way your horse moves under saddle is so important. As discussed in Chapter 10, in relation to the groundwork exercises, we need to include specific movement exercises into our horse's regime in order to keep them healthy and prepare their bodies for the demands we ask of them. This is even more important when we ride our horses because they have not evolved naturally to carry weight on their backs, since this is not something a feral horse would ever do. When we ask them to carry the weight of a rider, we need to teach them how to move differently so that they can do so comfortably and healthily. Without training, horses keep their weight on their shoulders and do not engage their core abdominal muscles fully. This leads to an unsupported back, which then dips and sags the more they are ridden. Tension and anxiety, as well as lack of training, can also lead to a high head, a bulging lower neck, and a contracted back. These body positions are uncomfortable for the horse and can lead to pain, injury, and lameness as well as behavioural problems. When a horse is schooled and is moving correctly, you will see a straight back supported by a strong abdominal core. Every ridden horse will benefit from being trained to carry more weight on her hind legs, engage her core abdominal muscles, and develop strength and suppleness evenly through her body.

Ridden exercises for improving strength and suppleness are certainly not new, and many have been around for thousands of years. You may already be familiar with lateral exercises, the use of poles and cavalletti, and concepts of collection. You don't need to take horses to a high level of dressage training for them to be happy, strong and sound when ridden. But we do recommend that they at least learn basic circles and lateral movements in walk, as well as steps towards engaged collection and lengthening in walk and trot, taking the groundwork exercises into your ridden work. Teaching these on the ground first is not necessary, but can be very beneficial as your horse already has the strength, understanding and ability of the movements before you ask for them when riding. This helps young horses carry a rider comfortably from the start, older horses learn to balance and bend for their health and enjoyment, and injured horses become gently rehabilitated back into work.

As in the gymnastic groundwork, the difference with riding with connection is *how* we teach these techniques. We want the horse to choose to learn each movement, genuinely understand it, and have such a positive association with it that he can't wait for you to ask him to do it again. The result is a light, responsive horse. You will not have to 'get after him', increase the pressure, struggle to get your horse to focus or feel like your horse would rather be anywhere but in the arena! Instead, you'll be working as a team to learn and perform these exercises.

CASE STUDY: EX-RACEHORSE GERTIE

Gertie came to her owner, Helen Gilbertson, after a short racing career. Typical in ex-racehorses, Gertie was stiff, one-sided and easily went lame. Because moving well was difficult for her, Helen found it hard to motivate Gertie in her training.

Helen began using Connection Training techniques. At first, she rewarded Gertie for simply bending a little or stretching down towards a target, both on the ground and ridden. The exercises were at the right level for Gertie physically, and she began to enjoy being ridden as she was successful and rewarded.

Gradually, Helen could ride for longer and add in more exercises, such as circles, lateral work and pole-work. All her work at this stage was

done at walk. Because of the rewarding nature of the training, Gertie was also mentally engaged and began to offer more of her own accord as she was physically able, such as flexing at the poll, collecting her movement and willing forwards energy.

In just a few months, Gertie had changed both physically and emotionally. She was relaxed and enthusiastic when ridden and staying sound. Helen and Gertie perfectly demonstrate our Riding with Connection approach, as they worked together to build Gertie's physical health in a way which was clear, relaxed and fun for both of them.

TACK AND EQUIPMENT FOR RIDING

The saddle and bridle you ride in will have a direct impact on your horse's ability, enjoyment and communication under saddle.

Finding the best saddle to fit your horse can be a difficult (and expensive!) process, but a well-fitting saddle is paramount to your horse enjoying being ridden. As well as getting professional body workers and saddle-fitters to help you make the best decision for your horse, listen to your horse, too. Your horse is the only true judge of which saddle is comfortable If he's moving away or pinning his ears when you tack up, it's likely that the saddle is uncomfortable, even if you've been told that it fits your horse. Test your horse's emotional reactions to different equipment, such as different saddles, saddle pads, surcingles and a variety of girths. Work your horse in each one for a few sessions and it will soon become clear which he likes and dislikes if you give him choice and watch his behaviour.

Choosing the right bridle is just as important. One of the main questions is whether to go bitted or bitless. Even though bitless bridles are seen as less aversive than using a bitted bridle, some horses find the pressure of bitless bridles highly aversive. Bitless bridles come in many designs and some have thin, tough nosebands which apply a lot of pressure on the nose. Many also use poll pressure, which can also be highly aversive for some horses.

Our approach is to treat each horse as an individual and choose the tack accordingly. You may need to do a lot of trial and error with different types of bridles and bits before you are sure your horse is happy. You can use your knowledge of tiny signs of stress from your horse to help you in this process. You can also use the concept of "preference and avoidance". In other words, teach your horse to put his head low and forward and to put his nose into the bridle. That way, if your horse hesitates, then you can assess whether he is finding it aversive. If, on the other hand, he keenly sticks his nose in and practically puts the bridle on himself, then you know that he is happy with it. We generally tack up at liberty to encourage our horses to communicate how they are feeling at that moment about the tack.

Ensure the bridle fits well with ample space around the ears and a comfortable noseband. Be careful to ensure the noseband sits on the correct part of the nose for the bridle you've chosen. They must always be higher than the soft part of the nose, on the bony nasal plane.

Hannah gives all of her horses the choice between bitless or bitted bridles, as well as a variety of bits, to establish their preferences. Freckles and Rowan have always loved their bitless bridles, Toby was happy in either and India prefers a narrow bit. This sits nicely in her small mouth and Hannah always uses the reins lightly. Although Hannah rides India from time to time in a bitless bridle, India tends to shake her head and rub the noseband on her legs occasionally when wearing it. Hannah has also removed the noseband from India's bitted bridle as she prefers it without one. Here, Hannah is holding out the bridle and India is dropping her head into it and picking up the bit herself.

The old recommendation that you need to be able to fit "2 fingers" between the noseband and your horse's nose is still the best guideline. If the noseband is tighter than this, then the horse's licking, chewing and yawning responses will be inhibited. If your horse can easily take treats and chew them happily, then the noseband is likely to be loose enough.

We don't recommend restrictive tack such as flash nosebands or martingales. These are designed to prevent the symptoms of the horse opening their mouth or raising their head against the bit. However, when you address the cause and make being ridden comfortable, clear, positive and enjoyable, your horse won't try to evade your aids or show these signs of tension and distress.

VIDEO RESOURCE

CHOOSING TO BE TACKED UP AND RIDDEN

See Hannah's mare, India, choose to be tacked up and line up for mounting and learn how to improve this with your horse.

www.connectiontraining.com/video-resources

THE MOUNTING BLOCK: STAYING CONNECTED

Before you can train any ridden behaviours, you need to ensure your horse is relaxed and connected as you transition from the ground to the saddle. Many horses 'lose' their human when they mount because this step has been missed in the training. If that's the case, the horse is likely to be much more anxious and distracted when being ridden than when the human is on the ground. As you work at the mounting block, you're teaching your horse that the only thing that has changed is your position. This creates a horse who is focused on you even when you're on his back, which of course leads to more relaxation and responsiveness to your ridden cues or aids.

If you're working with a horse who has already been ridden, his behaviour at the mounting block will tell you a lot about how he feels about it. Does he stand calmly and relaxed for you to mount, or does he fidget? Does he come to the mounting block or move away from it? Does he swish his tail or lift his head high when you mount? Does he rush off as soon as you get on? If your horse is happy to come to the mounting block and stand calmly as you get on, that's great—you can move on to training other ridden behaviours. If your horse fidgets, tries to move away from the mounting block, or shows tension as you mount, you'll need to find out why and remove the source of the anxiety.

To teach your horse to line up at a mounting block, use a target to show where you'd like him to stand. Then spend a lot of time in this position just standing calmly and rewarding your horse. This establishes place preference and builds relaxation associated with mounting. You can practise leaning and lying over your horse's back, feeding him from both sides, and asking for stationary behaviours such as lateral flexion (bending the head to each side) and targeting your feet. Gradually introduce actions such as flapping the stirrups, lifting your legs towards the stirrups, and waving your arms over your horse. All of these will prepare your horse for being ridden and enable him to be relaxed and confident about your movements before you even get on. When your horse is truly relaxed about all the things you're doing at the mounting block, mounting will be an easy next step.

Use a target to teach your horse the position you need to her to be in at the mounting block. Reward her highly for standing at the block as you lean over her and prepare her for riding, creating strong place preference with the mounting block. As you practise lining up at the block and standing in position, you can fade the target and your horse will line up willingly in position for you to mount.

Once you've mounted, spend time marking and rewarding your horse by asking for behaviours such as rein flexions and simply standing quietly with you in the saddle. This keeps your horse connected with you and ensures he waits quietly for you to ask him to walk on. If your horse has a history of rushing off as soon as you hit the saddle, spend extra time at this stage, ensuring he's truly relaxed and happy to stand when you mount. You can support the standing behaviour by having a nose or mat target in the correct position for your horse while you reward from the saddle. Then you fade these prompts as your horse learns to stand still instead of rushing off.

Each time you do this, you're building your horse's positive associations with mounting, helping him to be more joyful and relaxed about it each time. Many riders rush this mounting block work in their eagerness to get on. You're looking for a relaxed ride, so this work at the block will ensure your horse is relaxed from your very first step together each time you ride.

And when your horse voluntarily comes to the mounting block and asks you get on, it's the best feeling in the world!

By training in this way, we are sure that our horses love to be ridden. They participate willingly while being tacked up at liberty; they come to the mounting block at liberty and present themselves in the correct position for us to mount and they express positive emotions while they are being ridden.

However, as we've emphasised throughout, this is a partnership between you and your horse, so we never take it for granted. If a horse hesitates to come to the mounting block, for example, we question why and don't ride until they willingly present themselves to be ridden. That was why Rachel retired Roisin. Roisin stopped a few feet out of position of the block. The second day it happened, Rachel realised that she needed to stop even trying to mount and find out what was wrong. After months of investigation and physical rehabilitation, it was clear that Roisin could no longer carry herself correctly under saddle, leading to pain and discomfort when ridden. Rachel made the decision to retire her from riding. The clear communication and consent that Rachel had created at the mounting block enabled Roisin to express her discomfort long before it became externally visible.

By working with our horses and allowing them to say 'no' and communicate in this way, it is always a great honour that they say "yes" almost all the time.

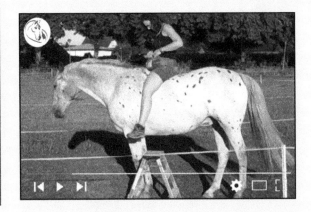

VIDEO RESOURCE

CT HORSES CHOOSING TO LINE UP AT THE MOUNTING BLOCK

Learn more about our mounting techniques and see loads of CT horses line up willingly at the mounting block, keen to be ridden.

www.connectiontraining.com/video-resources

VIDEO RESOURCE

TOP TIPS TO TEACH YOUR HORSE TO BE EASY TO MOUNT

Get some top tips on training your horse to line up at the mounting block in this video.

www.connectiontraining.com/video-resources

PRIORITISING RELAXATION

Relaxation is just as important when riding your horse as it is on the ground. As you monitor his emotional responses to being ridden and various exercises, you will notice which behaviours he loves and where he shows tension. Just as you've worked on helping your horse to relax and soften at the mounting block, you need to ensure your horse is relaxed and connected to you in basic movements, such as walk, halt and turning, before working on teaching or refining more advanced movements.

Prioritise relaxation and connection in basic movements such as walk, halt and turning before moving on.

Since you are always rewarding the emotional state as well as physical behaviour, you can mark moments when your horse feels more relaxed or tuned into you. This will be progressive, so if your horse is very uptight to begin with, you won't get to true relaxation in one session. Reward 'better' not 'perfect' and you will see improvements over time. When your horse is relaxed, he'll be able to respond well to cues and challenges.

As you increase the pace or difficulty of the work, it becomes harder to maintain relaxation. Ensuring that your horse is truly soft and relaxed in basic behaviours first will help you to stay calm and connected as you advance. Canter, especially, is an emotional gait for many horses. Naturally, they only canter when they are excited or scared, so these emotions tend to be linked to this gait. We have to teach our horses to be able to canter calmly, which begins with relaxation at the walk and trot. From here, you can begin to ask for the canter transition, then come back to trot and establish relaxation again, which you can mark and reward. With a little repetition, your horse will soon stay relaxed and eager through the canter transition and you can build from there. As you work together, this connection and relaxation will only get stronger and are fundamental to a great ridden partnership from the basics to more advanced work.

The next Chapter covers techniques to help you relax and connect with your horse as a rider, using your internal cues, such as breath and alignment to help your horse soften. If your horse shows extreme signs of tension and is a very long way from relaxed, you can find out more on overcoming problems in Chapter 13.

Relaxation is necessary for connection and enjoyment, even at higher paces. Hannah's mare, India, was prone to getting easily over-excited in canter, leading her to disconnect, speed up and buck. Hannah worked on relaxation in canter first on the ground, establishing calm transitions from the trot, and gradually asking India to maintain the canter for longer. Once it was solid on the ground, Hannah repeated the process in the saddle. This could only be successful once the walk and trot were relaxed and balanced, and rushing into the canter too soon is the cause of much tension in many horses. This process was slower, but resulted in calm, connected, balanced canters right from the start. This was important to keep Hannah's confidence levels high and India's canter experiences successful and enjoyable.

IMPROVING RESPONSIVENESS

Improving responsiveness to your aids helps many situations, such as slowing down when you ask, creating soft and accurate turns or going forwards willingly. Once you've worked at the mounting block to get connected in the saddle, you can begin to improve responsiveness to any existing aids (cues).

First, pinpoint areas where you'd like your horse to respond better to your cue. Begin to mark and reward each time your horse responds more quickly or more softly than usual when you give an aid. For example, if it usually takes your horse five steps to make the downward transition from a trot to a walk, begin to mark and reward as soon as your horse slows slightly - this is the first approximation towards a downwards transition. As he realises that the downward transition is getting rewarded, he will begin to offer improvements himself, coming down to a walk more promptly until you get the transition immediately from the lightest of cues.

As well as improving specific cue responses, you can also improve general responsiveness across all ridden movements. Ask for varying behaviours and mark and reward every time your horse responds well to your cue, regardless of what you're asking for. You might reward a prompt downward transition, then an accurate turn, then a moment of collection. These great moments will come among many other behaviours. When you mark the best responses from your horse and reward highly for them, your horse will begin to eagerly pay attention to your cues and respond better each time. The 'behaviour'

you're working on here is *responsiveness to your cues*, whatever they are, rather than a specific movement from your horse. If you reward a left turn too many times in a row, your horse may well think that you really want him to turn left today and begin to offer that movement more enthusiastically and determinedly. You need to keep your clarity that you are rewarding cue responsiveness in this session, not working on specific behaviours. This exercise builds better communication between you.

When you're assessing your horse's responsiveness to existing aids, take into account his emotional response, as well. If your horse pins his ears, swishes his tail or resists your aid, he either doesn't understand it or has negative emotions associated with the cue and/or the behaviour. By observing your horse and monitoring his emotional response, you will be able to pinpoint which areas need addressing to help your horse be relaxed and happy. Many horses have underlying tension associated with riding due to past experiences, which causes them to be tense, resistant and less responsive than the rider desires. In order to get soft, prompt responses to your ridden requests, you need to address the underlying emotional cause of the tension and counter-condition it to replace it with feelings of joy, willingness, relaxation and enthusiasm.

Your horse will be highly responsive to your aids when he is mentally connected with you in the saddle. As you now know, that connection comes from positive emotions, so you will see good changes in your horse as you prioritise clarity, relaxation and fun in your ridden work.

VIDEO RESOURCE

STAYING CONNECTED THROUGH TRANSITIONS

Watch this video on how to improve transitions, to stay soft, connected and balanced with your horse.

www.connectiontraining.com/video-resources

USE OBJECTS FOR CLARITY

Just like in the groundwork, you can use objects and specific exercises to help your horse give you the response you're looking for. For example, if you're training your horse to go forwards more willingly when you ask, you'll have a much higher chance of success if you ask your horse to go towards a target as you're asking for it. This will create more joy and enthusiasm in your horse and he'll be moving *towards* something, supporting the response you're asking for. You will use your marker and rewards to pinpoint better responses to your forwards aids.

For example, if you're riding your horse towards a target, you can ask him to increase his speed. He'll be drawn towards the target, which will increase the likelihood he'll go forwards enthusiastically when you ask. As you gently give your aid to go faster, mark and reward your horse as soon as he responds - the target is helping to create the movement, but you use your marker to explain to your horse which response is the one being rewarded, which will happen *before* he reaches the target. Don't wait until he reaches the target to mark. By then, he is probably at a halt! Mark and reward the increase in impulsion when it happens. This process will build more positive emotional associations with going forwards and responding promptly when you ask, so you will see it improve over time.

Use objects to guide your horse and set him up for success. Here, Rachel is riding towards a stationary target to encourage more forwards motivation from Heather over the poles.

TRANSFERRING CUES FROM GROUNDWORK TO RIDING

Training behaviours from the ground first is a great way to introduce exercises to your horse and it's a simple process to then transfer these to your riding, without having to train them again from scratch.

To do this, keep as many cues and indicators of the exercise consistent from the ground to the saddle. For example, if you had a particular pole set-up when you taught your horse to leg-yield in the groundwork, set it up again as you first ask for it when riding. Any cues, such as voice and rein, that you can keep consistent as you transition to the ridden work will also help your horse understand which exercise you're asking for.

Practise the exercise first on the ground, then mount and repeat immediately in the same location, keeping as many of the cues as consistent as possible. Often, because you've just been working on that behaviour and it's at the forefront of your horse's mind, she'll offer that most recent behaviour. If your horse even gives you an inkling of the behaviour on the new cue, mark and reward! If she doesn't, you might have to dismount and try again. Your horse will probably get it next time.

This process works beautifully for most behaviours you've trained on the ground and now wish to ask for when riding. It often takes only a few minutes, especially if your horse is really tuned in to the training. You can make the process even easier by having a person on the ground cue the horse for the behaviour while you're in the saddle. Gradually transfer the cues from the ground handler to the rider until the horse is responding only to the rider's cues.

CASE STUDY: TEACHING A CUE FOR REIN BACK

Here's an example of how Rachel taught rescue pony Rowan how to rein back with a rider.

The pictures show the first time Rowan ever reined back with a rider on board. You can tell from the position of her ears that she's listening. Her muscles look relaxed and the movement is soft and light. There is no use of the reins from the rider, it's a response to the voice and body cues alone.

Rachel began by letting Rowan practise backing up using the cue she already knew. She put her hand on Rowan's chest and said 'Back'. Rowan backed up nicely, which Rachel marked and rewarded.

Next, Rachel stood at Rowan's shoulder and again said 'Back'. Rowan backed up immediately, which Rachel marked and rewarded highly. Rowan clearly understood the cue when Rachel was in different positions.

The final transfer Rachel needed to make was to change her body position from the ground to the saddle. So, she hopped on board and gave her cue, saying 'Back'. Because Rowan had just practised backing up and had been rewarded highly for it, and because many elements of the cue remained the same, it was the first behaviour she offered. Rachel marked as soon as Rowan began to step back and gave her a big reward.

VIDEO RESOURCE

TEACHING REIN-BACK

Watch Rachel teach Rowan to rein back as she transfers the behaviour from the ground to the saddle.

www.connectiontraining.com/video-resources

You can use this technique to transfer any behaviours your horse knows on the ground into the saddle. In addition to targets, you can use objects such as poles, obstacles, barriers, mats, and jumps to explain to your horse what you'd like him to do. Once your horse understands the behaviour and the new cue, you can fade these tools completely. Your horse will now understand your new cue, and you can use it from then on.

Once your horse understands the new cue, you can refine the cue and the response to it. Maybe you want to add another element into the cue or remove your voice. Maybe you want your horse to respond more promptly, for a longer duration, or with more energy. When you shape the behaviour by marking and rewarding the best attempts from your horse, you will see the behaviour improve.

TEACHING NEW MOVEMENTS FROM THE SADDLE

You can also teach your horse new movements directly from the saddle. Once your horse has a basic understanding of some cues from the saddle, you can combine these cues to teach new movements. The technical term for this is 'behavioural adduction'. For example, if your horse already knows a voice cue for lowering his head and a cue for walking forward when you're riding, you can combine these by asking your horse to lower his head while he's walking. Combining these two cues will teach him to stretch and lengthen his body in movement.

Most ridden movements are a combination of more basic ridden behaviours, such as bending laterally, moving the quarters or shoulders sideways, and changing head position. If you teach these elements separately to begin with, just as you did in the groundwork, it is much easier to combine them to create new movements. For example, in leg-yield, you ask your horse to move forwards and sideways at the same time. If you have cues for teaching your horse to go forwards and move his shoulders and quarters over, you can ask for them at the same time to create a leg-yield. Teaching them in this way also makes it easier to refine and improve the new movements, since you can always isolate and work on the necessary part.

Let's say you're working on shoulder-in and your horse is drifting his quarters in off the track, rather than continuing to move along the track laterally. Simply go back to halt and ask him to move his quarters over an easier behaviour he knows well. Mark and reward this movement to draw your horse's attention to it. Then try your shoulder-in again, focusing on your cue to ask your horse to step across with his hind legs. When you feel any increase in his lateral step with his hind legs, mark and reward it. This is when the pinpoint precision of a marker is extremely beneficial. With a few repetitions, your horse will be very aware of what he's doing with his quarters, and the shoulder-in will improve.

You can combine cues to teach new movements, such as shoulder-in.

VIDEO RESOURCE

TEACHING THE WALK PIROUETTE

See how you can combine a set of cues into a new behaviour in this video, where Hannah is teaching her horse the first steps of a walk pirouette.

www.connectiontraining.com/video-resources

SHAPING ENGAGEMENT

Using a marker gives you the ability to improve the way your horse moves to ensure he stays sound and comfortable under saddle. This is a great way to increase engagement in your horse's movement as you can pinpoint the exact stride that you feel your horse step underneath you and lighten his shoulders or stretches through his back. By stopping to reward it, you will make it very clear to him exactly what he did to earn the reward and he'll be keen to try again next time.

Again, this builds on the gymnastic groundwork exercises, teaching horses to change their balance and lengthen or collect their frame. Once your horse understands how to change his balance in this way, you can use a rein or a voice cue to ask for it. This transfers directly to the ridden work.

Hannah on her horse, Freckles, showing lengthening and collecting at the trot. As you saw from Chapter 10, Freckles can offer these changes of balance at liberty as well. Both on the ground and in the saddle, it is clear that he understands what he's being asked to do and, though Hannah explains and refines it through a variety of cues, Freckles actively creates the movement himself.

.THE SLIDING SCALE OF POSTURAL ENGAGEMENT

Moving with postural engagement is a sliding scale, or continuum, from high levels of collection to full extended movement. Every horse will benefit from being taught basic changes of balance within walk and trot, learning how to collect and lengthen his strides a little, while staying engaged and balanced. You do not need to train full extension and collection to keep your riding horse healthy and sound, though these are the foundation lessons of that if you wish to train it to those levels.

The Sliding Scale of Postural Engagement

Collecting Lengthening

Every horse starts in the middle, showing small changes of balance towards both more collected and lengthened movement, while maintaining engagement. You will gradually work towards each end of the scale as your horse builds strength, suppleness, awareness and control.

VIDEO RESOURCE

TEACHING ENGAGEMENT UNDER SADDLE

Watch this video to learn more about changes of balance and how to shape your horse's movement when riding.

www.connectiontraining.com/video-resources

REFINING MOVEMENTS

Nothing beats the use of a marker for precision. You can accurately explain to your horse exactly which stride you liked best, giving your horse clarity and enabling you to refine movements with great accuracy.

2.Hannah uses cues India knows to help guide her into a better position. This is a conversation between them as they work out which cues and subtle shifts will make the difference. India is an active participant here, consciously trying different positions and balances to see which will be rewarded. Because of her history, she loves to problem-solve and learn new exercises, and it is this two-way communication that riding with connection creates. When India finds the right position, Hannah clicks to pinpoint that moment.

1.Here, Hannah is improving the half-pass in trot with her mare, India. At first, India struggles to find the right position.

3.Hannah rewards India and the break helps them both consolidate their learning, before they come around to try again. Once Hannah and India could float easily into the correct half-pass movement, then they could work on duration and refine the half-pass further.

VIDEO RESOURCE

TRANSFERRING LATERAL WORK IN-HAND TO UNDER SADDLE

You've seen this video already, from Chapter 10 but now you can look at the ridden portion of it. You can see how groundwork transfers to the saddle, how it's a conversation between you and your horse to work out the movements and how you can use your marker to teach and shape lateral movements when riding.

www.connectiontraining.com/video-resources

A PROGRESSIVE PROGRAMME

Creating a happy, healthy ridden horse takes consistency. You need to choose appropriate exercises for your horse's level and progress systematically as your horse builds physical straightness, suppleness and strength. The speed you can progress will also be dictated by your horse's emotional state. Some horses will physically be ready for more challenges but are still tense or unmotivated and will need help to find joy and enthusiasm before moving on. Other horses will be emotionally balanced but need the time to build up their strength. This is often the case when rehabilitating a horse from an injury, and it can be a challenge to keep the work mentally interesting while your horse recovers physically.

As you progress, you will be able to ask more from your horse and fade the prompts you used for teaching. If you have been using targets to teach your horse to go forwards more willingly or turn more softly, you want to fade those out as your horse learns to perform movements easily from your ridden cues only. Once your horse understands how to do a certain lateral movement, you no longer need to reward each step; gradually ask for more until you can fade the mark out completely. Then you will only reward your horse occasionally for the best moments to keep the movement strong.

As you're working on these ridden exercises, remember to keep it fun for your horse as you focus on his movement. The same principles apply in the saddle that you have used on the ground to keep your horse relaxed and motivated in his work. Use your horse's natural preferences as you train him in the saddle.

BUT MY HORSE PREFERS GROUNDWORK!

As you begin to observe your horse's emotional response to riding, you might notice that he seems much more enthusiastic in the groundwork than the riding. This could be a natural preference, dislike of tack, pain or due to his ridden history. First get him examined professionally to rule out pain and tack discomfort problems. Horses often find it easier to connect with you on the ground partly through evolving and living in a herd with their companions all around them, and partly due to the fact that they have usually had much more time spent with them by people handling and training them on the ground. Preferring groundwork over riding could also be a reflection of being asked too much in the ridden work, making it difficult, uncomfortable or worrying. It could even be a reflection of your own feelings if you feel anxious or confused in the saddle compared to the clarity and confidence you feel on the ground.

Whatever the cause, you need to make the riding more rewarding than the groundwork. For example, you can make riding more rewarding by using special treats your horse only receives for ridden work; keeping the riding sessions short and highly reinforcing; and even jumping off to do some groundwork with your horse after a moment of great effort in the riding. If you tend to work on the ground first before riding, try switching it around. That way, your horse will be rewarded for his ridden work with a groundwork session and it can have a big impact on your horse's enthusiasm.

As you move on with your horse, introduce new and more challenging exercises in between more relaxed work. Your ridden sessions should develop a natural ebb and flow as you work with more focus and energy and then relax with an easier one. What counts as challenging will depend on your horse. For a green horse, working on basic transitions or turns could be challenging, interspersed with easier behaviours such as touching targets, standing on mats and boards and walking on a long rein. As you progress, you can work on more difficult behaviours such as canter, lateral work and collection, though

Make being ridden as rewarding as possible through variety, working on your horse's favourite exercises, keeping the sessions short and saving your best rewards just for riding.

your horse will still appreciate breaks with fun, easy and well-known behaviours.

These training principles apply to all ridden situations. If you're hacking out, begin by riding a known route to keep your horse relaxed and reward for moments when your horse tunes into you or responds well when you ask her to wait or slow down. If you're opening a gate, use your arena lessons of moving the quarters over and reward your horse for responding to your cue in a new situation. If you're working over poles or cantering through a field and your horse has a tendency to get excited, begin by setting your horse up for success. For example, work over poles or canter only the final few strides of the field so your horse is expecting to stop, and reward your horse for slowing down and staying connected.

Variety in your ridden training sessions will also keep your horse interested and motivated. Include object work, lateral exercises and hacking with friends, as well as fun ridden sessions such as bareback riding, jumping or even training your horse to be ridden bridle-less.

Variety in your ridden sessions will keep your horse interested and motivated. Include exploring new places with friends and even train your horse without tack (progressively and safely!).

CHAPTER 12

THE CONNECTED RIDER

When riding your horse, you want to feel the same mental and emotional connection as you do on the ground. This means that your horse is relaxed, tuned in, responsive and an active participant, clearly understanding the exercises and working with you in order to problem-solve together. To become the best rider for you horse, you need to understand your own emotional state when riding and how you connect physically with your horse through your seat. When you work on yourself in these areas as you are training your horse under saddle, your partnership will deepen and you will reach a new level of communication with your horse, allowing your ridden work to progress beautifully.

In your training sessions, prioritise relaxation, communication and joy for both of you. You'll have more fun and make more progress when you both look forward to your ridden sessions.

CONNECTION IN THE SADDLE

The "Connected Trainer" lessons from Chapter 6 are directly applicable to your ridden training. As a rider, you have to do your part to be someone your horse trusts and wants to connect with. Ask yourself how you can create clarity for your horse, to help guide him to the answer. Respect and respond to his emotional state in order to set the right challenge level for you horse. Give your cues softly and gently and be consistent in what you ask for and how you ask for it. Stay positive, calm and focused to be a rider your horse can rely on. Riding should be a joyful experience for both of you and it's your responsibility to create the best environment in which your horse can thrive. Sometimes this means you may have to progress more slowly than you'd like or adapt your plans to suit your horse. Despite all this, you will still have rides which didn't go so well, either through training mistakes (we all make them) or external influences. Just like on the ground, your job is to then rebuild the confidence of both you and your horse to get back to a happy working partnership. Prioritising relaxation and communication over external training goals will pay off in the long run as your horse builds trust in you as a rider and joy in the work you do together.

WORKING TOGETHER

As a partnership, you and your horse should be communicating with each other in order to problem-solve together. In practice, this is shown by the horse understanding what behaviour you're working on and offering that behaviour herself. Your horse will offer suggestions as you work on teaching or refining a behaviour, such as moving into different positions or trying different paces. She will sometimes pause as if to say, "that was

right, wasn't it? Surely I deserve a reward for that?" Although you don't want your horse to stop and demand treats when she feels like it, this is a fantastic sign that your horse clearly understands what you are both working on and when she has made a good effort towards it. If she does this, just quietly praise her and ask her to continue on until you are ready to stop and reward her. Occasionally, however, you may see that she was right - she did try really hard and deserve a reward for it. You can reward her now and again at times like this because it keeps your horse communicating with you and participating in the riding with you as you both work towards the same goal.

Your horse should be working with you towards the same goals when you're riding. Here, Hannah is teaching India Spanish Walk under saddle. You can see India is turned to Hannah as she offers a leg lift for the first time, as she asks, "Is this what you want?"

STAYING FOCUSED

As a rider, you will feel your horse's attention and know whether he is focused on you, or not. Horses will disconnect from their rider when they are anxious, over-excited, confused or simply have never been truly connected to a rider before. Begin with simple exercises such as walk, halt and turn and mark and reward your horse for those moments when he really tunes into you and focuses on the task at hand. This means you need to stay focused, too, so keep your attention on what you want your horse *to do*. It's easy to get distracted by all the things you don't want, but your horse will learn to follow your focus if you keep your concentration. As you reward your horse for staying with you, you will find that he will tune in more easily and stay focused, even after a distraction or as you're working on more difficult exercises.

Pay attention to your horse's emotional state and which situations, exercises or aids cause him to disconnect from you as well as when he softens and tunes in. Set him up for success by working mostly on exercises that enable him to stay focused and reward him for those moments when you feel he is most connected with you. Intersperse it with short bursts of asking for the more challenging behaviour until he can stay relaxed and focused as you work through the challenge together.

Working with objects is a great way to bring clarity and fun into your ridden work and your horse will quickly show that he understands the exercises by choosing to step over the poles or move towards the stationary target. However, you can find that your horse starts to focus more on the objects than you, the rider. While working with objects, reward your horse for those times when he's listening to you and responds well to *your* aids, rather than taking the presence of an object alone as the cue to that behaviour. This will bring his focus back to you and help to stay connected and responsive to your cues.

BUILDING TRUST
Another sign of connection between horse and rider is your horse tuning into you in difficult situations, just as you have been working on from the ground. For example, if your horse gets spooked when you are riding, you want him to stop and turn to you rather than bolt away. Or, if he is struggling with a difficult ridden challenge, he should feel confident to turn to you for help instead of, say, running off in his own direction. Just as on the ground, building this trust and communication takes time. You can begin to train it by setting small challenges in a safe environment, such as your arena. For example, ask your horse to pass a spooky object, rewarding all those moments when he tunes into you and you feel him asking you what he should do. Of course, part of the connection is two-way communication so if your horse is telling you that he is too scared to pass it, you must respect that and help him to feel more confident by making the situation easier. You could take him a further distance away, not asking him to step any closer until he's calmer or dismount and lead him from the ground. When he knows that he will be listened to by you, your horse will stay more connected to you as a rider, rather than disconnecting and making his own decisions.

PROGRESS, NOT PERFECTION
Work with your horse towards your goals and remember that it takes time and consistency to see big changes. Aim to make every ride as positive and fun as possible for both of you. Not only will this create great reinforcement history for your horse, building his willingness and enjoyment of being ridden, you will both enjoy your time together and deepen your relationship.

Keep your focus on what you want your horse to do and mark and reward him for tuning in and working with you.

Achieving your goals is easiest if they align with what your horse loves most naturally. For example, if you want to do long distance rides and your horse adores exploring the world, you are likely to be successful fairly quickly. On the other hand, perhaps your horse gets fearful when hacking out, but loves focused movement work like dressage or pole-work. All relationships require some give and take and playing to your horse's strengths will make the journey smoother for both of you. This doesn't mean you need to give up on your goals, but you could adapt them to make it easier for your horse. For example, Hannah's mare, India, does not like to be the lead horse, so finds hacking out alone very challenging. Hannah continues to work on this in a number of ways, such as leading past scary areas and taking her out in the horsebox and riding her home. However, for the most part, Hannah arranges to ride out with someone else, which India is very happy to do. This means that India builds fitness and they both have a more enjoyable time.

Another example is Hannah's horse, Freckles, who loves flatwork but wasn't so keen on jumping. Since Hannah wanted to jump Freckles (and it's a great exercise for him), Hannah compromised by doing lots of flatwork with the occasional small jump each session. This kept the challenge low and achievable for Freckles and it enabled Hannah to work towards her goal of jumping with Freckles. This approach actually worked so effectively that Freckles is a very enthusiastic jumper these days, as long as the jumps stay small!

Celebrate your small successes and enjoy your time in the saddle, while slowly and steadily working towards your goals. When you both look forward to riding sessions, you will progress much faster as your

horse will truly be working with you. And that is an amazing feeling.

Work with your horse's preferences and strengths to build a successful and happy ridden partnership. Although anxious hacking alone, Hannah's mare India is confident riding out in company.

CONNECT THROUGH YOUR SEAT

As well as specific training techniques, connection in the saddle requires an awareness of your internal cues, too. They are even more important when you're riding than when you're working on the ground because your horse responds strongly to any tension, stiffness, or imbalance when you're in the saddle. Everyone has some imbalance or stiffness, and your horse will compensate for this in the way she moves. For example, if you sit more heavily on your right side, your horse will tend to move underneath your weight to keep you in balance, which means he will tend to fall in to the right. If you are tight through your hips and pelvis, which is common in riders, you will inhibit your horse's ability to fully lift his back and engage his hindquarters.

A lack of awareness of your internal cues can often cause conflict and tension in your horse. For example, if you are unaware that you sit to the right when riding, you will struggle to train your horse to turn left in balance, no matter how much you mark and reward it. Your external rein cue will be telling him to turn left, but your internal weight aid (sitting to the right) will be telling him to go right. If you cannot release the muscles in your back or shoulders, your horse will struggle to stretch down and move freely through his back. If you are out of balance and get left behind whenever your horse moves forward, you will struggle to teach your horse to move forward willingly.

Since healthy movement is fundamental to a positive ridden experience for your horse, it's important to work on your ridden posture to enable him to move in balance and with engagement, supporting his back to carry the rider.

Sophie Pickard demonstrates ridden tension with her horse, Elfine. You can see Sophie's back is arched and contracted, her knees have gripped and her heels come up because of the tension in her seat and hips and she has tension in her shoulders and down her arms. Elfine responds in kind, hollowing her back, lifting her head and taking short, tense strides. You can see her facial expression is not relaxed, either.

As Sophie released her back and pelvis, Elfine was able to do the same. Sophie is no longer braced through her back, but sitting with a neutral spine, enabling her to stay balanced and follow Elfine's movement. She has released the tension in her buttocks and pelvis, allowing her legs to hang softly under her seat. Likewise, she has dropped her shoulders and softened her arms, now following Elfine's movement with a soft contact. This has enabled Elfine to lengthen her stride, lift her back and stretch her top-line. You can see how much more relaxed her facial expression is in this more connected, comfortable position.

RIDER BODY AWARENESS EXERCISES

There is a huge amount of information available regarding rider biomechanics and the correct use of the seat and aids, with some teachers dedicating themselves to teaching people how to be balanced and effective in the saddle. As a rider, you will continue to study and improve the way you ride, but there are some basic exercises you can try, which create a great foundation of better body awareness, balance, and engagement in your riding and can have a profound effect on your horse.

DISMOUNTED EXERCISES

Before you even get onto your horse, you can work on your own posture and alignment. Regular Tai chi, yoga, Pilates and dance will keep you flexible, strong and improve your own body awareness and control, which will have a direct influence on your riding. Taking the time immediately before you mount to find your own alignment and become aware of your body is a great way to set yourself up for success in your ridden session.

BREATHING

So many riders hold their breath when they ride. Doing this causes and holds tension in the body, preventing you from moving freely with your horse. If you have a tense or excitable horse, you can often calm him down effectively by taking long, slow, deep breaths. Studies have shown that horses match their breathing and heart rate to that of their handler or rider, so this exercise is simple but powerful for a range of situations.

You can do this exercise when walking beside your horse or from the saddle. Breathe in for a count of 3 of your horse's steps. Then breathe out for 4 steps. Then breathe in for 4 steps and breathe out for 5 steps. You can play with how many steps to match your breath with, but the key is to always breathe out 1 step more than you breathe in. The longer your breaths, the calmer you and your horse get. The

shorter, the quicker you both get. So, this is a key to increasing and decreasing energy through your breath alone.

Once you've found your rhythm on the ground, it's time to mount and repeat the exercise ridden. In both situations, watch your horse's response. Does he give a long sigh out? Does she lower her head? Does his jaw relax and his lips loosen a bit? These relaxation signs show that your horse is responding to your breathing alone and becoming more relaxed.

VIDEO RESOURCE

BREATH CONNECTION IN THE SADDLE

Learn how to use your breath to keep your horse calm and connected right from the mounting block.

www.connectiontraining.com/video-resources

BECOME AWARE OF YOUR SEAT BONES

Increasing your body awareness helps you pinpoint problem areas and change them accordingly. As you're walking around on your horse, feel your seat bones in the saddle. Do they feel the same, or there is some difference in them? If there is a difference, it means you are heavier or tighter on one side or you have one hip further forward than the other. As you breathe in, just think of directing your breath more to the lighter side. This will change your diaphragm and increase the pressure slightly on that side. Your seat will become more even.

Also feel the rise and fall of your seat bones. As your horse moves, your seat bones will move with his hind legs. That is,

as the right hind leg pushes off the ground, your right seat bone is lifted; as the hind leg steps under, it drops. The same happens on the left when the horse moves his left leg. It feels like his ribcage is rocking side to side. Allow your seat bones to follow the movement so that they stay in equal contact with the saddle, both rising and falling. If you have tightness in one side, you will often feel the horse drop out of contact on that side as he places his foot. At this stage, just become conscious of it. If you try to alter it, you will add tension. Simply relax, breathe and wiggle your toes. Yes, we really mean that! Wiggling your toes in your boot helps to release tension in the hips. But it must only be your toes, not your ankle or foot. So, wiggle your toes and concentrate on your breath. Your hip will release as much as it can. If the stiffness is still too much for the hip to follow the hind leg movements, then you know you need to work on releasing that hip with bodywork and exercises.

Spend time working on feeling the rise and fall of your seat bones. This rhythm gives you information about where your horse's hind legs are. This will enable you to feel when your horse stops square or when to apply cues for transitions and lateral work. For example, applying a leg cue for stepping the hind leg under is ineffective if you apply it when the leg is on the ground as the horse cannot move that leg at that moment. You need to give the cue when the leg is lifting so the horse can place it correctly in response to your cue.

FIND YOUR NEUTRAL SPINE

Without training, many riders—just like horses—have a weak core and a tight back. If this is the case for you, it causes you to tighten up against big movement, such as the sitting trot, because the spine isn't supported enough to absorb the movement freely. Also, when you are tight in your back, you are unable to be truly balanced in the saddle and will often find yourself being thrown off balance. If your horse loses rhythm or spooks, your back will tighten further, and you'll get left behind or thrown forward or sideways. However, if you engage your abdominal muscles instead, your spine will have freer movement and your core will tighten to keep you in balance when the unexpected happens.

The process of finding a neutral spine is the same in the saddle as it is on the ground (see Chapter 10). It involves engaging the abdominals and lengthening your spine. Engaging your abdominals is a small movement: bring your belly button towards your spine and drop your tailbone down. If you put your hand in the small of

your back while you do this, you will feel your back press into your hand slightly (it's the opposite of arching your back). You need to engage your abdominals only slightly in walk, but you will need more in bigger movements. The engagement should not be forced and held tight; you should still feel your pelvis and back moving in rhythm with your horse.

Elongate your spine by lifting the back of your head. Feel that slight lengthening from your tailbone to your 'poll' (base of the skull). Many riders have been taught to sit up straight with the effect of contracting their back. If this is you, you might also have to lean your chest forward slightly as you engage your abdominals. This will prevent you from leaning back and being behind the movement (which causes you to get that slight jolt when your horse moves forward, especially unexpectedly).

Check that, when you lengthen, you lower and release your shoulder blades. Many of us habitually hunch one or both shoulders and you need to be aware of when you do that and actively drop your shoulder blades down your back. This will also soften your armpit and bring your elbows slightly forward, softening your hands and improving your sensitivity down the reins.

LENGTHEN YOUR LEGS

Tight hips and knees are common. They prevent the pelvis from moving freely and prevent you from being able to keep your heels down. If you have repeatedly been told to put your heels down but they always creep back up again, chances are a tightness in your hips is the problem. Allow your buttocks to relax and your legs to hang heavily from your hips. Really feel the weight of your feet in your stirrups. Feeling and keeping the weight in your seat bones and stirrups will keep you balanced over your horse's centre, especially through rising trot and unexpected spooking.

SOFTEN YOUR ARMS

Allow your shoulders to soften and hang freely and pay attention to what you can feel down the reins. This is your connection to your horse's very sensitive head or mouth. Your rein cues and communication should always be soft, light, and giving; by keeping your awareness in your hands, you'll improve your sensitivity down the reins.

Your arms should move with your horse's head. In walk and canter, your horse's head moves forward and back; your hands should follow this movement to keep the contact consistent and comfortable. The more engaged your horse becomes, the smaller this movement will be. In rising trot, your horse's head doesn't move much, but you do. Your arms must bend and straighten as you sit and rise to keep consistent contact down the reins. Soft shoulders and awareness of your hands will enable you to do this. A feeling of 'openness' in the armpits is a great way to ensure you have relaxed your arms and shoulders.

COMBINING INTERNAL AND EXTERNAL CUES IN YOUR TRAINING

The above exercises are the foundation of the rider's part of riding with connection. They are simple, but not necessarily that easy, especially when you try to do them all together! As you are practicing, remember to train yourself, too. Just pick one or two areas to focus on at a time, keep your sessions short, and repeat until you feel confident. Then add another area, and so on, until you can focus on them all together. This process will make you more balanced, softer, and more effective in the saddle.

Once you are connected through your seat, there are many different ways you

In a relaxed walk, focus on your internal cues. Here, you can see that Hannah's left seat bone has dropped as Toby steps under with his left hind and his barrel has rocked to the right. Allow your seat to gently follow this movement, rocking your pelvis from side to side each stride. You can also see that Hannah's shoulders are relaxed and her arms and hands are soft, following the movement of Toby's head and maintaining a light connection on the reins. She's also smiling – don't get too intense when you're doing this as that can create tension, so remember to breathe, smile and enjoy your ride!

can use your internal and external cues to help your horse through different movements. These include weight aids, positioning of your shoulders and hips, how you use your arms and reins, your focus and leg aids.

You can combine this work with the exercises training your horse. For example, if you're working on encouraging your horse to relax when ridden, take the time to use your breath and body to help your horse soften, too. If you feel your horse respond to the internal changes you make, you can mark and reward it. Or, if you're working on teaching your horse to bend around your leg on a circle and he's tensing up as you ask, bring your awareness to your body. Experiment with shifting your weight slightly in the saddle, release any areas of tension in your back or legs and focus on maintaining the rhythm of your seat bones as you ask your horse to turn. This will often be the key that enables your horse to turn smoothly, rhythmically and in balance and which leads to the moment you can reward. Understanding how to use your seat and cues effectively when riding is especially important as you progress to faster paces and more advanced movements.

You cannot separate your internal and external cues as your horse will be responding to your breathing, weight distribution and tension naturally. By rewarding your horse at moments when you notice him respond to the positive changes in your body will draw the attention of both of you to that moment and help you re-create that feeling together. In time, you will both become more tuned in to each other and will be able to respond

to increasingly subtle changes. This is a key element of true connection in the saddle.

Your internal and external cues need to be in alignment to give clear ridden signals to your horse.

VIDEO RESOURCE

STAYING CONNECTED THROUGH TRANSITIONS

With this new understanding of the rider's internal cues, watch this video again to see the difference this awareness makes to the quality of transitions.

www.connectiontraining.com/video-resources

THE ANXIOUS RIDER: CONNECTION CREATES CONFIDENCE

Understandably, many riders lack confidence in the saddle. This could be due to a previous fall or simply the fact that horses are large, powerful, and sometimes unpredictable animals. Just as you can build your horse's relaxation and confidence, you can build yours, too.

Riding a horse who is connected with you is the best way to feel safe in the saddle. It is the feeling that your horse won't respond when you ask him to slow down that makes riders feel anxious. A connected horse who is tuned in, enjoying being ridden, and is responding to your cues will certainly make you feel more confident when riding. However, this connection takes two. We've discussed techniques to boost your horse's confidence and enable him to stay soft and present in training sessions; as a rider, you need to do the same for yourself.

You will feel safe and confident when your horse is relaxed and listening to you, no matter the situation. Even without tack, Freckles is calm and connected to Hannah as she asks him to rein-back.

The most important thing when working on confidence is to be aware of your own emotional threshold. Pay attention to what makes you start to feel anxious, get butterflies in your stomach, and breathe more shallowly. It could be when you think about cantering or jumping or simply mounting. Wherever it is, you need to keep yourself below your threshold point so that you don't feel overwhelmed.

When changing your own emotional associations, the key is to make the experience successful and positive. If you push yourself and are anxious the whole time, getting off your horse will be a relief ('Phew! I made it!') and your emotional memory will be one of tension. You want to change this around so that you can't wait to ride and the memories associated with it are of relaxation and fun. Which means that you need to find ways to make it relaxing and fun, just as you do for your horse.

Our first suggestion for dealing with your fears is a meditation exercise. By reflecting on what scares you and focusing on your breathing, you slowly rewire your brain to build associations which are positive. The second method is a bit more cognitive. You also identify your scary situations but match them with when you are relaxed and create your own "comfort zone" map. This helps you to learn what relaxation feels like for you and your horse and helps you to practice feeling that way until it becomes your habitual feeling when riding. Both are highly successful techniques. You can choose which approach you prefer or try them both together.

MEDITATION EXERCISE

Perhaps there's a particular aspect of working with your horse that causes you to feel nervous, worried, and afraid. You don't want to be anxious about it, but you are! Just as you can train your horse to be calm in a fearful situation, you can train yourself, too. This meditation exercise can help you desensitise your brain to the cause of your fear.

1. Identify the situation that you're fearful about—for example, mounting your horse.

2. Write down your level of fear about doing this on a scale of 1 to 10, with 1 being totally relaxed and happy and 10 being terrified and feeling almost nauseous.

3. Sit down and take ten deep breaths. Each time breathe in for five counts and breathe out for six counts.

4. After ten breaths, continue to breathe deeply as you start to think of the scary situation you identified. Really explore the situation: Where would it happen? Who would be there? What sounds would you hear? What would you see? What would you feel?

5. As you think these scary thoughts, become aware of your breath. Breathe in for a longer count—perhaps six, seven, or even eight counts. Breathe out for one count longer than you breathed in. Take at least twenty breaths. Do NOT try to relax. Just breathe and count.

6. Return your breathing to normal and sit for another ten breaths.

7. Think of your fearful situation again, and score how anxious you feel about it now on the 1 to 10 scale.

You'll probably find that at the end of the exercise, your anxiety level stays the same as it was in the beginning or even goes up. This reflects your brain feeling anxious about the mental picture of the fearful stimulus. Just let it be until the next time you come back to the exercise (ideally, the next day). Go through the exercise again and check your anxiety score. It's likely to be lower than it was the first time. This is because the brain has processed the memory and stored it again with less fear attached to it.

WORKING ON THE FEAR FOR REAL

The next step is to start doing real things that engage your brain with the scary situation. You can start this after your first meditation session so the two will work side by side.

Let's take the mounting fear as our example. This was a real fear Rachel experienced after some serious falls. This is her story:

A couple of years after breaking my back from a fall, I started to learn tai chi for riding. This taught me to be aware of my breathing. Was it shallow or deep? Was it in my chest or in my belly? Was it fast or slow?

At the time, I was working on my rescued mare's saddling issues. Roisin would not stand still to be saddled and would turn her head and snap at the saddle, girth, and me. I had stopped trying to ride her and was using clicker training to help her overcome her problem.

The first morning I went to get the saddle after the tai chi course, I realised that I stopped breathing (held my breath) at the thought of getting the saddle. No wonder Roisin still had saddling issues! Without being aware of it, I was trying to retrain her when my anxiety was way over threshold. I was amazed and immediately realised that I had to work on myself first.

Using the meditation exercise outlined above, I started to identify the point where I actually felt calm. It was when I was doing sessions where I was not going to ride. So, I identified the first point of anxiety as the intention to saddle up.

I did the meditation again. The next day, when my anxiety level was normal while thinking about the saddle, I decided to go and look at the saddle but do nothing else. I became aware that even doing that raised my anxiety levels, so I went back to the meditation and worked on that. When that was okay, I then went to the tack room with no intention except to touch the saddle. I continued working this way. It took about two weeks of nearly daily practice until I was calm enough to bring the saddle out to Roisin.

Then I discovered an amazing thing. When I was truly totally relaxed in this way, Roisin displayed no anxiety at all about the saddle. She did not have an issue at all! She was simply reacting to my anxiety.

That was such an amazing revelation, and it gave me confidence to move forward more quickly with the saddling. But within a few days, Roisin was back to displaying anxiety, nipping at me again. What had happened? I checked my own anxiety levels but felt very confident. Then I realised I had made one change. I had put the girth on top of the saddle. It was bringing the saddle with the girth on top that had set Roisin's anxiety off again. She didn't have an issue about the saddle, but she had a huge fear about the girth and being girthed.

I then had to start working on her girthing issue, but since I had no anxiety about that, it was only her fear I had to deal with.

I'm sharing my story because it shows that horses are so sensitised to fear that they will easily pick up on your fear and start displaying fear behaviours. That's why it is vital that you sort out any fear you have in training. You MUST truly be relaxed when you train in order to see clearly what is going on with your horse. Otherwise, it is easy to believe that it is your horse's fear and not your own.

Rachel riding Roisin. Both were happy and confident by then, with Roisin standing at liberty to be tacked up and willingly presenting herself at the mounting block.

STAY IN YOUR COMFORT ZONE

In Chapter 1 we talked about the Connection Zone, when you and your horse are below threshold for fear, anxiety, rage, or excitement. You are both relaxed, in your comfort zones, and can think through problems without getting too anxious or frustrated. Keeping your horse in his comfort zone and below threshold is important for his enjoyment and confidence. The same is true for you.

The horse community in general urges riders to go out of their comfort zone as a matter of course. We've all heard advice along the lines of 'Ride him through it,' 'Get back straight on,' and 'Don't let him win.' In these situations, both horse and handler are often well over threshold, and neither is building positive associations or memories about the situation.

If you're over threshold, you will be unable to think clearly, and therefore will be reacting to the situation impulsively. This, of course, doesn't make you the best trainer for your horse in that moment, and there is little to be gained by pushing through it. In order to be the best possible trainer for your horse, you need to feel calm, confident, and clear. You can then set yourself up for success by making decisions that you feel comfortable with. For example, you can decide to work your horse in protected contact for a while or lead him out rather than ride him. You can choose to stay home rather than push yourself to take your horse to a clinic or competition. You can make sure you've got someone you trust to help you, and you can take the training slowly, proceeding only when you're comfortable.

A good connection relies on *both* of you being relaxed and joyful. This means you have to progress at the right speed for your partnership, ensuring both you and your horse are comfortable and confident with the situation. In some cases, you may have to slow down to help your horse build confidence. In others, you may have to make different decisions to ensure that your confidence remains strong. As you make the best decisions for both of you, your training will be increasingly successful. Your bond will become extraordinary too, as you learn to have complete trust in one another.

Since many of us have been involved in or witnessed horse accidents and near misses, it isn't surprising that we may feel anxiety when handling or riding horses. However, the key to confidence is identifying where you are confident and relaxed, then building from there in steps as small as you need to stay confident. Just like building your horse's confidence, you'll expand your comfort zone as you build new and positive experiences.

THE COMFORT ZONE EXERCISE

Here's a practice that will help you identify what being in the Comfort Zone feels like for you. You want to know this good feeling so well that as soon as you start to lose it, you pull back until you are back in the zone. This is the best way to learn how to keep you and your horse safe. It's also the best way to build that connection and have all your behaviours associated with feeling calm.

First, think of an activity you are working on, such as mounting. Then write down two easier steps that you do before you actually mount, and two steps you'll take after mounting. You will end up with five levels of difficulty. For example:

1. Stand at the mounting block.

2. Put weight in the stirrup.

3. Get on the horse.

4. Do rein flexions while mounted.

5. Walk a few steps to a cone.

Now we're going to fill in this diagram with these steps:

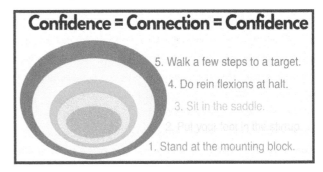

The easiest level is 'in the pink'. Pink is a soft and relaxing colour. The phrase 'in the pink' means being happy, healthy, and relaxed. The centre point is green. Green is also a relaxing colour, but we have associations with traffic lights and 'green for go', so there is more arousal associated with green than pink. The outermost layer is red—the universal warning colour, like the stop signal of traffic lights. Looking at red will actually increase your heart rate and blood pressure, so it indicates a place where you are heading to the edge of threshold.

Now think of the activity you placed in the green zone—in this case, mounting. As you think about the green layer, be aware of your breathing. Is it low and relaxed, or high and a bit anxious? Be aware of any thoughts in your mind. Do you have some breakthrough anxious thoughts, like 'What if something bad happens'? If so, just be aware of them.

Then think about the activity in the pink zone. Sit a few minutes thinking of that and be aware of your breathing and thoughts. What is the difference between this zone and the green zone? Remember, the green zone is where you thought you'd start training today. Do you have any anxieties about it at all? Or does it feel the same as the pink zone?

Often, we think we are starting at a point where we are completely relaxed. But when you do this exercise, you may realise you are more anxious about it than you thought. You feel calmer thinking about the activity in the pink zone. If this is the case, start with the activity that's in the pink and stay in the pink! Start where you are truly comfortable in that session. Progress through the session while keeping that feeling of being 'in the pink'. You may find you have a 'pink area' to work in, such as the gate end of the arena. You may feel you have 'pink circumstances' you need, such as no other horses in the arena. The aim of this exercise is to learn what it feels like to train while feeling truly comfortable.

It may be that you've overestimated the pink and need to go back a few more steps. That's great! The aim is to find the place where you are relaxed *and to learn how it feels*.

Do this exercise as often as necessary until you know how the pink zone feels for you and your horse. Notice the signs of relaxation your horse gives you when you're in the pink. Notice your own signs. Maybe you smile more; maybe you slow down; maybe you get more creative.

When you know how good it feels in the pink, you will train more and more with this relaxation, and then the magic happens. You have gone slower and—wow! —you are getting there quicker. More and more situations feel fine and comfortable. More and more times, your horse calms down quickly and tunes in to you.

Your pink area will expand as you progress, and you will also feel more comfortable moving into the blue and green areas. You have created a good buffer around your threshold. The red is far away! Very quickly, though, the activity that you had put in the red will appear in the green and then the pink zones. You will progress with great connection. But on the bad days, the difficult days, you will have a pink zone to retreat to and can finish on a good note.

VIDEO RESOURCE

SUCCESS IN YOUR COMFORT ZONE

Rachel explains how you can best create success from within your comfort zone.

www.connectiontraining.com/video-resources

Rachel and Hannah living a dream - cantering calmly on a beach! It took a combination of horse and rider awareness to ensure that no-one was pushed over threshold during the training or on the beach trip. The training steps worked with this awareness to build confidence and trust in both horses and riders.

VIDEO RESOURCE

CANTERING ON THE BEACH

Rachel and Hannah discuss all the steps it took for them canter calmly on the beach.

www.connectiontraining.com/video-resources

DISMOUNT TO FEEL SAFE AND RELAXED

As you're creating a bonded partnership between you and your horse, you need to stay within your Comfort Zone. So, no matter what anyone else says, you need to learn what truly feels comfortable and relaxed to you. From there, you can work to desensitise and counter-condition your horse's fears, knowing that you are not adding to them, but are the source of calmness and confidence for your horse. While you are riding, if you have any doubt about the way things are going, dismount! This is key to building your confidence and enjoyment in riding. Perhaps you get on and everything goes well for a while, until it doesn't. Maybe something startles your horse or one of you begins to get confused and a little worried. Whatever the cause, if you start to lose that connection and feel at all anxious, hop off immediately.

There is a lot of pressure in the traditional horse world to stay mounted no matter what. If you dismount, you are often told you are 'letting the horse win'. Well, first, that assumes your horse doesn't want you on his back in the first place and will find it more reinforcing if you're on the ground. Second, we feel that everybody wins if you take the steps needed to keep both you and your horse calm, safe, and tuned in. Conversely, everybody loses if the situation turns into any kind of fight. So be a winner—do whatever you need to make it

another successful ride for you both. You will find this approach gets you much further faster and makes the journey enjoyable, too.

You can also make the decision not to mount at all. Maybe you make your plans, tack your horse up but find that he's excitable, disconnected or reactive in the session. To prioritise the success of the session for both of you, it might be best to work on the ground until next time, when you can have a more connected and positive ride.

In time, you and your horse gain confidence, maintain balance, and stay connected in a wider range of situations. As you improve your horse's responsiveness to your ridden cues and understand how to calm and rebalance him, you'll also be able to get that connection back if you start to lose it, without having to dismount. Give yourself and your horse the time and tools to have fun together, and your confidence will grow naturally.

VIDEO RESOURCE

CONNECTION CREATES CONFIDENCE

Watch this video to see Rachel work with CT Coach, Claire Waldron, to keep her horse's focus when riding outside of the arena, building the rider's confidence.

www.connectiontraining.com/video-resources

CHAPTER 13

SOLVING RIDDEN BEHAVIOURAL PROBLEMS

Behavioural problems under saddle include everything from pulling, shying, spooking and napping to rushing, bolting, bucking, and rearing. When addressing ridden behavioural problems, we like to strip the behaviour down to find the root cause: at what point did the horse begin to show tension? From here, you can work out the triggers of the horse's fear and begin to change those emotional associations to relaxation and enthusiasm. In this Chapter, we will address some common causes of ridden issues and explore training solutions.

CAUSE: PAIN AND DISCOMFORT

Pain, or the memory of pain, is the most common cause for any behavioural problems in horses and is especially relevant to ridden issues. If your horse is showing any tension when being tacked up, mounted or ridden, a physical check up by a vet or healthcare professional is the first step.

Well-fitting tack is of the utmost importance. An uncomfortable saddle will prevent your horse from moving correctly and will make being ridden unpleasant, no matter how many extra rewards you give.

We don't recommend tack that inhibits your horse's communication with you. Gadgets such as flash nosebands, long shank bits, martingales, and side reins all prevent your horse from moving and expressing himself freely. They can also cover up the symptoms of a problem, making it more difficult to find the root cause.

If your horse is showing avoidance or tension around a certain piece of equipment, he could be telling you it's uncomfortable. If that's the case, you will need to replace it with something your horse prefers. If discomfort doesn't seem to be the issue, you'll need to take the time to rebuild more positive associations with the equipment.

When positive associations have been developed effectively, horses show a lot of enthusiasm when presented with their head collar or tack. We have seen many horses trained with Connection Training come straight over when they see their tack, stick their head into the bridle, and grab the bit themselves. This is a great sign that they are happy in their tack and keen to be ridden.

Does your horse show tension when being tacked up? This could be a sign of uncomfortable tack. Ensure your horse is happy to stand calmly while you tack up before working on ridden issues.

When you're re-training your horse to be relaxed and confident after pain issues, take the time your horse needs at each stage, such as tacking up, mounting, different gaits, different riders etc. It will take many positive experiences to change those negative emotions and for your horse to trust that being ridden will be pain-free, relaxing and fun.

This is Leonera, a rescued mare, being re-trained at the mounting block, learning that it's now a relaxing and enjoyable experience.

The rider also has a strong influence on the comfort of the horse. Riders who are too heavy for the horse to carry comfortably, or who are unbalanced, tense or in the habit of giving heavy aids, will cause discomfort and fear for the horse, leading to potential behavioural problems. As discussed in the previous Chapter, the rider's physical role is important in creating a positive experience for the ridden horse.

Horses may also experience pain when being ridden at certain times, such as when a mare is in season or if they are suffering with metabolic issues. If your horse's behaviour changes suddenly, it is usually due to pain. For example, if a horse who usually lines up happily to be tacked up and mounted, displays tension such as nipping when being girthed or avoiding the mounting block, she is likely in some discomfort. By listening to your horse in these moments, you will prevent unintentionally causing more problems by pushing on through the pain.

RE-TRAINING AFTER PAIN ISSUES

Once you are sure your horse is not currently feeling any pain or discomfort, your horse could still demonstrate tension due to the memory or pain and the negative associations with riding. For example, a horse who bucks in canter may be found to be suffering from back pain.

Once he has received treatment, he may still be tense in canter as he now associates canter with pain. This will still cause his FEAR system to be triggered when asked to canter, even though there is no longer any pain.

Through training, you can replace your horse's anxiety with more positive emotions, using systematic desensitisation and counter conditioning techniques (Chapter 5). In practice, this means that you will expose your horse to the lowest level possible of the negative stimulus and begin to weigh the scales towards more positive emotions.

In the canter scenario, you could begin by lightly giving your cue for canter. This could be enough for the horse to show signs of tension such as lifting his head, pinning his ears or swishing his tail as he anticipates going up into the painful gait. Instead, don't let him complete the transition; instead, just ask him to continue trotting. Once he's relaxed, you can stop and reward him. Repeat this sequence, hinting at the canter but not transitioning up to it, until your horse remains relaxed as he even thinks about going up into the canter - and, of course, reward him highly. This process is beginning to change your horse's emotions at the prospect of canter from fear to relaxation.

Don't move on from this stage until your horse is showing you that he wants to go up into the canter. As you make thoughts of canter rewarding, he will begin to ask if he can transition upwards - this is the point that you know you've tipped the scales in favour of canter and your horse is ready for the next stage.

Hannah's pony, Toby, started bucking in canter when he developed some pain in his back. After fixing the physical cause, it still took some time for Toby to trust that canter was going to be comfortable, so Hannah had to re-train the canter slowly. As Toby had more positive canter experiences, he became confident and willing to canter once again.

The key in overcoming negative emotional associations like this is to take it slowly. In order for your horse to show extreme behaviour in response to a specific situation, he has either had many negative experiences with that stimulus or a highly traumatic one. If your horse has been feeling pain in canter for weeks or even months before it is addressed, you will not overcome his fear in one session. Regardless of the memories of pain or discomfort you are helping your horse to overcome, take your time to thoroughly change the emotions at each stage. Go slower to get there faster.

CAUSE: LACK OF UNDERSTANDING

One of the potential causes of behavioural problems is confusion. So often when horses are described as 'difficult', 'stubborn', or 'balking', they simply don't understand what you're asking for. Increasing the pressure is like shouting in your own language to foreigners; it's not going to help them understand and will only cause you both to get frustrated, scared, or angry. Even if your horse has responded correctly a few times, it doesn't mean that the cue and the behaviour are linked strongly enough for your horse to be able to do the behaviour every time you ask. You may think the horse understands what is being asked, but the horse is confused.

TRAINING SOLUTION: CLARITY

In this case, you want to bring clarity to the horse. You can do this by re-establishing the behaviour on the ground first, using objects or an extra person to help explain to the horse what you'd like him to do. Break it right down to the smallest steps and ensure your horse is clear and confident at each stage as you build it back up. If confusion is the cause of the problem, once he understands, he'll be happy to do as you ask.

Hannah has a story from one of her clients to illustrate this:

I was called out to help with a child's pony who was new to this family. The pony, Lily, was only six years old and quite green. She was great when hacking out with other ponies, but when her young owner tried to ride her in the field she would ignore the rein cues, take off to the edge of the field, and sometimes even just lie down!

When we broke the behaviour down, it turned out that Lily simply didn't know how to turn from a rein cue. We guessed that she'd only been hacked out in her previous home, where she was able to follow the horse in front. So, her rider dismounted, and we taught Lily how to bend her head from a rein cue on the ground. Then we used targets to help give Lily focus and guidance as she learned what the rein cues meant in the saddle. Gradually, we moved her away from the targets until she didn't need them anymore. Now that she understood what was being asked, she stopped running off and lying down and was happy to be ridden in the field.

CAUSE: LACK OF BALANCE OR PHYSICAL ABILITY

Balance in horse and rider is essential to enable the horse to move comfortably and confidently when ridden. Because horses are prey animals, being fully in control of their balance and movement is of the utmost importance to them so they can escape predators. Losing that balance and control is scary to them, which is why it leads to behavioural problems.

Horses usually respond to lack of balance in one of two ways. The first is speeding up, which includes rushing, bolting, and bucking. The other is to slow down and be reluctant to go forward. The horse who does this is protecting himself from losing his balance, since he knows that going forward is likely to be uncomfortable and unnerving. This resistance can escalate into planting, running backwards, and even rearing. However, a loss of balance can be subtle. A horse who struggles to slow the walk could easily be out of

balance and falling on the shoulders. On circles, the horse will fall out or fall in. The trot will be out of rhythm and rushed. In canter, this loss of balance often leads to bucking through the transition.

TRAINING SOLUTION: BUILD PHYSICAL FITNESS

If lack of balance is causing the problem behaviour, you can solve it with exercises that teach your horse to become more body aware, supple, and collected (see Chapters 10 and 11). Often the best approach is to first teach and establish balance on the ground, since the horse doesn't have to worry about the weight of the rider or be anxious or tense about being ridden. Once your horse is calmer and moving more in balance on the ground, you can begin to introduce these exercises in the saddle. Since your balance greatly affects your horse, work on your riding technique to help your horse out, as well (see Chapter 12).

For your horse to be successful, you need to choose exercises appropriate to his fitness level. If you suspect he is not fit or strong enough to easily complete your requests, make it physically easier and see

This mare came to her owner, Sophie, with a lot of issues regarding riding. She was very tense and would often pin her ears, throw her head up and rush forwards. She was unbalanced and uncoordinated and this loss of balance would cause anxiety leading to her tension and rushing.

As Sophie worked through exercises to build her horse's balance, body awareness strength, the horse relaxed and stopped rushing off. Because she found this process quite challenging, we used objects and rewards to give her clarity and motivation.

if he becomes more relaxed and willing. Gradually increase the challenge level of the exercises as your horse's fitness level builds.

CAUSE: LACK OF MOTIVATION

Boredom, drilling, lack of choice and consistent mild punishment can create a lack of motivation in many riding horses. They will drag their feet to the arena, step away from the mounting block, do as little as possible in their ridden sessions and constantly nap to the gate.

Hannah experienced this with her own pony, Toby:

After years of traditional schooling, Toby had come to see arena work as no fun at all. Although he would light up at the prospect of hacking out or jumping, he had no enthusiasm at all for schooling in an arena. He would not go forwards at all unless I was carrying a whip - I didn't have to use it but I did need the threat of it to coax him into reluctant work. It wasn't a joyful experience for either of us and we made very limited progress as he consistently did as little as he could in our schooling sessions.

TRAINING SOLUTION: FIND THE FUN

In this situation, you need to build your horse's motivation and enjoyment of being ridden. Add in games, such as riding to targets and through pole exercises to add interest. Keep your riding sessions short and rewarding - perhaps you simply mount, walk a few steps, give your horse a big reward and jump off to end the session there. This will take your horse by surprise and begins to tip those scales towards

Use poles, objects and stationary targets to add interest and variety to your sessions and increase your horse's motivation. Reward your horse highly and with the best treats for ridden behaviours. Keep your ridden sessions really short and highly rewarding. All of these techniques will increase your horse's joy, enthusiasm and willingness to be ridden.

enthusiasm as your horse discovers that being ridden is the easiest and more rewarding behaviour. If your horse prefers hacking or groundwork to being ridden in the school, an effective approach is often to switch your training sessions around. Begin with riding and, when your horse has given you some good work under saddle, hop off and do some groundwork, or leave the arena and hack out. By doing this, you are rewarding your horse for the ridden work with an exercise he prefers, which will build his enthusiasm and enjoyment of the ridden work itself.

Many horses who shut down when ridden also need to know they've got a voice in the situation, so giving your horse choice when you ride instead of insisting on a specific response can boost his enthusiasm and willingness to participate. It was certainly a key element for Hannah and Toby:

As I began to use more reward-based training with Toby, other behaviours were improving hugely but riding wasn't, which really highlighted just how shut down and uninterested he was in being ridden in the arena. I decided to change everything to see if I could change how he felt about it. I stopped nagging him to respond. Instead, I would mount, gently ask him once to walk on... and then wait. He didn't move and I didn't insist. This was new for him and he would stand for ages, sometimes seeming to doze for a while. He would then abruptly wake up again and deliberately take a step or two forward. At which point, I would jackpot him, jump off and end our ride for the day! This was really hard for me because if I nagged and insisted, we could do some passable dressage, but I didn't want it to feel like a fight any longer. It was very disheartening to only walk a step or two each session. I also found his dozing off frustrating and wanted to wake

him up and insist he paid attention. However, I felt it was very important at the time to let him choose to engage or not and I now know that he was showing signs of stress in relation to the riding which had been suppressed.

We continued with this for a couple of (very long!) months, gradually seeing more prompt responses and enthusiasm from Toby. In the end, it felt like a switch as he suddenly became animated and enthusiastic. In fact, once he realised he wasn't going to be coerced, he threw himself joyfully into the work and he spent a few weeks just wanting to canter everywhere!

This profound turnaround in Toby's emotions regarding riding lasted until his retirement from riding when he was 25. Those few months were extremely difficult at the time, but they gave us years of fun together that we wouldn't otherwise have had. Toby came to love dressage and the strength and suppleness he gained through it gave him a new lease of life in his late teens.

For your horse to say a true "yes", you have to let them say, "no". This can be hard to do but is certainly worth it because when your horse wants to ride as much as you do, there is no better feeling in the world.

*Toby became highly motivated in his ridden schooling in his late teens,
thanks to reward-based fun and choice under saddle.*

VIDEO RESOURCE

FROM PROBLEMS TO PERFORMANCE

Hannah tells her story with her pony, Toby, who led her journey through best management and training techniques. This culminated in Connection Training – it wouldn't exist without Toby!

www.connectiontraining.com/video-resources

CAUSE: FEAR

A frightened or overexcited horse is much more likely to be unpredictable, spooky, or explosive. In addition, riding often takes your horse to unfamiliar territory loaded with scary triggers, from spooky objects and traffic on the trail to crowds of people, loud noises, and strange horses at shows.

TRAINING SOLUTION: RIDDEN DE-SPOOKING EXERCISES

De-spooking exercises will help enormously. Chapter 5 explained de-spooking exercises you can do on the ground and we recommend you work on these first. These techniques can transfer to work in the saddle too. As your horse relaxes, stays tuned in to you, and becomes emotionally and physically balanced, he will be a much safer and more fun ride.

Since fear issues are so common, we will explain different exercises you can use to build your horse's confidence under saddle in different situations.

DE-SPOOKING UNDER SADDLE

NOVEL OBJECTS

When de-spooking your horse for riding, you want her to feel relaxed when you encounter novel objects from dressage markers at a competition, to spooky objects you might need to pass when out hacking. The more confident your horse is when exploring and passing novel items, the calmer she will be in general. When working on ridden de-spooking exercises, begin in your own arena or field. Start small and build from there. You will be more successful if you don't overwhelm your horse, but instead build her confidence progressively.

First, let your horse explore new objects while you're leading her. For example, you might place some traffic cones in your arena or set up obstacles such as a tarpaulin or a pile of logs.

After your horse gets used to the objects, mount and repeat the exercise. Even if she seemed confident when you were on the ground, she can become more anxious when you mount because it's a change in context, so take it slowly.

India spooked at the rolled-up tarp at the side of the arena, so Hannah quietly asked her to approach it. Because India is a naturally reactive and spooky horse, Hannah has done a lot of de-spooking exercises over the years.

This history gave India the confidence to explore the tarp, although she was wary. Close up, India realised what it was and immediately offered to stand on it since she has done a lot of work walking over tarps as part of her de-spooking training! After this, India was happy to be ridden past the tarp for the remainder of the session.

Reward your horse for approaching scary objects, but don't push her to get so close that she panics and wheels away. Instead, take her to the point where she's looking at the object. Then, at halt, ask for small behaviours such as rein flexions, targeting your feet, a rein-back step, and so on. These behaviours will help your horse focus on you instead of the object. You will feel when she relaxes. Reward that relaxation, then take her away before returning to the object again. Repeat until your horse is confident to explore the object calmly while you are mounted.

As your horse becomes more confident while exploring the objects, you can begin to ride around them. Reward your horse for ignoring the objects and listening to you instead. This process builds well for being able to pass spooky items in future.

Throughout all of India's de-spooking training, Hannah has worked on keeping India under threshold. India has had a tendency to go up to spooky items too fast and then scare herself and spin away from them. Now, Hannah knows when to stop India a little distance away and help to relax at that point before approaching any closer. The de-spooking work on the ground has been invaluable for teaching this safely before transferring to de-spooking under saddle.

HACKING OUT

Once your horse is comfortable doing these exercises at home, it's time to venture out on the trail. When you begin to take your horse out into the world, the context shifts again, so you need to make it easier for your horse to be successful while he gains confidence. Your aim is to change your horse's emotions associated with leaving his home from fear to fun. Therefore, you need to build it up slowly and create positive experiences for your horse when he leaves his yard.

Rachel hacking out on Heather.

When you first start this process, take your horse on lots of mini rides. Horses usually get increasingly anxious as they get further away from home. So, to prevent trigger stacking, you might begin with taking your horse just outside the gate and playing his favourite games and giving him lots of rewards. When you feel him settle somewhat, turn around and take him back home. By doing this, you won't overwhelm your horse and he will have had a positive experience in leaving home, beginning to tip the scales in favour of hacking out. He will be more eager the next time you go. Gradually increase the distance you venture as your horse gains confidence.

Your horse will be more confident going out when following a lead. If you can ride out with a calm lead horse and supportive friend, that's great. But, if you don't have that opportunity, you can be the lead for your horse by beginning to build his confidence exploring world by leading him rather than riding him.

Following an older, calm lead horse can be a great way to build your horse's confidence when hacking out. However, if this isn't possible, you can be the lead for your horse, instead, by dismounting until he gains confidence.

As you lead your horse out, look for any object that you can ask your horse to explore. Make it a game for you and your horse and reward him for playing. Target road signs, dustbins or garbage cans, and tree branches. Turn speed bumps, road markings, puddles, and rocks into mats by asking your horse to stand on them. Lead him up and down banks, circle around trees, and ask for lateral movements along the road or in a field. All these activities change both your and your horse's perception of the world: instead of being filled with scary objects, it's filled with potential games and opportunities for reward.

Look for opportunities to make going out fun and build your horse's confidence. Freckles was worried about this new road sign until he realised it was a target!

As you and your horse grow in confidence while leading, you can begin to mount. Because of all the work you've done at the mounting block, your horse will line up for you to get on anywhere—tree stumps, benches, stone walls, or whatever you happen to find.

Thanks to all the work you've done building connection at the mounting block, your horse will now line up for you to mount, no matter what you find to stand on.

If your horse is reluctant to line up at any point, it could be a sign that she is not feeling confident enough for you to ride right now. This is a great way for horses to communicate that they are feeling anxious and preventing themselves from going over threshold. If this happens, spend some more time on the ground working on relaxation and connection and try again later.

DISMOUNTING CAN BUILD CONNECTION AND TRUST

Ride as long as you and your horse feel confident but get off again if you encounter something spooky or you feel your horse is disconnecting. Remember, you want to create positive emotional associations with hacking out for your horse, so pushing him on when he's worried will work against your training. However, if you dismount and lead him from the ground, you will build his trust in you, making a stronger partnership and creating a positive experience. This increases the likelihood your horse will have the confidence to be ridden past the scary thing next time.

It is common for riders to be told that they must stay on or the horse is 'winning'. In our view, you and your horse are working together, not against each other. A negative experience for either of you results in you both 'losing'. Making the decision to dismount to keep you both calm, safe and confident will create a positive experience and a big 'win' for both of you.

Leading your horse is a great way to build confidence and trust. If either of you get tense, dismount and reconnect until you are both calm enough to continue riding on calmly. Success is a positive experience for both of you!

ENCOURAGE EXPLORATION

A great way to make going out both enriching and enjoyable for your horse is to encourage him to explore his surroundings. He will love the opportunity to smell strange horse droppings and browse plants he doesn't have access to at home. It is a lovely way to bond with your horse, as well, as you explore the world together. This is one of the most natural ways to provide enrichment for your horse.

Exploring the world is enriching for your horse and promotes his health, happiness and well-being.

CALM AND CONNECTED

The more positive experiences you both have while out and about, the calmer you will both become. You'll be able to stay connected as you go out longer, further, and into gradually more challenging environments. You won't need to keep your horse's focus by asking to him to do lots of different behaviours or rewarding him all the time, as he will be able to stay relaxed and connected as he continues along the trail. As you progress into more difficult situations, you may need to go back to easy behaviours with him in order to help him stay calm and relaxed.

For example, Hannah's horses, Freckles and India, were used to hacking along roads, tracks and fields but the first time they set foot in a stubble field got them very excited. To prevent them going over threshold and disconnecting from their riders, she worked on relaxing them through circles and bending at walk, rewarding them for moments of softness and connection. They quickly calmed down, tuned in and stopped pulling for a gallop. The riders repeated this for a few days until the horses expected to stay calm and relaxed in the stubble field - then they could canter calmly while staying connected.

Hannah and her friend worked on rewarding the horses for walking calmly in the stubble field to keep them relaxed and connected in this environment. Once they could stay relaxed in walk, they were able to move up to trot and canter without the horses getting over-excited .

VIDEO RESOURCE

BUILD CONFIDENCE AND CONNECTION HACKING OUT

Learn how to keep your horse relaxed and tuned in when hacking out on the trail.

www.connectiontraining.com/video-resources

TRAFFIC TRAINING

If you're training your horse to get used to traffic, repeat the process of setting up a training session at home where you can manage the environment before taking the training into the real world. Have a friend drive a vehicle at a slow speed and safe distance from your horse. Reward your horse for staying calm and responding to your cues instead of getting worried about the vehicle.

Gradually, your friend can drive closer and make the vehicle spookier by having the radio blaring, revving the engine, and even honking the horn. If you have access to bigger vehicles, you can practice the same exercise with trailers and tractors.

Training a horse in your own arena means you can manage the situation as you build her confidence. Melanie Watson, of Instinctive Horse Training, is helping this mare to overcome her traffic fear.

Throughout this process, progress only when your horse is truly confident, not just holding it together. Practice this exercise until your horse actively enjoys traffic training at home. Then you know you've counter-conditioned it properly!

When your horse is ready to venture out onto the streets, have a helper on the ground to give your horse extra guidance as she builds her confidence. Although you can mark your horse for standing quietly as she is passed by traffic, it is good practice to wait until the vehicle has passed and your horse is relaxed before you feed. You don't want your horse to spook away from the traffic when you're in a vulnerable feeding position. If you reward your horse regularly when passed by traffic, she'll learn that coming traffic is an indicator of good things. This is a great way to change your horse's emotions from fear when she hears a car to pleasant anticipation.

Feed your horse only once the traffic has passed and your horse is relaxed so that you're not in a vulnerable feeding position when your horse may spook.

Even if your horse is confident in most traffic, there may be occasions when you need to dismount in order to keep her calm. This is often the case as you encounter unusual traffic such as lorries, tractors, quad bikes and motorbikes. If you hear or see a vehicle coming and you are worried about how your horse might react, dismount and stand quietly between your horse and the traffic; this will both give your horse confidence and keep you out of the way if your horse spooks away from the vehicle. As your horse experiences a greater variety of vehicles and discovers that they all result in rewards, he will lose his fear and will be safe to ride as they pass.

This horse, Bobby, had an extreme fear of large vehicles. When she heard this one coming, his owner, Lorna Butterworth, dismounted. The friendly driver could see Bobby's anxiety and kindly waited a few minutes to allow Bobby to explore it and pass it quietly. This created another positive experience for Bobby and large vehicles to help him overcome his fear.

VIDEO RESOURCE

TEACH YOUR HORSE TO BE CALM IN TRAFFIC

Watch CT guest, Melanie Watson of Instinctive Horse Training, teach an anxious horse to be confident when ridden in traffic.

www.connectiontraining.com/video-resources

SHOWS AND OTHER EVENTS

Gradually prepare your horse for events so that your horse remains calm, confident and connected without going over threshold. This rescued mare, Elfine, used to get very worried about travelling and going to new places. Her owner, Sophie, worked with her through exercises such as de-spooking, loading and travelling and calm groundwork and riding to build Elfine's confidence and their communication together. When Sophie started to travel Elfine, she would go just a short distance to a quiet location or friend's house and make it a positive experience for Elfine, working in-hand, allowing her to graze and spend time with friends' calm, older horses. As Elfine became more experienced and confident that it would be a fun experience, they were able to go further afield and to more high energy situations. Here, they are competing in an endurance competition – this is enjoyable for both of them as Elfine arrives calm, is happy to stand quietly at the trailer and stays connected to Sophie throughout. They both love to do this together.

To help a green or anxious horse become confident in a show environment, begin by finding the smallest approximation of an event and create connection and confidence there. For example, you might take the horse to a friend's yard to experience being in a different environment around strange horses. For a green horse, this is often enough to cause excitement and anxiety. Your job is to help the horse have a positive experience he will want to repeat. Practice asking for all his favourite behaviours in this new environment, rewarding him for listening to you instead of being distracted by what's going on around him. Anxious horses often calm down once they are allowed to move around a little, so lead or lunge your horse rather than insisting that he stand still.

Practice visiting your friend's yard until your horse is calm and connected as soon as he unloads there. Then it's time to take him to a slightly busier event, such as a low-key competition, and repeat the same steps there. You won't be competing yet; you are there to help your horse relax in a show environment. Simply lead him around or find a quiet corner for groundwork. As your horse gains experience in being calm and relaxed in different, busy environments, he will grow in confidence and be ready to stay connected no matter where you take him.

Freckles became very anxious and excited when taken to a small local competition yard for practice. There were lots of strange horses and people around and different activities in each arena. Hannah dismounted to give him more confidence and, since Freckles was high energy and unable to stand still, asked him to settle while lunging. Because he has a strong reinforcement history with working calmly on the lunge, this helped him to relax and tune in. Once he was calm, Hannah mounted and was able to ride him and stay connected and safe.

CASE STUDY: PREPARING FOR AN EVENT

Hannah was asked to attend a St George's day event with her horse Freckles. Hannah was to be St George, and Freckles was to be her noble steed. This was to be a family event with lots of children, crowds, and noise. The organisers wanted Hannah to ride up on Freckles and for him to stand on a pedestal and wave a flag.

Although Hannah had previously done some work getting Freckles out and about to horsey events, they had never done anything like this before, and he was still young and green. So, Hannah worked through a series of steps to prepare him for the event. She began this de-spooking work at home using flags, bunting and loudspeakers. She then took him on regular outings to local venues which simulated a large family event, but where she could take Freckles to a safe distance and introduce him gradually. These included riding through local villages, visiting the local country school at break time, taking him to her local town on market day and, finally, riding up and down a bridleway alongside a theme park (next to the rollercoasters!).

Throughout, Hannah's aim was to help Freckles enjoy these outings, so she worked on keeping him under threshold, staying focused on her and practiced many of his favourite behaviours, such as playing fetch, targeting and letting him graze lush grass verges.

Her work paid off and Freckles was calm and connected throughout the madness of the St George's day celebrations!

VIDEO RESOURCE

TRAINING FOR AN EVENT

You can find out more about Hannah's process to de-spook and prepare Freckles for the event, as well as the event itself in this video.

www.connectiontraining.com/video-resources

RESTARTING UNDER SADDLE

If your horse's ridden behaviour problems are extreme or dangerous and you feel your horse is not able to connect with you at all when you ride, you may need to strip everything down and restart your horse under saddle from the very beginning. Maybe your horse had an accident under saddle that has destroyed his ridden confidence completely. Perhaps you have a rescued horse, or one whose history is unknown, who is clearly terrified of anything related to riding. Maybe your horse didn't have the best start under saddle and is tense and disconnected when ridden, leading to extreme behaviours. Whatever the cause, you can use Connection Training to restart your horse in a way that is calm, relaxed, connected, and enjoyable for both of you.

Restarting a horse involves the same process as starting a horse under saddle for the first time (as discussed in the next Chapter.) The only difference is that restarting often takes a little longer because you must overcome the negative emotions that your horse already has about riding. Take the time to retrain each step along the way until your horse is no longer afraid, but relaxed and enjoying the process instead. With patience, you'll have fun and strengthen your bond with your horse in the process.

VIDEO RESOURCE

FROM RESCUE TO RIDDEN

Claire Waldron, a CT Coach, shares her story of re-starting her rescued mare under saddle and overcoming their fear together.

www.connectiontraining.com/video-resources

CHAPTER 14

STARTING YOUR HORSE UNDER SADDLE

Traditionally, starting a young horse under saddle (also known as 'backing a horse') is seen as a difficult and dangerous process best left to the professionals. But the Connection Training way is calm, relaxed, progressive, and easy all the way through. You shouldn't see any dramas like rearing, bucking, or running around in terrified circles, with the horse way over threshold. This means you can start your own horse and keep her at home throughout the process. This prevents bad lifetime associations with riding that could be created by the separation anxiety of being trained away from her familiar environment and herd.

If you're re-starting your horse due to problem-behaviours and high levels of tension or fear under saddle, going through this process at home allows you to take all the time your horse needs to become calm, confident and happy to be ridden.

PHYSICAL MATURITY

Horses take a long time to mature physically and carrying a rider puts extra pressure on their body. You need to wait for them to reach physical maturity before riding them regularly to avoid joint injury. Use their earlier years to prepare your horse for a smooth transition into being ridden. The more you teach him, the better he'll be at problem-solving and impulse control, so train easy handling, in-hand leading out, de-spooking, long-reining and lunging before riding him. When working with young horses, keep the sessions short to help keep them focused and ensure you don't overwork immature joints.

As you work with your youngster, you'll create a great relationship with your horse on the ground. Young horses, trained through Connection Training from the start, feel confident with people, are great at solving problems, and love to learn. This sets your horse up to be a fantastic ridden horse.

Begin riding your horse when she's physically mature to ensure she stays sound and comfortable for years to come. In the meantime, preparatory work with your youngster will build confidence, communication and physical fitness to make a smooth transition to riding. Here, Hannah works on some body awareness exercises with 3-year-old India.

Working through some gymnastic groundwork exercises is the best way to prepare your horse for being ridden. Improving your horse's balance, body awareness and control will help him to feel confident with new sensations of carrying a rider. Teaching your horse how to move with relaxation and engagement will make being ridden comfortable from the start. Working at a trot and canter on the ground first will teach your horse how to stay connected at these higher paces. This work combines to make the transition to being ridden smoother, easier and safer for both of you.

INTRODUCING SADDLES

Introduced in the right way, you can create positive emotions associated with tack from the very start. Unfortunately, it's common to see young horses galloping around on a lunge line, bucking in terror, as someone straps a saddle to them for the first time. Instead, take your time with your young horse. Gradually introduce ropes, stirrups, surcingles and saddle pads, asking your horse to target them and to stand quietly while you rub her all over with them. You can practice dropping them on the floor around your horse's feet, walking with them laid over her back and making them trail and jangle. Pay attention to your horse's emotional state to keep her under threshold and enjoying the experience. Reward her highly - you want her tack to be associated with feel-good emotions.

Once your horse is completely relaxed at this stage, you can introduce the saddle. With this preparation, your horse should see the saddle as an extension of the work you've done already and be relaxed and happy for you to place it on her back.

You can take your de-sensitisation work a step further and practice sliding the saddle around on your horse's back, even under her stomach. By building up to it through positive, systematic training, your horse will learn that it is nothing to be worried about. If we wanted our horses to carry their saddles under their belly, we'd all train for it - your horse doesn't know that it's supposed to be on her back, except that that's what she has been trained for. Taking the time to teach her that it's nothing to worry about when it's underneath her instead will prevent her from being frightened if it ever happens by accident in future. You can even train the saddle slipping as a cue to stop for extra safety.

Hannah at a live demonstration with her mare, India, who was 3 at the time, demonstrating training her to be calm and relaxed in the event of the saddle slipping.

VIDEO RESOURCE

TEACH YOUR HORSE TO STAY CALM IF THE SADDLE SLIPS

In this video, Hannah demonstrates teaching horses to be relaxed as their saddle slips and even how to turn saddle slipping into a cue to stop.

www.connectiontraining.com/video-resources

INTRODUCING BRIDLES

We always start horses and do the basic rein work using a soft, flat headcollar. These are the ones we use every day for leading. If you then intend to use a bridle, bitless or bitted, you need to train those positively.

When introducing bits, allow your horse to explore the bit and teach him to mouth it while you hold it out until he's happy to take the bit *himself*. When he holds it in his mouth happily for a few seconds, you can slip the headstall over his ears. You need to reward this process all through the stages. Once it's on, leave it on for short periods of time, rewarding him highly and giving him time to work out how to take treats and chew with a bit in.

Whichever bridle you choose, get your horse to wear his bridle during your training sessions but continue to work him from his headcollar as he gets accustomed to wearing it. When you do come to transfer the reins to the bridle, you will have to go through a process of transferring the rein cues from the headcollar. The reins may feel the same to you, but it's a very different sensation for your horse.

TEACHING BASIC CUES FROM THE GROUND

Teaching your horse how to walk, halt and turn from your voice and rein cues from the ground first will make it a smooth transition into the saddle. The more consistent you can keep these cues, the easier it will be for your horse. For this reason, we teach them in a short-reining position, where you walk at your horse's saddle area.

WALK ON AND HALT
Begin by strengthening your voice cues for walk on and halt while leading your horse.

Establish distinctive and clear cues such as, "walk on" and "whoa", said in specific, consistent tones. Also practice transferring these cues to a feel on the rope as you ask your horse to halt, so that he learns to stop from the rein too. Once your horse responds well to these cues when leading, you can begin to ask for them in a short-reining position. This is where you stand at the saddle area and work the horse from the ground as if you were in the saddle.

When you're in this position, most horses are initially reluctant to walk forwards because they are used to you in front or at their head in leading position. They need to learn to go ahead and follow your cues from behind. Even if your voice cue alone does transfer well and your horse walks on when you ask from this new position, you haven't yet taught him how to turn from this position, so he will most likely try to turn back to you. Instead, we use an object to guide the horse forward, such as a mat or stationary target.

Begin by using your voice cue to ask your horse to walk only a few steps to a known object such as a target or mat, while you're in the short-reining position. It's best to have no contact on the reins at this stage to make it really clear for your horse when you're asking for forwards, compared to when you ask for a halt transition.

Lead your horse towards an object he knows and halt him a few steps away from it. Step back into your short-reining position and give your 'walk on' voice cue. The object should be a strong enough draw that your horse steps forwards towards it – mark and reward this decision. Gradually begin further and further from the object until your horse is responding to your voice cue without the need of the object.

Alternatively you can ask another person to guide them forwards instead of an object, which can be an effective way to begin the process. However, in this set-up, it's easy for the horse to only focus on the person in front and disconnect from the person short-reining, which can work against you as you want the horse to be really tuned into the 'rider'. If you do use two people, ensure that the lead person is interacting with the horse as little as possible so that the horse is really listening to and working with the person who is short-reining.

You can use a second person to help guide the horse forwards as you begin to work from a short-reining position, just ensure that the horse is mostly connected to the person who is short-reining as that is the 'rider' in this situation. Fade out the guide person as quickly as possible; they can always be ready to step back in and help in moments of confusion as the horse is learning.

Once the walk is established, you can introduce halt. Your cues are very similar from the ones you've taught from a basic leading position; a voice cue, such as the word, "whoa" and a slight feel on the rein. Asking for the halt initially as you approach an object helps to set your horse up for success because they will naturally stop at the target or mat anyway. After a few repetitions, you can try asking for the halt away from an object. Reward your horse for any attempt at halting, even slowing the walk initially, and it will soon become a strong behaviour. We like to give extra rewards for halting when preparing horses to be ridden because it is a safe default behaviour. If your horse gets worried or confused at any point during the early stages of being ridden, halting is a good solution. It keeps you both safe and allows you to reconnect before continuing on, or dismounting if necessary. Reward it highly so that it's something your horse loves to do and offers readily!

TURNING WITH A TARGET SQUARE

Turning begins by teaching lateral flexions from a rein cue. This simply means that the horse knows to turn their head to each side as you lift that rein. Once your horse knows this in halt, you can begin to teach them to follow a rein cue and turn in walk.

Our favourite exercise for teaching turning is the target square, made up of four stationary targets. These will guide your horse around the turn as you teach the rein cues. Begin by teaching your horse to turn towards the side you're on. For example, you will walk around the target square on the left rein (anti-clockwise), and you will be short-reining from the left side of your horse. As you prepare to walk from one target to the next, you will lift your rein gently to ask your horse to flex in that direction and give your 'walk on' voice cue. The next target will also be only a few steps away, giving extra guidance for your horse. If he even thinks about stepping forwards in the direction of the bend, mark and reward him highly! This builds easily into light, simple turns.

As you prepare to move onto the next target, lift your inside rein to ask your horse to bend in that direction and give your voice cue to walk on. The combined cues will result in your horse taking a step in that direction and the stationary target will draw them forward, too.

You will also need to repeat the exercise from the outside of the turn, so your horse is following your rein cue and turning away from you. This is slightly trickier for your horse as they naturally want to turn towards you, but it's a vital step to ensure your horse is truly understanding and following your rein cues, rather than any subtle body cues you might be giving.

Following the rein cue to turn away from you is harder. You can do this towards a stationary target, again using your target square. Here, a second person is helping to guide Leo with a target, instead.

The handler who is short-reining gently gives the rein cue and quietly waits as Leo works out the answer. As soon as she takes a step in the right direction, she gets marked and rewarded.

MOVING ON

These exercises teach your horse how to walk, halt and turn from voice and rein cues that you can bring directly to the saddle. Take your time practicing these lessons until you can easily walk, halt and turn your horse in both directions, and that you can do this while short-reining from either side of your horse. If your horse gets worried or confused at any point, simply go up to his head and lead him through the exercise to give him confidence and clarity before trying again from a short-reining position.

You can build on this exercise by enlarging the target square, varying the patterns such as adding in circles or turning across the diagonal of your target square and incorporating other objects such as poles or boards. When you're leading your horse out on the trails or roads, occasionally move back to a short-reining position and practice it there. Because your horse will suddenly feel they are in the lead, rather than following you, it's an effective way to gradually build their confidence exploring the world before you ride out. It is also an easy progression to move behind your horse into a long-reining position, which is another great exercise working on your horse's movement and preparing him for riding or driving. You will also need to return to these exercises if you change your horse's tack, such as moving from a headcollar to a bitted bridle, to ensure the cues remain clear for your horse.

Moving into long-reining is a fairly simple process once your horse is comfortable short-reining. Here, CT Coach Gesine Jimenez-Martinez, is long-reining her horse, Diesel, over cavalletti.

MOUNTING FOR THE FIRST TIME

You can begin the mounting block work long before you are ready to ride your horse. Teach your horse to line up at the mounting block as discussed in Chapter 11. As well as being a necessary skill for a ridden horse, this exercise will help you to stay connected with your horse as you move from the ground to the saddle. It also gives you the opportunity to teach your horse how to turn around and take treats when you are at the saddle. Most horses want to move back to get the treats, so you have to teach them to stay still and bend their head round. This can be unbalancing, so take time to get this solid as you will need it for ridden training.

Then start lying over your horse and give rewards from the other side too. Work on de-spooking him at the mounting block—touch his ears and tail from the block, jump up and down on the block next to him, wave your arms above his head. It often takes time for horses to understand that you on their backs is the same you as on the ground! It's amazing how disconnected most horses are with their riders, so this time at the mounting block builds the connection and communication you need while riding.

When it comes time to sit on your horse for the first time, you may want to have a friend at the horse's head for extra support, but it should go smoothly from all your preparation. Since your horse is relaxed as you lean over, simply just slide onto his back, mark that moment, slide off and feed the reward from the ground. It can be easiest to begin this process bareback so that you can dismount quickly if your horse begins to move. As you slide on and off, you are training your horse to stay relaxed and connected as you move from the ground to the saddle and he should stay relaxed throughout. Marking while mounted and then feeding when you're on the ground helps to train your horse to stand still and wait for the treat while you dismount. This creates a really good safety mechanism for dismounting.

Once you're on, don't rush to start moving. Gradually increase the time you stay mounted and mark and reward from there. Before you even take a step, practice sitting on your young horse many times until he is totally relaxed about you getting on and his default behaviour is standing still.

This was the very first time someone sat on this young horse. Because of all the previous work at the mounting block, he was relaxed and connected throughout.

This is also the time to embed an "emergency dismount" routine too. You have started this with marking and then rewarding after dismounting. Make sure you can do this from both sides and that your horse just stands still, waiting for the treat. Then start messy dismounts, sliding clumsily off your horse instead of dismounting neatly. Mark as you are "falling" if your horse stays still, and reward when you're on the ground. Start dismounting awkwardly and then rolling on the ground, preparing your horse in case you trip, stumble or fall as you dismount, or a rushed leap off. Again, you are looking for your horse to stay calm and still while you do these crazy things. The more you practice different things, in different places, the safer your horse will become as it's all just routine and it won't spook him when things are done differently or something unexpected happens. It's better to have a horse whose default is "stand still and wait". It's easy then to develop the forward you want from a place of calm connection.

FIRST RIDDEN STEPS TO A TARGET

The preparatory exercises should progress smoothly into the first steps of riding your horse. Once again, we're using a stationary target to make the first steps easy, clear and positive for your horse. Set up the target a few steps in front of your mounting block. Begin by mounting and dismounting at halt at the block. Then, using your short-reining voice cue, stand by your horse's saddle area and ask her to walk on to the target. This should be a very easy exercise for your horse at this stage and is used here to give your horse clarity about the exercise in preparation for asking for it while riding for the first time.

Bring your horse to the block again and mount. This time give your voice cue to walk on, while sitting on your horse. It may take a few moments for your horse to try to take a step, but reward her highly if she even *thinks* about going forwards. Since

the target is only a couple of steps away, it should draw your horse towards it, which will help her learn to walk on with you mounted and means you don't also have to worry about steering at this stage. When your horse reaches the target, jackpot and dismount. With a few repetitions, she should be walking on promptly to the target with you on her back.

Your horse will likely feel unstable at first as she learns how to move with the weight of a rider on her back. You can make it easier for your horse by staying as balanced in the saddle as possible. With practice, your horse will quickly gain stability and confidence at moving with a rider.

This was rescue pony, Rowan's, first ever step with a rider on board. You can see the portable mounting block Hannah has mounted from.

Rowan moved forward from Hannah's voice cue to the yellow stationary target. Rachel held the end of the rope as a safety precaution and was there to guide Rowan if necessary, though she stayed connected to Hannah on her back throughout.

You will repeat the same steps on board as you did on the ground to teach walking and halting. As you progress, you can introduce a gentle squeeze with your legs along with your 'walk on' voice cue and take a slight feel on the reins when you ask your horse to halt. By using existing known cues and gradually changing small elements as you progress, you will make it a smooth transition to teach the ridden aids as your horse has understood your cues at each stage from leading, through short-reining to riding

RIDING THE TARGET SQUARE

Following the work you've done on the ground, we return to the target square for the ridden training. Through your short-reining training, your horse should understand to turn, change directions, walk and halt from your voice and rein cues. You can use the target square to transfer these cues to the saddle, re-tracing the short-reining lessons.

First, practice on the ground, short-reining your horse from one target to another. Begin with the simplest pattern of walking directly from one target to the next around the square. Make the target square small again, so that it is only a short distance between them. Ask your horse to line up when you get to the mounting block and ride to the first target, as in the above exercise. As you prepare to ride to the next target, add in your rein cue as you ask your horse to walk on. Through short-reining and with the guide of the targets, your horse should respond to this - you can mark and reward any steps in the right direction. When you reach the second target, reward your horse highly and dismount, ready to repeat that stage until your horse is clear and confident before moving on.

Rowan is learning to turn from a rider's cues with the aid of a target square.

Reward your horse for calmly responding to all your cues or trying to work out what you're asking for. Ensure that you stay calm, relaxed, focused, and confident so that both of you increase your skills and trust in each other in this new situation.

As you progress over subsequent sessions, you can ask for more changes of direction between the targets, transitions to halt and gradually move away from the targets completely as your horse learns to respond to your ridden cues and is ready to move on to more advanced ridden exercises. Although you use large, clear cues when you're first teaching your horse, as he progresses you can make your cues increasingly subtle until you only need a small weight shift and squeeze of a rein to turn.

VIDEO RESOURCE

STARTING YOUR HORSE UNDER SADDLE THE CT WAY

Watch the Connection Training process for starting a horse under saddle with Hannah and Rowan.

www.connectiontraining.com/video-resources

YOUNG HORSE VARIABILITY AND IMPULSE CONTROL

Compared to adult horses, young horses are generally more variable in their behaviour and have more energy and less impulse control. Take this into account in your training to set your young horse up for success. This might mean that you start each session by working him in movement on the ground to allow him to use his energy safely and productively. Then work on stationary or slower behaviours, such as mounting and walking, later in the training session when he feels calmer and is more likely to be successful at them.

Set up your training area to help your young horse be able to focus and stay relaxed. Perhaps you have an older horse who can stand quietly at the edge of your arena to give him confidence. You could fence off a smaller portion of the arena or field to work in or always have an extra person on the ground for guidance and safety. If you feel at all unsure, seek the help of a professional.

If you begin to work your young horse on the ground and find that he's spooky, anxious, or excitable, work on exercises to help him calm down, but leave riding for another day. Again, you want to set him up for success and ensure that his experiences with being ridden are positive ones. That means adapting your training depending on what your young horse brings to the session each day. This will help to keep both of you safe, happy, and confident as your horse takes his first steps with a rider.

CALMNESS AND CONNECTION WHEN RIDING FROM DAY ONE

Our step-by-step process is kind of obvious when you know it—it makes a lot of sense to both humans and horses, which makes progress easy. It follows all of our training principles to break down the exercises so it's easy for the horse to learn and prioritise calmness and connection throughout. Anyone can follow it, even if you've never backed a horse before and we have many students who have successfully backed their horse at home following our online course. It's wonderful to see so many horses around the world experience such positive riding from day one.

Hannah teaching Freckles how to turn from a rider's cues using the target square. He is highly focused on Hannah and calmly working out this new exercise, though you can see how big and obvious the cues are at this stage.

As you can see from the more advanced pictures throughout this book, he has progressed well from these early ridden days!

CHAPTER 15

JUMPING AND OBSTACLES TRAINING

Jump and obstacle training builds on the gymnastic groundwork and ridden exercises as an effective way to improve strength, balance, body awareness and co-ordination. Whether you're asking your horse to jump a grid, walk under a curtain or stand on a pedestal, you are challenging his brain and body in different ways, and you can adapt the level of the challenge to suit any horse. You can train both jumping and obstacles on the ground and ridden, and you will build your communication and your horse's confidence as you do so. Incorporating some jump or obstacle work into your training regime adds variety, exercise and should be a lot of fun for both of you.

A range of competitions are based around jumps and obstacles, both mounted and dismounted, such as show jumping, cross-country, horse agility, TREC, working equitation, handy pony, and trail classes. Even if you don't intend to compete, replicating these obstacles and exercises at home is a fantastic way to bring all your training together and build on your horse's skills in a wide range of situations. And, if you're out on the trail and need to pop a fallen log, open a tricky gate or squeeze under some low hanging branches, you and your horse will be well prepared to do so!

FREE JUMPING

You're probably familiar with loose jumping, where the horse jumps without rider or equipment. This is usually done by setting up a channel, or chute, creating fences that enclose a series of jumps so that the horse cannot run out. Unfortunately, this approach can often make the horse feel anxious about being chased or trapped, and they often worry more about being chased forward than focusing on what and how they are jumping.

In Connection Training, we prefer free jumping. This is where the horse has the choice to go over the jump and is moving towards something, such as a person or target, instead of being chased over the fence. This approach means that your horse is taking an active role in the training, so they must clearly understand

the exercise and be confident and motivated to choose to jump. Trained progressively, this is an effective way to build confidence and joy over jumps and is an exercise most horses love to do! If your horse has fear over poles and jumps, shown by rushing, jumping overly high, refusing, running out or other signs of tension, re-training it in this different way will change his associations until he, too, enjoys jumping calmly and confidently.

There are many physical benefits to jumping, too, as it's a dynamic and gymnastic exercise. It builds your horse's strength in his core and hindquarters as he pushes over the jump, stretches out his top-line, improves his body awareness and builds fitness. Free jumping also allows your horse to learn how to use his body in this way, build strength and navigate jumps before adding in the weight and balance of a rider.

Hannah and India demonstrating Recall A-B free jumping. India is free to choose to go around the jump, but knows that going over it is rewarding and fun.

TRAINING FREE JUMPING

A-B free jumping is a technique we learned from trainer Shawna Karrasch, where the horse goes between person A and person B over a jump that is placed in the middle of the arena.

Rachel (Person A) is sending Selena to Claire Waldron (Person B). Rachel puts her target away and sends Selena to Claire. Claire uses her target to draw Selena towards her and explain the exercise.

To begin, you will only ask your horse to walk a short distance between you to teach the concept of moving from person to person. As you progress, you can increase the distance and introduce poles, jumps and faster paces.

We have adapted this basic A-B exercise in various ways to suit different horses and enable trainers to do it alone, without the need of a second person. The most common approach we use is Recall A-B free jumping. This builds on your 'stay' training from the Foundation lessons (Chapter 3). You ask your horse to stay at a stationary target or on a mark until you are at the other side of the jump and can then call your horse to you over the fence.

Horses usually find it easiest to stay at an object in this exercise, so, to begin, ask your horse to 'stay' at a stationary target or on their mat or board. From just a few steps away, call your horse to you. Make sure that this cue is very different from your 'stay' cue as it needs to be clear to your horse when to stay put and when to come to you. For example, Hannah's stay cue is to put her hand up in a 'stop' position and say, "stand" in a low, drawn-out voice. Her recall cue is holding up a target and trilling (rolling her R's) in a high-pitched way. As well as being distinctive, they also help the horse intrinsically because this stay cue is low energy, helping the horse to stand still, and the recall cue is high energy, a motivating noise, encouraging the horse to move.

Gradually increase the distance you can walk away from your horse and call her to you. There are two elements to this; the stay and the recall, and you will need to reinforce both parts. If you only reward your horse for coming to you, you will most likely lose the stay, so sometimes walk away from your horse and, instead of calling her to you, mark and run back and feed her in the stay position. This will ensure that she waits for your recall cue before leaving her target or mark. If your horse does start to come to you before you've called her, quietly reposition her at the target or mark and repeat the exercise,

rewarding when she stands well. It's also effective to pause if you see your horse thinking of leaving the stay position, and only continue backing away when you see your horse has recommitted to the stay position. Even though you're working your horse from a short distance away, the communication is still strong.

Once you've established stay and recall, you can add in a pole. Use your target to encourage and guide your horse over it initially. Mark as soon as he steps over the pole to clarify that's what you want him to do. To increase the speed, use your existing voice cue (trained in-hand or on the lunge first) and gently run back as you call your horse to you. You can mark the decision to move into trot, even if you reward your horse when she gets to you. You can then start to raise the pole into a jump and build the behaviour from there.

India 'stays' on her low pedestal while Hannah walks to the other end of the arena.

When Hannah gives the cue, India leaves her pedestal, turns and canters over the jump to Hannah.

Most horses will quickly figure out how to step and then jump over the poles, though there might be some clumsy attempts during the learning process! Reward your horse for all attempts while she is learning and building confidence, especially since the first time your horse knocks down a jump is often worrying to your horse. You can refine the technique to create clean, neat jumps at a later date, but confidence, enthusiasm and joy is most important at this stage.

As the jump becomes higher and you increase the distance between the stay point and yourself, continue to mark right at the moment when your horse goes over the jump. Don't worry—he won't stop in mid-air! The mark tells your horse what's important. He'll remember that and will continue to you to get his reward.

There are other ways to include free jumping in your training, too. One exercise is to send your horse over a jump to a stationary target. This keeps your horse forward and straight as he focuses on the target beyond the jump. By having multiple stationary targets at different points in the arena, such as set up in a square pattern, you can create different exercises and courses of multiple jumps.

You can also include poles and jumps in your work on the lunge. This is effective whether you're lunging on a line or at liberty. By incorporating changes of direction and cues for circling and going straight, as taught through the lunging exercises, it's possible to build this up into a full free jump course, similar to dog agility.

VIDEO RESOURCE

HOW TO TEACH FREE JUMPING AROUND A TARGET SQUARE

Watch this video to learn how to teach A-B Free jumping using stationary targets.

www.connectiontraining.com/video-resources

IMPULSE CONTROL AND GOOD DECISIONS

All of these free jumping setups give the horse a choice of whether to go over the jump or around it. As you know by now, training is more effective when the horse is relaxed and has freedom of choice. Free jumping allows your horse to communicate with you freely and learn the behaviour while experiencing feel-good emotions.

Free jumping also improves your horse's impulse control as he must learn to raise his energy to go over the jump without getting over excited, disconnecting or going over threshold. If you're working on A-B free jumping, your horse will have to slow and calm down again as he reaches you or the target, which can be difficult for many horses after trotting or cantering over a fence. If you're lunging your horse over poles or jumps, he may struggle to come back down to walk after jumping. Reward highly for relaxing with you after jumping, and spend time working on downward transitions and calm behaviours between jumps. Ask for higher paces and longer distances gradually, so that your horse is able to stay calm and connected while jumping.

Maybe you need to work on the other end of the scale because your horse is reluctant to put much effort into going forward or jumping. In that case, you can help him by calling him energetically, rewarding him as soon as gets to you, and drawing attention to any moment when he goes forward more enthusiastically. Reward highly for increased effort and keep your jumping sessions short so that you don't overface or tire your horse while you're building his motivation and enthusiasm.

If your horse has existing fear regarding poles and jumps, take this training very slowly to build confidence. You will reward moments of brave attempts, confident approaches and enthusiastic effort.

As always, ensure that the challenge level is right for your horse so that he *can* be successful. This process helps your horse to make good behavioural decisions to help his emotional balance, finding relaxation and motivation from wherever he starts.

Free jumping also gives you other opportunities to improve your horse's decision making within sessions, since he will have the choice to go around the jump instead of over it. If he does go around it, quietly re-set him and ask again. Reward him highly for choosing to jump – that's a good decision!

However, it's important that you mark decisions that are sensible in the moment. If a jump is too high or scary or your horse is uncharacteristically resistant, listen to what he's telling you—that he *can't* jump, not that he won't. Even incorrect responses are useful information as they can help you work out how your horse feels about a certain situation, whether he understands the behaviour, and what your next training steps will be. If the jump is too difficult, make it smaller or easier, or come back to it on a different day when your horse is feeling back on form so that he can stay successful and fully enjoy the game.

ADVANCED FREE JUMPING

Once your horse understands the concept of free jumping and is performing it over small fences willingly, you can introduce new exercises and refine your horse's jumping technique.

Giving your horse the space and time to learn from her jumping experience will naturally improve her ability. She'll become more adept at hitting the jump on the right stride as she'll discover it's more difficult if she takes off too far away or too close. She'll learn how high she needs to jump to not knock the fence and learn to find the best balance and momentum to make jumping easiest. Support your horse through this learning process and keep the jumps small while she builds competence.

You can also draw attention to the best moments with what you choose to mark and reward. Perhaps your horse just trots into it instead of canters and has to haul herself over the fence. Maybe she's a bit careless and knocks it down. Not receiving a reward from you gives your horse just as much information as when you do give a reward. Acknowledge that she did the general right thing with a stroke but save your marks and best rewards for the times when she jumps best. In this way, you can give your horse valuable information to improve her jumping technique and ensure that balanced jumps and good impulsion are most rewarding.

Using a variety of jumping exercises will improve your horse's ability and keep the training varied and interesting.Grid work (a line of jumps) is one of the most beneficial exercises and is commonly known as gymnastic jumping due to the physical benefits it brings. Introduce your horse to different kinds of jumps, including various fillers, spreads and narrower fences. The aim is to gradually build your horse's skill, confidence and joy so that they can tackle any new fence competently and willingly.

You can use free jumping to teach your horse how to confidently navigate difficult jumps like skinnies. This can both overcome and prevent problems with tricky fences. In free jumping, you can gradually make the jump narrower, rewarding your horse for choosing to jump the centre of the fence.

VIDEO RESOURCE

LIBERTY FREE JUMPING COMPILATION

Be inspired by a variety of free jumping exercises with Hannah and India, using Recall A-B's and Free Jumping when liberty lunging.

www.connectiontraining.com/video-resources

OBSTACLE TRAINING

Obstacle training is a great way to bring movement, interest, and fun into your sessions with your horse. Obstacles are any items which your horse can engage with such as cones, poles, bridges, flags, tires etc. They give you and your horse focus and train a wide range of skills. They can be done dismounted so can be adapted for young horses, older horses and un-rideable ones.

Horses tend to love obstacle training. They like the clarity and focus of moving between obstacles, and they enjoy solving the puzzle of each one. Different obstacles require you to improve different skills in your horse.

BODY AWARENESS

Building on the body awareness work in the gymnastic groundwork exercises (Chapter 10), obstacles can bring more variety to tactile awareness exercises. These include obstacles such as see-saws (teeter-totters), wooden bridges and passing through narrow gaps, archways and hoops.

Using a target to guide the horse through the hoop. This exercise incorporated body awareness and de-spooking as this horse was very afraid of anything behind his withers when his owner, Ceska Grosvenor, began training him. It is also a preliminary step to jumping through a hoop.

DE-SPOOKING

Many obstacles are designed to increase your horse's confidence and build on your de-spooking work (Chapter 7). These include obstacles such as a water splash, the curtain and flags.

Curtains make a great de-spooking obstacle. When you begin, make it easy for your horse by tying the strands to the side. You can see that Khalil is very worried about going any closer to the curtain, even to touch the target. Seeing this tension, Hannah made this exercise easier, rewarding Khalil for touching the target as he approached the curtain to build his confidence.

Khal's confidence grew through subsequent training sessions. Hannah released the strands one at a time until Khalil was happy to push through the curtain fully released. Because she took this process slowly and made it highly rewarding, this actually became one of Khalil's favourite exercises!

CUE CLARITY

Obstacle courses are fantastic for improving your cue clarity. You will have to work out how to explain to your horse that he needs to leave you, go around a barrel, and return, or navigate an S-bend of poles alone. Sometimes, you will need your horse to do different behaviours with the same obstacle such as targeting a flag or walking past it. Obstacles, such as opening, passing through and closing a gate while mounted, require a combination of cues and behaviours to complete the obstacle. This encourages you to become clear in your cues to explain each behaviour to your horse.

IMPULSE CONTROL

As you work through obstacle training, you will be improving your horse's impulse control. He will learn to wait for your cues as you guide him through the obstacles. This can be challenging at first as most horses love obstacle work and can easily disconnect from you in their excitement about the objects. As he improves, he will need to stay calm and focused to navigate through the obstacles when you cue at trot and canter.

CT Coach and Horse Agility Champion, Judith Edel, works with her rescue pony, Pip. She has combined Recall Free Jumping with obstacles – Pip has to wait at a stationary target, his traffic cone, until Judith calls him. He then trots the poles, jumps through the hoop Judith holds up, canters the white pole and stops at another stationary target. This exercise combines cue clarity and impulse control.

Rachel working with Leo through the S-bend. This is a great exercise for body awareness and cue clarity as Rachel guides her between the poles.

VIDEO RESOURCE

HORSE AGILITY TRAINING

See horse agility in action with Judith Edel, CT Coach and horse agility champion and teacher.

www.connectiontraining.com/video-resources

RIDDEN JUMP AND OBSTACLE TRAINING

Taking the free jumping and dismounted obstacle lessons into the saddle follows our general principles of transferring groundwork to ridden work. We use the dismounted lessons to teach the horse the concept of the behaviour and to find the best emotional balance, increasing motivation and relaxation and finding joy in the exercise. It allows you to safely help your horse reduce reluctance, fear or excitement about the behaviour before riding the exercise.

Transitioning to the saddle requires going back to basics in the exercise and setting it up so that it's easy for the horse to understand, using poles, targets or other guides to explain the exercise.

Once your horse realises that it's the same exercise they love to do on the ground, they usually gain joy and confidence, quickly performing the behaviour with a rider. It's a much quicker process progressing through the stages of the behaviour this time because your horse already knows it and is confident to do it on the ground.

Once your horse has some experience being ridden over jumps or obstacles, you can introduce new variations and continue his education directly from the saddle.

For example, with a green horse, you will introduce walking over a wooden bridge from the ground first, ensuring he's confident before riding over it. However, if you have worked with your horse over platforms and different surfaces in the past, you may choose to ride over the wooden bridge without doing any dismounted work. Depending on the level

Here, Hannah is introducing Freckles to jumping with a rider. Although confident cantering small jumps and grids when free jumping, Hannah goes back to basics when she begins to ride him over the jumps. The jump is very small, she approaches in trot and sets up a stationary target, the blue cone, to help guide Freckles forward and make it clear for him.

Here CT Coach, Kristen Vanderpool, is teaching her horse Aslan to step on this high platform. This was Aslan's first attempt and you can see that he's showing some signs of worry in his facial expression and posture. Of course, he gets rewarded highly and with a few repetitions gains confidence until he loves to stand on the platform.

After working at the platform dismounted until Aslan was truly confident, Kristen was able to ride him onto it confidently and calmly.

of your horse, you might still need to break the behaviour down, rewarding him from the saddle for first approaching it and then stepping on it. You can expect an advanced horse to be able to confidently tackle a new obstacle, receiving a reward after the obstacle or at the end of a course.

This generalisation happens once horses have had enough positive experiences with a range of similar objects or situations, in this case, standing on different surfaces. This is also important for jump training if you plan to compete, because you need your horse to confidently jump any new fence on sight. In order to do this confidently, your horse must gain enough positive experiences with all kinds of jumps until he sees any jump-like obstacle, understands what to do with it and feels good about jumping it. This creates a willing and enthusiastic partner, keen to tackle novel fences.

Once your horse understands the concept of jumping over certain obstacles, you can tackle novel ones directly from the saddle.

Our Riding with Connection (Chapter 11) principles apply to jump work and obstacle courses, too. You can refine your horse's responsiveness and technique from the saddle by marking and rewarding best moments. Highlight and reinforce good decisions, clean jumps, balanced turns, confidence tackling a new obstacle and moments of relaxation or tuning in. You and your horse can work as a partnership to improve your ridden work *together*, making it an enjoyable and fun journey for both of you.

You can refine obstacles and jumping directly from the saddle. Here, Hannah is working India over a 3-fence grid (the final element is out of shot), working on India maintaining rhythm and impulsion throughout the combination.

RIDER CONFIDENCE OVER JUMPS AND OBSTACLES

Riding over jumps is a common concern for many riders, due to past experiences or simply that feeling of power and movement as the horse pops over even a small fence. The same is true for certain obstacles, such as cantering through water, riding up and down banks or steps or underneath an archway (an obstacle found in TREC competitions to mimic low hanging branches). Overcoming this anxiety requires you to slowly and systematically build up both your and your horse's confidence over jumps or obstacles.

If you have any anxiety about the fence or obstacle, we always recommend training your horse from the ground first. You can build up your horse's confidence and skill

using a variety of exercises, without worrying about riding any spooks, leaps or miscalculated strides.

Hannah works with India on building her confidence over novel or spooky jumps. She begins with free jumping and you can see from the way India is jumping that she was a bit worried and therefore clumsy at first. However, the jump itself is small enough for India to manage easily on the wrong stride or even walk over it, so there are no additional challenges to the de-spooking lesson.

Hannah repeated it until India was confident jumping it on the ground and then rode her over the fence. To start with, they went right back to walk to give Hannah confidence riding it and India confidence going over with a rider. From here, they built up to trotting and cantering over the fence.

The more you do of introducing your horse to different jumps and obstacles in this way, the more generally confident your horse will become when faced with novel or unusual challenges. The next case study shows this in action.

PANDORA AND OSCAR

CT Member, Pandora Maund, first came to us because her young horse, Oscar, was highly reactive and tense, just doing basic schooling and hacking out. Pandora had lost her confidence following some falls. Hannah assessed the anxiety levels of both horse and rider and recommend dismounted work first. Oscar was able to take more reassurance from Pandora on the ground and Pandora was able to stay fully calm, confident and therefore competent when dismounted. The process began with simple exercises such as leading a circle while Pandora focused on her breathing and her own levels of relaxation. She rewarded Oscar for tuning in and settling down until Oscar was able to stand still (even for a few seconds to begin with).

From here, Pandora worked on de-spooking exercises with Oscar in the arena and leading him out in-hand. These gave them tools to communicate and stay connected even when faced with exciting or scary situations, such as open fields or a novel object. She also spent plenty of time working at the mounting block, focusing on keeping their connection and calmness as she moved into the saddle. She taught Oscar to line up at anything she climbed onto – gates, fences, tree stumps and walls. This enabled her to continue leading Oscar out in hand, mounting when he felt calm and dismounting when either of them began to get worried.

Their trust built over time and Oscar became a much calmer horse generally, so it was time to revisit some of these exercises over jumps. Due to all of their previous work on breaking down scary situations so that they could tackle them successfully together, they had the tools to do this over jumps, too.

Once they were confident jumping plain fences, Pandora worked on de-spooking Oscar over jumps. This photo was taken at the Connection Training Conference 2016, where spooky objects were gradually added to the jump as long as Oscar remained confident. He was rewarded each time and was soon enjoying jumping the previously spooky fence.

Continuing this work in gradually more challenging situations and generalising their confidence over novel jumps in practice sessions, Pandora and Oscar were able to put it into practice in competition, staying calm and connected cross-country.

VIDEO RESOURCE

DE-SPOOKING YOUR HORSE OVER JUMPS

See how this technique works in action as Hannah works on jump de-spooking with India.

www.connectiontraining.com/video-resources

As you both build in confidence together, you can begin to make the obstacle challenges more difficult. This might include making the jumps higher, riding the obstacle at a faster pace or riding in a open space or new environment. When you do increase one area of challenge, remember to reduce another. For example, if you're jumping higher than you have previously, do it at home or in a known environment where your horse is relaxed and confident. If you're planning to ride obstacles or jumps in an open field for the first time, start in walk over small, easy obstacles to ensure you both stay calm and connected at that level before moving on.

No matter what stage you're at, you can gauge your horse's emotional state each day in order to make the right decision for both of you. Hannah discusses making these decisions with India: *Because India can be an anxious and reactive horse, I'm still careful about deciding when I'll ride her over jumps or what exercise we'll do each day. For example, if she's generally more 'up' than usual, I'll ride on the flat or maybe free-jump her instead. Although she's had a lot of jumping practice now, and very rarely spooks as she's grown in age and experience, it's taken a lot to build my own confidence over jumps and I'm just as careful about maintaining my own calm joy as I am about ensuring India has a good experience! So, if I'm anxious, we won't jump. It's about making the right decision for both of us, so that we continue to have fun jumping together.*

Trained at the right pace, riding jumps and obstacles can be a lot of fun for both of you, as well as building strength, fitness and confidence.

Hannah jumping India with no hands.

Hannah jumping Toby with no bridle.

Hannah jumping Freckles in an open field.

CHAPTER 16
TRICK TRAINING AND BRAIN GAMES

The more variety and fun you can bring into your horse's life, the better. This Chapter is all about some more ways you can do this. These exercises stretch your horse's brain power and boost your training creativity. This will strengthen your connection, increase your horse's problem-solving skills and keep him fresh and interested for all your training.

Hannah and Toby in a Halloween photoshoot, showing Toby's 'smile' trick. He loves to do this and offers it very readily, often when you're just gesticulating! Having fun together is an important part of bond-building (though you don't have to dress as a zombie!).

WHAT IS TRICK TRAINING?

You might have a clear idea of what trick training is and why it is different to other behaviours you may train, such as husbandry tasks. However, to your horse, there's not really any difference between the process of learning to lunge or pick his feet up and learning to fetch an object. It's all just learning behaviours. From the

Toby loved to rear and posture when playing and trick training with Hannah. Advanced tricks like rearing require strength and balance, as well as strong cue control so your horse never offers it unasked.

human viewpoint, however, tricks tend to be behaviours that serve no useful purpose. They are just for fun. They make us smile, and our horses often surprise us with their cleverness.

Common trick behaviours include 'smiling' and kissing; fetching an object; playing catch, nose ball, or football; shaking and nodding the head; pawing, painting, and bowing; rearing and doing the jambette and Spanish walk.

Trick training often divides people. Some believe that reward-based training is useful only for teaching tricks. (By this point in the book, we hope you know that's not the case!) Others believe that tricks are in some way demeaning to the horse.

However, we find trick training is a brilliant opportunity to have some no-pressure fun with your horse and to get creative with

your training. It's also an opportunity to play to your horse's strengths and ingenuity and improve your communication and relationship.

Freckles fetching a horse-ball with Hannah.

WHAT ARE BRAIN GAMES?

Brain games—behaviours that work on the horse's cognitive abilities—are less well-known in horse training. They include exercises such as object differentiation, in which the horse must pick the right object from a selection based on colour, word, or visual cue; scent detection, in which the horse must find or track a specific scent; and creative games such as '101 Things', in which the horse has to come up with a different behaviour each time you mark. These are quite advanced exercises, though there are people across the world who are getting creative and pushing the boundaries of the cognitive abilities of horses in this way. Just like people, different horses respond differently to this type of mental challenge. Some find brain games hard; some prefer to be physically active and don't seem to find them that interesting; others absolutely love these types of games.

Teaching colour discrimination - the horse has to touch the yellow cone.

BENEFITS OF TEACHING TRICKS AND BRAIN GAMES

You can reap many benefits by adding trick training and brain games into your horse's repertoire. This type of behaviour:

BUILDS BONDS

Many tricks are small, discrete behaviours that are easy for your horse to learn. This means trick training offers moments of pure fun together, which gives a big boost to the relationship between you and your horse.

HAS NO NEGATIVE ASSOCIATIONS

Typically, horses have no prior unwanted emotional associations with tricks because most have never been taught them before.

PROVIDES FREEDOM OF CHOICE

Trick training is a time when you can give your horse completely free choice. It doesn't really matter if she doesn't want to engage in trick training on a certain day. You can let her decide what tricks she'd like to do, rather than rewarding her for following your decisions all the time. Most horses love this chance to call the shots, and it usually creates an enormous amount of joy and enthusiasm about the trick training sessions. Being given free rein during trick training also means your horse will be happier to follow your lead when you're working on other behaviours that require more cooperation, such as riding, handling, and healthcare tasks.

IS ENJOYABLE

Everyone loves to see joy in their horse. Because the training is fun and simple, and because they have free choice, horses are often most enthusiastic about their tricks. A horse who enjoys fetching his toy and handing it to you or goes off on his own to stand on his pedestal or is waiting eagerly for you to throw something for him to catch makes everyone smile. In turn, your horse will pick up on this relaxation and joy, making him love his tricks even more. We've even seen horses bring their learned play behaviours, such as carrying items in their mouth, into their regular play with their herd mates.

IS APPROPRIATE FOR SMALL SPACES

Many tricks and brain games can be done in a small space, so they are perfect for entertaining your horse while on box rest or when in a confined space. This mental engagement helps your horse to relax, settle, and build bonds with you while limited in movement.

OFFERS ALTERNATIVES TO PHYSICAL PLAY

The natural way horses play with each other involves galloping, bucking, rearing, play-biting, head-tossing, and striking out. Plenty of horses enjoy this type of play with their humans, too, and are able to tone it down at these times. But many horses get overexcited, tense, or even dangerous if you try to play in this way with them, and that's not enjoyable for anyone. Also, some horses are too old, lame, or disinterested to play in this way. Teaching horses tricks gives you an alternative way to play with them.

CAN EXTEND TRAINING SESSIONS

There may be times, at the end of a more formal training session, when your horse wants to continue. That's a great opportunity to offer playtime. You can be quite spontaneous, offering certain games to your horse but also following his lead. You'll often find that games naturally change and develop between you and your horse. Horses enjoy play and creativity, and it's wonderful to have a way to explore this with your horse and let their ideas shine through.

CAN BE USED AS A REWARD

When you spend this kind of playtime with your horse, you'll find he builds a highly positive association with tricks and games. You'll then be able to use these behaviours as rewards in other areas of your training. For example, Hannah had great results teaching Toby to go forward more enthusiastically under saddle by using the pedestal as a reward. After he gave a good try for forward movement, he could

go and stand on his pedestal and get rewarded for that. When a play behaviour is associated with free choice, joy, and pure fun, it's a powerful reward. Just be careful not to overuse it, or it won't be fun for your horse any more.

IMPROVES OTHER SKILLS

Trick training and brain games can help your horse improve in *everything*. Since your horse has no concept of the difference between learning a trick and learning any other behaviour, you can improve her general problem-solving abilities by teaching her tricks. The more problem-solving she does, the better she gets at it, so teaching her tricks will improve her focus and ability to learn.

Painting is one of Toby's favourite behaviours and, as he's got older, it's become an especially good exercise because he can do it on days when he's a bit stiff and movement is limited. It's fun for everyone and painting a picture for guests makes everyone smile! Learning to paint is fairly straightforward; once the horse has learned to hold an object (in this case a paintbrush), you ask them to target the paper with that object. However, it's a co-ordination challenge because they have to learn to reach forward with the brush lightly so that the brush doesn't get knocked out of their mouth or the paper ripped.

VIDEO RESOURCE

TOBY THE PAINTING PONY

Watch Toby create a masterpiece in this video!

www.connectiontraining.com/video-resources

TRAINING TECHNIQUES FOR TRICKS AND BRAIN GAMES

SHAPING

The most common way to train tricks or brain games is to shape them. This is exactly what we've described throughout the book; breaking the behaviour down to small steps and rewarding successive approximations towards the desired results.

For example, if you are teaching your horse to play catch, you will first reward your horse for mouthing the catch toy, then holding it, then grabbing it as you hold it out in front of him. Once he understands to reach for it and hold it in his mouth, you will gradually swing it to him from an increasing distance away.

When you are shaping behaviours, you will use all the tools you have to explain to your horse what you would like him to do. For example, you can use a leg target to train Spanish Walk, hand targets to teach head nods or a combination such as playing fetch and targeting to teach your horse to paint. This approach is the most practical and you can teach your horse many tricks in this systematic way.

Freckles has learned that the stick target held in front of him, combined with a specific voice cue, mean that he is to touch the target with his front legs instead of his nose, creating the steps of the Spanish Walk.

VIDEO RESOURCE

HOW TO TEACH YOUR HORSE TO PLAY CATCH

See the shaping process to teach your horse how to play 'catch'.

www.connectiontraining.com/video-resources

FREE SHAPING

Free shaping is a technique where, rather than prompting or guiding your horse, you wait for your horse to offer behaviours and then reward the ones you wish to see more of.

For example, if you were to free shape your horse to back up, you would stand back and see what your horse offers. He might walk forwards, sniff the floor, or turn around. You would ignore all these movements. When you noticed your horse even look behind him, or shift his weight backwards, you would mark and reward. It is then up to the horse to figure out what behaviour is earning the reward and repeat it.

This process differs hugely from the guided shaping we've described in previous Chapters, where you would shape a back-up using a target, or your hand on his chest to guide your horse towards the correct answer.

You can also use free shaping to give your horse a chance to be creative - what behaviours can he come up with? One free shaping exercise is called 'show me something new', where the animal has to offer a different behaviour after every reward. As you can see, free shaping can be a fantastic brain game as it stretches your horse's mental skills.

Some horses love free shaping as they enjoy the freedom to problem-solve and figure out the answer. However, some horses really struggle with free shaping as they get very anxious or frustrated with the lack of guidance. If you want to try free shaping with your horse, keep your sessions really short and reward your horse highly for small tries to prevent him getting too anxious or frustrated. You can also have a specific location or set-up for free shaping sessions to explain to your horse what kind of training you're doing. You will quickly see whether this is a game your horse loves and you can include it in his training, or whether it is a cause of tension in your horse.

Hannah's mare, India, loves to be stretched cognitively and enjoys figuring out the answers with little guidance, so free shaping is a good exercise for her. Here, she's playing "Show me something new" where, without guidance from Hannah, she has to offer a different behaviour at the barrel after every reward.

VIDEO RESOURCE

SHOW ME SOMETHING NEW

Hannah's horse, India, plays "Show me something new", coming up with lots of creative ways to play with a barrel.

www.connectiontraining.com/video-resources

CAPTURING

Capturing is a process where you mark and reward your horse for behaviours he is already offering on his own. This is the final behaviour, without successive approximations.

For example, suppose you want to teach your horse to whinny on cue. If he often whinnies when you approach with the feed bucket, you can mark the moment when he does it and reward him. Next, strengthen the behaviour by waiting to put the feed bucket down until your horse has whinnied at you. From there, use cue transferral techniques (explained in Chapter 5) to put the behaviour on a different cue so you can ask for it at a different time of day.

Rebecca Musselwhite, founder of the Jive Pony Equestrian Display Team, used this technique to teach her miniature pony, Hobo, to whinny into a microphone. Her cue was to hold the mic towards him and say, 'What do you think, Hobo?' Rebecca began by holding the mic out as she approached Hobo with his feed bucket. With repetition, her pony learned to whinny as she held the mic out, before she presented his bucket—he was beginning to associate the behaviour with the new cue. It took a bit more practice for him to generalise the behaviour so that he would whinny whenever and wherever he was presented with the microphone. Once he learned the trick, he was happy to offer it anywhere, much to the delight of his audiences.

Hobo whinnying into a microphone on cue with Rebecca Musselwhite, founder of Jive Pony Equestrian Display Team.

Capturing is our recommended way of teaching your horse to lie down on cue. This is a trick behaviour that many people would love their horse to do, but lying down is a vulnerable position for a horse and it can cause stress if not trained sensitively. A benefit of teaching the lie-down through capturing is that the horse lies down in a way which is natural to do,

ensuring no unnatural strains on his body which can often occur when the lie-down is taught using other techniques. Just as in the whinnying example, you need to find times when your horse is already lying down comfortably when you're around, such as if he regularly rolls after a ride. Begin to reward him when he's down and gradually transfer it to a new cue so that you can ask for it at any time.

Capturing is the best technique for teaching your horse to lie-down on cue. India regularly enjoyed a roll in the arena sand. Hannah started to notice times when India was preparing to roll and added her cue in at those moments. She rewarded highly when India was down. Soon Hannah could initiate the behaviour at any time by giving that cue.

Capturing behaviour can also be a way for you and your horse to collaborate. If you're training your horse to do a certain trick, but your horse would rather do it a different way, you can capture that moment. This is a great way to boost your horse's creativity and imagination. Hannah did this with Toby when she was teaching him to fetch. Instead of bringing the tea towel to her, he started waving it about madly. She quite liked this behaviour, so she began to reward that instead. Waving a cloth or flag is still one of Toby's favourite behaviours, perhaps because he came up with it!

VIDEO RESOURCE

HOW TO TEACH YOUR HORSE TO LIE DOWN

See capturing in action as Hannah teaches India to lie down on cue.

www.connectiontraining.com/video-resources

WORKING WITH MULTIPLE HORSES

Horses love to do things as a herd, so including work with multiple horses together can be a fun exercise for everyone. In order for this to be successful, there are some key points to bear in mind.

Firstly, it's much harder to teach new behaviours to multiple horses at once as you will find your attention gets pulled in different directions and you can miss pivotal moments to mark, leading to confusion and frustration. The easiest way to avoid this is to teach the behaviour to each horse individually first and then combine them. For example, if you want to begin working with two horses working at liberty together, ensure that each horse is solid with leading, halt and turn cues on their own before trying it together. Gradually increase the complexity and duration of the behaviours you're asking for, returning to work with the horses individually if you need to clarify any behaviours and avoid confusion.

Another useful technique is to use your 'stay' behaviour. Again, ensure you've taught this to each horse alone first and then add it into your training session together. Ask one horse to stay on their mat or at a target while you work the other. Remember to run back and reward the one staying patiently to ensure that behaviour stays strong. Switch regularly to start with so that you're only asking each horse to wait patiently for very short bursts, as it's quite a test of impulse control! Gradually build the duration and solidify your cues so that both horses know when it's their turn to stay and wait or when to come with you to work.

Hannah is working with Khalil and Rowan alternately. Here, Rowan is asked to 'stay' on her pedestal while Hannah works with Khalil through the curtain. This is hardest for the waiting horse and you can see that Rowan's attention is back on Hannah, waiting for her cue to come and join in.

Our whole herd working together for our Christmas video.

When working multiple horses, work with the natural friendships within the herd. It can be stressful for the horses if you're asking two horses who don't get along to work in close proximity to each other. For example, when we trained for our Christmas video, all nine members of our herd came into the arena and stood on pedestals next to each other. We arranged them next to their favourite herdmates to make it a positive experience.

Having said that, working with multiple horses can also be an effective way to help horses relax and get along with each other, even if they don't naturally. Hannah did this with Freckles and India because she wanted to travel them together, a stressful experience for horses who don't like each other. To begin with, Freckles was wary of India, who would threaten him when he got too close. Hannah worked on gradually bringing them closer and rewarding India

for softening and staying polite. Freckles' confidence around her grew and he became less anxious. With practice, Hannah was able to travel them happily together, lead them out together and even ride Freckles while leading India. This also affected their relationship in the field, as they began to spend more time in close proximity with each other, seeking out each other's company.

Working together can give guidance and confidence to young or anxious horses, too, as they gain an experienced lead from the older horse. If you have multiple horses, we recommend to try training them together. Start with just two horses with simple exercises and build from there – in time you can work up to advanced behaviours and working with many horses at once.

VIDEO RESOURCE

MERRY CHRISTMAS HORSES ON PEDESTALS!

Watch our festive fun video with our whole herd of nine horses working together!

www.connectiontraining.com/video-resources

GET CREATIVE TO GET CONNECTED

Working with trick training and brain games brings variety to your horse's training and is a great way to boost your creativity in training. You can experiment with different ways to teach certain behaviours to see how your horse reacts best. Or, maybe you've seen a dog perform a behaviour and you'd like to work out how to train your horse to do it, too

(that's how horse agility came about). Or, perhaps your trick and brain training sessions are the time for you to foster your horse's creativity and imagination to see what he can come up with. Whatever you and your horse choose to work on, have the confidence to experiment. This type of play will be fun for both of you and strengthen your relationship even further. And, really, that's what Connection Training is all about.

JOIN THE CONNECTION TRAINING CLUB

We hope you've enjoyed our book and are inspired to bring more Connection Training into your horse's life. This book outlines our philosophy and practice, but we provide detailed video instruction on exactly how to do it in the Connection Training Club.

Membership of the CT Club gives you access to hundreds of videos, with step-by-step guides to everything we've discussed in the book. Videos are arranged into Home Study Courses, following the practical chapters in the book.

Members also have direct access to us through our regular members-only Live Q&A sessions. It's a great opportunity to ask your questions to us directly and we love to chat with you. Our global members are a close community and keep in touch with each other, and us, through our forum and our closed Facebook Group. Further inspiration and guidance is given through members' Training Journals, fun monthly Training Challenges and members-only content on everything from behind-the-scenes to trainer mindset.

Additionally, more personal instruction is available through one-to-one or small group coaching with us or one of our superb Certified Coaches. Live coaching is also available through lessons and clinics in the UK and abroad, and at our training centre, Positive Horse Training Spain.

Come and join in the fun! You will find yourself with the most positive, supportive group of people you can imagine, who will love to share your horsey journey and become your cheer-leaders and friends.

To find out more
and join the Club,
head on over to:

WWW.CONNECTIONTRAINING.COM

We look forward to
seeing you there!

ACKNOWLEDGEMENTS

Our journey into horsemanship has made us many friends. We've received support, ideas, advice and companionship all the way. We'd love to be able to thank each person individually, but the list would be too long, so our acknowledgements are for the people who most helped us with this book. For all the others, we are grateful for your companionship, teaching and support which helped us get to where we are now.

We have been blessed to work with some excellent professional photographers who provided pictures for the book. We would like to thank Meadhbh Dunne for providing the majority of photographs. We are also grateful to receive photographs from Donna Etherington, Pandora Maund, Cheryl McMurray and Ian Weston.

Our editor, Kathy Carter has been a lifesaver. Until she took a hand in it, we felt we had a tiger by the tail, trying to put all this information in some sort of coherent order. She cracked it on the first draft.

Special thanks go to Claire Waldron, CT Coach and Director of Positive Horse Training Spain, for providing many photographs, filming particular training sessions for us and letting us feature so many of her own sessions. Thanks also to Nina Sarkissian, for hours of filming and editing, while also providing excellent customer service to CT Members. We are grateful for the involvement of Shawna Karrasch for her participation in creating early drafts.

Our Connection Training Coaches feature in many of the photographs and stories and we are grateful to them for their active enthusiasm and contributions. They are Sarah Babcock, Venya Bonebakker, Belinda Daws, Melissa Deal, Suzy Deurinck, Judith Edel, Angelica Hesselius, Megan Hines, Gesine Jimenez Martinez and Kristen Vanderpool. Our Coaches, and additional readers Loni Loftus, Ella Dyer and Emma Blane, also read through the manuscript and pointed out errors, inconsistencies and recommended many improvements. It is a much better book because of their input!

Many of our students and colleagues have allowed us to use their photographs and we'd like to thank Jackie Atkinson, Lorna Butterworth, Hilary Cross, Rachaël Draaisma, Barbara Edwards, Susanne Eichelberger, India Evans, Helen Gilbertson, Ceska Grosvenor, Liz Hayden, Carolien Hendrikson, Lesley Holehouse, Sophie Kendrick, Elizabeth Lee, Rebecca Musselwhite, Sue Norville, Lily Perry, Sophie Pickard, Amy Sheddon, Helen Smith, Sue Sunley, Melanie Watson and Jan Wilkinson.

We have a special thanks to Jaak Panksapp, who sadly died while we were writing this book. His work gave us the scientific background we needed to explain our practise and to develop it further. We met him in Oxford in the Spring of 2015 and he was very interested in our book and massively encouraging. We are so sorry we can't show him the finished work.

Finally, we could not have written this without the great support and help of Maggie Roux and Ian Weston. They have been there when times have been rough, read first drafts, stood out in the cold taking photographs and listened endlessly to our discussions. They both now know more about horse training than they ever wanted to. We love you both.

INDEX

CPSIA information can be obtained
at www.ICGtesting.com
Printed in the USA
BVHW022016230520
579858BV00010B/150